Internships Through Employment

EDITORIAL ADVISORS

Deborah E. Bouchoux, Esq.
Georgetown University

Therese A. Cannon
Executive Associate Director
Western Association of Schools and Colleges

Katherine A. Currier
Chair, Department of Paralegal and Legal Studies
Elms College

Cathy Kennedy
Paralegal Program Director
Legal Studies Department
Globe University/Minnesota School of Business

Susan M. Sullivan
Director, Graduate Career Programs
University of San Diego

Laurel A. Vietzen
Professor and Instructional Coordinator
Elgin Community College

William I. Weston
Dean, College of Legal Studies
Kaplan University

ASPEN PUBLISHERS

Internships Through Employment

The Paralegal Job Hunter's Handbook

Deborah E. Bouchoux, Esq.
Georgetown University

Susan M. Sullivan
Director, Graduate Career Programs
University of San Diego

Wolters Kluwer
Law & Business

AUSTIN   BOSTON   CHICAGO   NEW YORK   THE NETHERLANDS

Aspen Publishers
Attn: Permissions Department
76 Ninth Avenue, 7th Floor
New York, NY 10011-5201

To contact Customer Care, e-mail *customer.care@aspenpublishers.com*, call 1-800-234-1660, fax 1-800-901-9075, or mail correspondence to:

Aspen Publishers
Attn: Order Department
PO Box 990
Frederick, MD 21705

Printed in the United States of America.

1 2 3 4 5 6 7 8 9 0

ISBN 978-0-7355-6247-9

Library of Congress Cataloging-in-Publication Data

Bouchoux, Deborah E., 1950-
    Internships through employment : the paralegal job hunter's handbook / Deborah E. Bouchoux, Susan M. Sullivan.
        p. cm.
    Includes bibliographical references and index.
    ISBN 978-0-7355-6247-9
    1. Legal assistants — Employment — United States. 2. Legal assistants — Vocational guidance — United States. 3. Job hunting — United States. 4. Law — Study and teaching (Internship) — United States. 5. Law — Vocational guidance — United States. 6. Legal assistants — United States — Handbooks, manuals, etc. I. Sullivan, Susan Moxon, 1949 — II. Title.

    KF320.L4B676 2008
    340.023′73 — dc22

                                                    2008010797

About Wolters Kluwer Law & Business

Wolters Kluwer Law & Business is a leading provider of research information and workflow solutions in key specialty areas. The strengths of the individual brands of Aspen Publishers, CCH, Kluwer Law International and Loislaw are aligned within Wolters Kluwer Law & Business to provide comprehensive, in-depth solutions and expert-authored content for the legal, professional and education markets.

CCH was founded in 1913 and has served more than four generations of business professionals and their clients. The CCH products in the Wolters Kluwer Law & Business group are highly regarded electronic and print resources for legal, securities, antitrust and trade regulation, government contracting, banking, pension, payroll, employment and labor, and healthcare reimbursement and compliance professionals.

Aspen Publishers is a leading information provider for attorneys, business professionals and law students. Written by preeminent authorities, Aspen products offer analytical and practical information in a range of specialty practice areas from securities law and intellectual property to mergers and acquisitions and pension/benefits. Aspen's trusted legal education resources provide professors and students with high-quality, up-to-date and effective resources for successful instruction and study in all areas of the law.

Kluwer Law International supplies the global business community with comprehensive English-language international legal information. Legal practitioners, corporate counsel and business executives around the world rely on the Kluwer Law International journals, loose-leafs, books and electronic products for authoritative information in many areas of international legal practice.

Loislaw is a premier provider of digitized legal content to small law firm practitioners of various specializations. Loislaw provides attorneys with the ability to quickly and efficiently find the necessary legal information they need, when and where they need it, by facilitating access to primary law as well as state-specific law, records, forms and treatises.

Wolters Kluwer Law & Business, a unit of Wolters Kluwer, is headquartered in New York and Riverwoods, Illinois. Wolters Kluwer is a leading multinational publisher and information services company.

DEDICATION

In memory of
Stephen Michael Sullivan
1971-1999

Summary
of Contents

Part I
Laying the Foundation for a
Successful Internship and Career   1

Part II
Finding the Right Job   77

Contents

Part I
Laying the Foundation
for a Successful Internship
and Career   1

Chapter One: Internship and
Career Strategies: The Preliminaries   3

Chapter Two: Internships: Setting the Stage 25

Chapter Three: Building an Effective Résumé and Cover Letter   39

Chapter Four: The Internship Experience   57

Part II
Finding the Right Job 77

Chapter Five: Revising Your Internship Résumé and Cover Letter for Permanent Employment 79

Chapter Six: Interviewing and Negotiating 99

Part III
The Workplace 129

Chapter Seven: The Law Firm Environment 131

Chapter Eight: Keeping Your Job and Advancing in Your Career 157

Chapter Nine: Quitting Your Job and Getting Your Next Job 179

Chapter Ten: Trading in Your Backpack for a Briefcase: Strategies for Success in the Workplace 201

Chapter Eleven: Alternative Career Paths 221

Appendices

List of Figures

Preface

Introduction

For some time now, the paralegal field has been growing rapidly and that trend is continuing, with the Department of Labor predicting that the profession is expected to grow much faster than the average for all occupations through 2016. Moreover, the value of paralegals to the legal profession is recognized by law firms, government agencies, the American Bar Association, and in numerous court decisions.

With that growth and recognition come additional responsibilities. Today's paralegals are expected to perform a wide variety of tasks and be ready to hit the ground running the instant they start work. Yet there is a significant gap between what is learned in the classroom and the way that knowledge is applied in the real world. Internships help "bridge the gap" and prepare students for their professional careers as paralegals.

Another transition occurs when students leave their internships behind and begin their jobs. The transition between internships and job hunting is a natural one because many of the same tasks and documents are needed. For example, you will need a résumé for both an internship and a job. Similarly, you will need to send cover letters and thank you letters for both internships and jobs. This text combines practical information with a variety of sample writings that pertain to both paralegal internships and job hunting.

The text is divided into three parts. Part I begins with an overview of paralegal internships and discusses the internship experience. Part II covers finding the right job, from revising your internship résumé for permanent employment through interviewing and negotiating a salary for your first job. Part III discusses the workplace, covering what paralegals do in "real life"; the various types of law practice, law firm, and other work environments; career strategies; techniques for success in the workplace; and alternative career paths for those with paralegal training and work experience.

Each chapter and section builds on the previous one. For example, once you understand how to prepare an effective résumé for your internship experience, you will be ready to modify that résumé for permanent employment. Similarly, once you read the information about the law firm environment in Chapter 7, you will understand how to keep your job and advance in your career, both of which are discussed in Chapter 8. The text concludes with pragmatic information on quitting your job, getting your next job, and strategies for success in the workplace.

A Real-World Approach

The book provides pragmatic and realistic information covering situations that occur in the real world of internships and law offices. For example, the following topics are covered:

- How to conduct a self-assessment before your internship experience
- How to make the most of your internship
- What to do if you're either underutilized or overworked during your internship
- How to handle sensitive topics, such as employment gaps in your resume
- Preparing for interviews
- Advocating for yourself in salary negotiations and annual salary reviews
- How and when to quit your job
- Strategies to improve job performance

Features of the Text

The text includes a number of features to enhance your internship experience and to improve your chances of finding suitable permanent employment. Chapters include the following features, as applicable:

- **Chapter Overview.** This chapter-opening section provides a brief introduction to the material to be covered in the chapter.
- **Chapter Summary.** This section, near the end of each chapter, provides a review of the material covered in the chapter and will help you refresh your recollection of the chapter before class.
- **NetWorks.** This list and description of Internet Web sites that provide information relevant to each chapter is included near the end of each chapter.
- **Case Illustration.** Some chapters in Part II and all chapters in Part III include a brief review of a case that illustrates one of the topics discussed in the chapter.
- **Key Terms.** The key terms and words introduced in each chapter appear with brief definitions as margin terms throughout each chapter and then in list form near the end of the chapter. The Key Terms are also collected together in the Glossary at the end of the book.

- **Bits and Bytes.** Chapters include some trivia or "fun" facts that relate to the topics discussed in the chapter.
- **Discussion Questions.** Questions are provided at the end of each chapter to enhance learning and illustrate some of the principles discussed in the chapter.
- **WebWork.** This is the very last section of each chapter and requires readers to access relevant Web sites to obtain information related to the topics discussed in the chapter. Students should use a general Internet search engine, such as Google (www.google.com), and type key words or terms into the search box to be directed to the pertinent site.
- **Figures, Charts, Tips, and Alerts.** Most chapters include useful figures and charts, as well as Practice Tips and Ethics Alerts, to illustrate the topics discussed in the chapter.

Although every effort has been made to refer to useful Web sites, those sites can change both their content and addresses without notice. References to Web sites are not endorsements of those sites.

Final Thoughts

Paralegals play a critical role in helping clients. Be excited about the challenges and opportunities that your internship and permanent employment will provide. Commit yourself to excellence both as an intern and as a practicing paralegal. You will be rewarded not only monetarily but also by knowing that you have performed your job to the best of your abilities.

Deborah E. Bouchoux
Susan M. Sullivan

April 2008

Acknowledgments

We would like to express our sincere appreciation to the many individuals who contributed to the development of this book. The various reviewers who reviewed the manuscript on behalf of the publisher offered instructive and insightful comments and advice. Throughout the combined total of more than 40 years that we have been involved in paralegal education, we have received valuable comments and feedback from our students on the paralegal profession, strategies for success as interns and as practicing paralegals, and the skills and attributes paralegals need to be valued members of the legal team.

Special thanks to Andrea Reedholm, Jennifer Trowbridge, and Gretchen Veihl from the University of San Diego Paralegal Program and Diane Petropulous, former director of the Sonoma State University Program.

Our sincere appreciation to our copyeditor, Julie Nahil, and to the following individuals at Aspen Publishers: Carol McGeehan, Publisher; Richard Mixter, Director, Digital Development; David Herzig, Executive Editor, Paralegal Education; Christine Hannan, Senior Editor; and especially Betsy Kenny, Developmental Editor. Everyone on the Aspen Publishers team offered encouragement and support throughout the writing and production phases of this book. We truly appreciated their thoughtful comments and suggestions, all of which contributed greatly to the text.

We would like to acknowledge the following publishers and legal associations for granting us permission to reproduce copyrighted material for this text:

Figure 6-2: Reprinted with permission. Copyright National Federation of Paralegal Associations, Inc.

Figure 7-2: ®2007 Sage Software, Inc. All rights reserved. Web page from www.timeslips.com is reprinted with permission. TIMESLIPS® is a registered trademark of Sage Software, Inc.

Appendix H: NALA Code of Ethics and Responsibility reprinted with permission. Copyright National Association of Legal Assistants, Inc.; NFPA Model Code of Ethics and Professional Responsibility and Guidelines for Enforcement reprinted with permission. Copyright National Federation of Paralegal Associations, Inc.

Laying the Foundation for a Successful Internship and Career

Chapter 1

Internship and Career Strategies: The Preliminaries

Experience is not what happens to a man; it is what a man does with what happens to him.
—Aldous Huxley

Chapter Overview

Before you embark on any pursuit, you must first consider your goals and then develop a strategy or strategies to achieve them. This is best accomplished by identifying manageable and achievable steps so that you can meet your overall objective. This chapter will provide a framework for you to assess your unique interests, examine your resources, and evaluate specific areas of the law that complement your interests or skills. By carefully analyzing the advantages and disadvantages in a variety of legal specialties, you will expedite your internship search and develop skills to assess opportunities in your geographic area that are most beneficial to you, thus maximizing the benefit of your internship experience.

A. Self-Assessment

1. Clarifying Your Objectives

The first step in setting objectives is to make a formal list. Whether you have 3 or 30 objectives, by writing them down you will clearly identify your goals and be more likely to achieve them. In formulating the list consider these specifics:

- Do you prefer to work in an office or do independent research without direct supervision?

Sole practitioner: An attorney who practices by himself or herself

- Are you able to contribute five hours per week over a long period of time or do you prefer to spend several intense training weeks at your internship?
- Do you envision yourself in a large firm/corporation or with a **sole practitioner**?
- Would you rather be supervised by an attorney, paralegal, or law office administrator?
- What, if any, compensation are you seeking?
- Do you need to acquire specific computer program skills such as Word, WordPerfect, Access, or Excel? Are you proficient using the internet and comfortable working with email?

2. *Evaluating Your Interests*

Fortunately for those pursuing a career in law, there are options for individuals with all kinds of interests:

- Are you particularly attracted to any social issues — for example, environmental causes, children's advocacy, elder care, or immigration?
- Do you enjoy working with people or do you prefer a quiet work space?
- Are you a leader or a follower?
- Are you an observer or an active participant?

Many high schools, adult education centers, community colleges, and career counselors offer standardized testing to determine your personality type, strengths and weaknesses, and skill interests. By taking an inventory of yourself you can better determine objectively where you would best fit in. Libraries and bookstores have numerous publications that can assist you in determining your "fit." Reference librarians can show you the appropriate sections in the library. At the bookstore, ask one of the clerks to direct you to the career or "self-help" section.

3. *Creating Your Personal Inventory*

Everyone has a unique set of skills and experiences. By creating a written inventory of your particular skill set, you can create a clear picture to ensure the best match possible when pursuing an internship.

- Do you speak more than one language?
- Do you have excellent computer skills?
- What types of legal experience do you already have?
- Do you have special certification in specific areas, for example, Notary Public or real estate license?
- Do you have proven writing or organizational skills?

Additionally, you must acknowledge any weaknesses that can preclude certain internship options.

- Is your commute limited by transportation issues?
- Is your schedule restricted by school, work, or family obligations?
- Do you have physical limitations?

If you have special needs, you need to plan in advance how you will approach the internship interviewer, anticipating any requests for equipment or variations in the normal office setting. For example, for a student in a wheelchair, it may be necessary to have additional space in the office or to obtain a special chair. Throughout your work or school experiences, you may have requested special assistance or been accommodated in a variety of ways. Develop a list of any needs and be sure to take them into consideration as you develop your internship plans.

4. *Changing Careers: For Those in Transition*

If you are already established in a career, you are most likely familiar with the steps necessary to secure a position. Don't think of this as "starting over," but instead put yourself in "career advancement" mode. One of the great things about the legal profession is that you can draw a connection from just about any other profession and build on it. In many ways, you are at an advantage because of your familiarity with the workplace.

For career changers this is a good time to make a list of all the transferable skills you have that would be needed in a legal setting. Teachers have excellent organizational, writing, public speaking, and people skills. Nurses have empathy, technical skills, and an ability to work under pressure. Human Resource personnel have knowledge of legal issues related to employment. Insurance personnel are familiar with policies, claims, mediation, and settlements. Escrow assistants know about real estate, title insurance, bank loans, and mortgages. No matter where you have worked, you have developed transferable skills that are highly valued in a law office.

However, you should consider the following:

- What do you really enjoy about your present career?
- What is it about your present career that dissatisfies you?
- What aspects of your current career have involved the legal field?
- Are you willing to take a pay cut or make other sacrifices to facilitate this transition?

5. *Being Realistic*

After you complete your self-assessment, read through it completely. Evaluate how accurately you've answered the questions and set your goals accordingly. The best way to ensure success in your internship and career is to work in an environment that maximizes what you have to offer and satisfies your goals, both personally and professionally. In some cases, law firms and companies do background checks. Government agencies almost always require that you go through their specific screening process. Criminal records may be a deterrent to being approved for internships. Contact your program director or internship coordinator if you have any questions.

B. What You Can Do While You're in School

Whether you're working while attending school or concentrating fully on your education, there are many things you can do to enhance and advance your path to an internship or job.

1. Attitude

We have all heard the old adage, "good luck is when preparation meets opportunity." Proper preparation is the key to your success in finding satisfaction in the opportunities open to you, and having a positive attitude is the first step. Once you've made the decision to attend classes, you must confidently embark on this career and remain positive about the subject matter and its importance in your overall education. For example, your self-assessment may point to an interest in corporate law. Your family law class seems to be of little relevance, but consider that assets divided in a marital dissolution often include business entities or financial issues. Always remember that you are in total control of your attitude. While you have no control over many events and situations that occur, you do have control over your response to those events. Be the person who makes the events work for you instead of against you. Prepare for your own destiny by always taking responsibility for your preparation.

A good attitude begins in the classroom. Get into the positive, cooperative mode by being on time for all classes and being respectful to faculty, administrators, and fellow students. Learn tolerance for other cultures, points of view, and teaching styles. React positively to new ideas, challenges, and situations in your classroom environment. Disagree without being disagreeable. Make up your mind to be positive and work on your attitude. It will become a habit that will serve you well as you begin the steps toward your new profession.

2. Work Ethic

By establishing a good work ethic as you proceed with your studies, you will position yourself with your instructors and classmates as a person of value. Students who study diligently, meet deadlines, and turn in quality work are most likely to receive helpful references when pursuing internships or employment. Furthermore, classmates who may know of opportunities are more likely to share them with someone they think is conscientious and will be dependable.

3. *Knowledge*

Although you will most likely learn far more about the legal profession once you are working in a job or internship, remember that your classes provide the foundation from which you will gain that knowledge. Take advantage of every class, every workshop, and every extracurricular activity offered by the program you're attending. You may even find yourself referring back to class notes or textbooks after you start working! Get in the habit of producing a work product in the classroom that would be acceptable in any legal work environment and that could be used during your job search as a writing sample. Take pride in your work and always do your personal best, no matter what the stakes.

4. *Network*

What better opportunity do you have for finding contacts in the legal field than when you're attending classes taught by legal professionals and when your classmates may also be working in the legal field? If you can, arrive early to class. You will find that advantageous exchanges occur between students who arrive early. Sometimes your professor will also be there. Discussions about classroom assignments and internship/ work experiences provide a forum for opportunities that go unnoticed by those who arrive late and are anxious to be the first to leave. If you are unsure of your particular interests, you may find interacting with experienced professionals will help you pinpoint your goals. Conversely, you may find that your interests change after you meet people who are working in specific areas of law.

C. Who Can Help

1. *Your Paralegal Program Staff*

When you researched your paralegal program, you obtained some knowledge of the program staff and their resources. Most administrators are readily available to students by appointment or "drop-in" hours. Take the time to meet the staff and let them know if you have special interests.

Position yourself as an eager student who is ready to take advantage of every opportunity the program offers. Many programs offer a classroom component to the internship experience. No doubt there are some established formulas and resources available that will be explained at class sessions.

2. *Paralegal Associations*

Paralegal association: Professional organization for individual paralegals—may be local, regional, statewide, or national.

Most major cities have **paralegal associations**. Even while you're a student, you should acquaint yourself with your local paralegal association. Attend sponsored events and meet people who are working in the field. Often, paralegal associations offer continuing education seminars, which may later be required in your state once you are working in a paralegal position. If you are already working in a legal setting, your employer may want you to attend seminars to keep up with changes in the law. The best benefit of paralegal associations is the opportunity to network: to find out about the legal community and opportunities for employment or internships.

3. *Bar Associations*

Bar association: Organization administered by a state; licenses attorneys and provides assistance to its member attorneys and to the public.

Bar associations vary in size and sophistication (many have subcommittees on various areas of law). Call the local bar association in your area and find out if they have a student section. If they do, you may meet attorneys and attend meetings where you can solicit internships. If not, they may refer you to other legal groups or clubs. They can also give you a list of legal clinics and other entities that might welcome interns. Bar associations can also be a resource for giving you the name of the legal newspaper in the community or other publications that advertise for paralegals.

D. Choosing an Internship Setting or Practice Field: The Major Specialty Areas

Once you have completed your self-assessment and set your goals, you will be better able to evaluate the advantages and disadvantages of specialty areas within the legal profession.

The following is a list of many of the legal specialty areas where paralegals work and that you will encounter when considering internship/employment opportunities.

1. *Administrative Law*

Administrative or regulatory law is the body of law created by the rules, laws, regulations, enforcement, and other dictates created by federal, state, and local agencies. Examples of those agencies include:

- Occupational Safety and Health Administration (OSHA)
- Securities and Exchange Commission (SEC)
- Civil Aeronautics Board (CAB)
- Internal Revenue Service (IRS)
- Environmental Protection Agency (EPA)
- Social Security Administration (SSA)
- National Transportation Safety Board (NTSB)
- Federal Trade Commission (FTC)
- United States Patent and Trademark Office (USPTO)

As you can see from the above list, these agency matters cross over into many legal disciplines, including tax, corporate, intellectual property, employment, securities, and environmental law.

Paralegals who are employed in these areas generally work for agencies in the federal, state, or local government sectors. Other paralegals work for private firms, corporations, and companies that interact with these agencies due to their involvement in banking, **copyrights**, utilities, investments, healthcare, or insurance.

The unique aspect of administrative law is that some states allow paralegals to represent clients and appear at administrative hearings. The work is diverse and interesting because it includes:

- Legal research
- Interpreting and analyzing laws and regulations
- Interviewing clients
- Appearances at administrative hearings
- Handling citizen concerns
- Dealing with the public

Copyright:
The exclusive right for a limited amount of time to print, copy, or sell an original work.

2. *Bankruptcy*

Bankruptcies are governed exclusively by federal law and are intended to help a debtor obtain a fresh start and to protect the rights of the debtor's creditors. All bankruptcy matters are heard in bankruptcy courts, which are units of the U.S. district courts. Bankruptcies are initiated by the filing of a voluntary petition (in which case the bankruptcy is initiated by the debtor) or an involuntary petition (in which case the bankruptcy is initiated by creditors). The three most common types of bankruptcies are those filed under Chapters 7, 11, and 13.

In a Chapter 7 proceeding, the debtor has no hope of financial recovery and the debtor's property and most of the debtor's assets are liquidated for the benefit of creditors. A Chapter 11 proceeding is usually referred to as reorganization because the debtor hopes to reorganize its debts and emerge from bankruptcy. A Chapter 13 proceeding allows individuals to adjust and repay their consumer debts. Once a bankruptcy is initiated, the court will appoint a trustee to collect the bankrupt's assets and pay the creditors' claims.

Paralegals involved in the bankruptcy field are very much dealing with finances and business matters. As an intern you may:

- Interview debtors
- Review lists of assets
- File petitions to initiate bankruptcy proceedings
- File notices of claims on behalf of creditors
- Prepare various documents related to bankruptcy matters

3. *Civil Litigation*

Most paralegals work in the litigation field. Civil litigation is such a broad topic that we can almost define it as "anything other than criminal law." It is the process that exists from the time that two people disagree and file a case until it is resolved. Civil litigation overlaps with many other practice areas because a lawsuit, among other issues, may allege breach of contract, patent infringement, or sexual discrimination. Most personal injury and medical malpractice work is litigation-oriented. A person who is injured by the negligence of or medical malpractice by another generally initiates a lawsuit to recover damages for the injury sustained. You may work with individuals filing law suits against neighbors, hospitals, and insurance companies, or you may work with doctors, business entities, or even government agencies defending themselves in unwarranted lawsuits.

Litigation is a very fast-paced environment with strict deadlines and volumes of paperwork, and litigation paralegals often work overtime. As a team player, the paralegal's role in litigation often involves trial preparation, client interaction, and assimilating information from a variety of sources to support a position. Paralegals may find themselves in warehouses sifting through boxes of dusty documents searching for the "missing piece of the puzzle" or a very specific document related to needed evidence. At other times paralegals number, organize, and index hundreds of documents under time constraints and great pressure. The entire process can be slow at times, sometimes testing the paralegal's patience.

Class action:
A lawsuit in which a specific number of people sue on behalf of an entire group.

Some litigation can last several years and involve hundreds of clients, as in the case of **class action** lawsuits. Even after the case goes to trial there can be an appeal process that delays the final outcome. However, there can be a great deal of satisfaction derived once a case is settled or decided by a jury, and it can be very gratifying to help clients win compensation for a wrongdoing. The process can be slow at times, calling for great patience, or it can be so frenzied that it seems like there is never enough time to get the job done.

Paralegals are involved in every stage of the process and can be called upon to:

- Review numerous documents, including medical and business records
- Assist at depositions
- Interview clients and witnesses
- Prepare motions, pleadings, proposed orders, and jury instructions
- Maintain the litigation calendar and note docketing dates for deadlines

4. Contracts

Contract law can be very rewarding for focused individuals who have a superior attention to detail. A contract is a promise that is enforceable in court. The word "agreement" is often used interchangeably with "contract." Attorneys and paralegals are frequently involved in preparing contracts, amending them, and then enforcing them through litigation. A contract may be a complicated agreement of merger between two industry giants, a simple partnership agreement, an employment agreement, or a one-page agreement not to disclose confidential information. Contracts are governed primarily by state **statutes** and case law and can be oral or written.

Statutes: Laws.

This area of law can be very interesting because it impacts all of us personally in many aspects of our life. While contracts can involve everything from corporate mergers and acquisitions to the leasing of commercial stores in large complexes, we as individual consumers are involved in contracts on a daily basis. Think of the times you have bought an appliance, rented an apartment, bought car insurance, agreed with your neighbor to build a fence, or the other times you entered into an agreement with another entity for a service or product. Each of these occurrences involve either a written or verbal contract. Contracts are governed by very specific rules and must contain certain elements. Paralegals are often called upon to review or draft contracts.

Failure to perform one's agreed-upon promise is a breach of contract, for which the law provides various remedies, including monetary damages, specific performance (or an order by a court to perform contractual obligations), **rescission** (or cancellation of a contact), or reformation or correction of a contract to reflect the parties' true intentions.

Rescission: The act of cancelling a contract.

If you work as a paralegal or intern in the field you will be called upon to:

- Draft, review, and proofread various agreements
- Conduct legal research to determine whether various terms may be included in an agreement
- Perform many tasks relating to litigation involving contract disputes

5. Corporate Law

After litigation, corporate work represents the largest specialty practice area for paralegals. According to the American Bar Association (ABA), more than two-thirds of attorneys who practice in the areas of business and corporate law use paralegals. There is tremendous opportunity for substantive work in this field. Although it is a deadline-driven field, corporate paralegals do not have the same trial pressures or the volume of paperwork that litigation paralegals often do and usually do not experience conflict situations on a daily basis.

In addition to forming various business entities, legal professionals maintain the entities by providing ongoing assistance, such as ensuring that annual filings and reports are timely made to the appropriate state agencies, meetings are held, and records are kept in good order. Business entities engage in transactions with each other. One may merge with another and buy another's assets or stocks. Working or interning for a publicly recognized company usually offers a reasonable work schedule and prestige. Work can be interesting because the intern is afforded firsthand knowledge about a client's business strategies, plans, marketing, and vision.

Paralegals involved in business and corporate law engage in the following activities:

- Meet with clients and obtain information so various agreements and filings can be prepared
- Conduct research regarding state and federal regulation of business entities
- File documents with state agencies to create and maintain various business entities to ensure they may transact business in other states
- Prepare stock certificates and maintain corporate stock ledger books
- Prepare notices and agendas for meetings, prepare annual reports, attend meetings, and prepare minutes of meetings
- Draft agreements to be used by business entities (e.g., draft employment contracts for key corporate officers)
- Participate in **due diligence** or review documents for business-related transactions

Due diligence:
A resonable effort to carry out a duty or direction.

6. Criminal Law

Criminal law generally covers all crimes committed by individuals. Paralegals may work for public prosecutors and assist in the prosecution of criminal defendants, or they may assist in criminal defense work, either by working for a public defender's office or for a private law firm devoted to criminal defense work. Most of the firms that employ paralegals or accept interns in this area of law are small- to medium-sized firms. Large firms generally refer out their criminal work or handle only very minor problems for their clients. The proliferation of television and crime shows has resulted in an increased interest in this area of law.

There are criminal law positions at the city, county, state, and federal levels. Paralegals conduct investigations, perform legal research, draft documents, assist at trial, and help with the appeal process, if necessary. Those who work in this field must have good people and interviewing skills. Often the cases go to trial and, with some variation, the paralegal will perform many of the same tasks as a civil litigation paralegal. As indicated above, paralegals who want to intern in a government office may have to undergo a background check.

Those working in this field have a choice of defense or prosecution and may do the following, depending on their choice:

a. **Defense**

- Review police and prosecutor reports
- Interview clients for factual information
- Organize files and evidence for trial
- Research and draft post-trial motions and appeals
- Obtain witness statements and relay bail information

b. **Prosecution**

- Conduct criminal investigations and interview witnesses
- Assist crime victims by referring them to the appropriate agencies
- Draft complaints and reports and prepare subpoenas
- Catalog and prepare exhibits for trial
- Act as a liaison among victims, law enforcement departments, and the prosecutor's office

7. *Elder Law*

Due to the "baby boomers," elder law has become an especially popular field, and the need for experienced legal professionals in this area will continue to increase as our society ages. The elderly face very complex issues, including medical insurance, living wills, Social Security benefits, conservatorships, Medicare and Medicaid, estate planning, insurance issues, long-term health care, financial planning, and retirement home contracts. Individuals who deal with the elderly must be especially sensitive to both family and individual needs and have good communication skills that convey a sense of caring.

The above description points out the various areas of law that could intersect in the elder law field. Some of those areas include litigation, real estate, criminal law, estates, trusts and wills, healthcare, insurance, contracts, and administrative law. Some prosecutors' offices now house special units that deal with elder care and abuse because of the increasing potential for criminal activity. A paralegal in those special prosecutor's units would routinely:

- Act as an advocate for the elderly at administrative hearings
- Confer with family members, health care professionals, and providers
- Be knowledgeable about administrative agencies and requirements
- Have the ability to explain complex issues to elderly clients
- Draft correspondence, make phone calls, and gather information about sensitive legal issues

8. *Employment and Labor Law*

The field of labor and employment law covers an array of employer-employee relations, including employee benefits (such as grants of stock options and employee retirement and pension plans), formation and termination of the employment relationship, claims of discrimination or retaliation by employees, sexual harassment, health care, and workers' compensation matters. Generally, law firms engaged in employment law represent either employees or employers, but not both. Paralegals may also interact with various federal agencies, such as the Equal Employment Opportunity Commission or the Department of Labor, and with state agencies as well.

There are now more opportunities in this area of law due to new federal and state laws that have been enacted to protect workers. While we have traditionally thought of employment law as strictly a human resource issue—dealing with hirings and firings and benefits—there are actually multiple opportunities for internships and employment in this area. Employment law covers working conditions, minimum age for working, discrimination issues in hiring and promotion, minimum wages, overtime pay, safety standards, unions, civil rights, workers' compensation, pension plans, benefits, and sexual harassment. Interns can assist with tasks that involve litigation, insurance claims, administrative law, and mediation; they can work in law firms, corporations, banks, and government agencies.

Employment and labor law interns can expect to do the following:

- Conduct legal research on labor law
- Review policy manuals and contracts for employers
- Inform clients on procedures involving administrative agencies
- Prepare litigation documents for lawsuits involving discrimination or other employment related issues
- Assist business clients with information on compliance issues

9. *Estate Planning, Wills, and Trusts*

When we think of an "estate," we often conjure up an image of millionaire holdings, multiple properties, and a grand inheritance. In fact, estate planning is the general term used to describe the way in which a person plans for the disposal of his or her property upon death. A **will** lays out the details of estate disposition, while a **trust** provides for the handling and disposition of property, either during a person's lifetime or after death. **Probate** refers to the court-supervised process of ensuring that a decedent's will is valid and that the decedent's estate is properly administered. Thus, because they are interrelated, the fields of estate planning, wills, and trusts are usually grouped together as one specialty field.

While a person may plan for distribution of his or her property with a will, there is more to estate planning than merely drafting a will and putting it in a safety deposit box. Individuals may use trusts and outright gifts as a means of distributing their assets to others. Paralegals who assist in estate planning often assist clients in gathering financial information, work with accountants, prepare tax calculations, and draft wills and different kinds of trusts. Each state has strict requirements for the contents and execution of wills and imposes guidelines for trusts.

Before working as an intern in this area, it is good to think carefully about the emotional impact this area of law can sometimes have on you. You will have the satisfaction of knowing you can handle the majority of the tasks involved in this area of law and get gratification from helping those in a time of need. However, this can also be very emotional for clients, so it is best to go back to your self-assessment and make sure you are equipped to handle situations that may be very sad and at times confrontational among family members.

With the exception of providing legal advice, paralegals can and do perform almost every task involved in wills, trusts, and estate planning, including the following:

- Drafting wills and codicils to wills
- Filing documents for probate of wills and supervising the probate process
- Preparing an inventory and appraisal of decedent's assets and estate
- Drafting declarations of trust and coordinating transfer of assets into trust
- Preparing and filing various tax returns
- Distributing trust assets to trust beneficiaries

Will:
A document that lays out the details of estate disposition.

Trust:
A document that provides for the handling and disposition of property, either during a person's lifetime or after death.

Probate:
The settlement of an estate.

10. *Family Law*

An intensely personal field, family law often concerns individuals at their lowest moments. However, there are also a few bright spots, such as finalizing adoptions and assisting couples with prenuptial agreements. The practice of family law includes activities related to marriage, divorce, child custody, spousal and child support, adoption, and juvenile law. In some cases, the activities are similar to those in litigation because a divorce or dissolution of a marriage is begun by the filing of a petition in court and a trial may be held (although there is no jury trial in such actions). Similarly, court matters involving juveniles sometimes share some things in common with criminal proceedings. Thus, there is overlap between family law and other practice specialties.

Family law is an interesting and challenging field, with a number of emerging issues, such as those relating to same-sex couples and grandparent visitation rights. But there can also be a significant amount of stress because clients are often highly emotional over the dissolution of their marriage, juvenile delinquency actions involving their children, or the difficulties inherent in the adoption process. Family law paralegals must be patient and understanding of their clients while maintaining their professionalism and integrity. Because you will interact with clients on an intensely personal level, you must be mindful of protecting your client's confidentiality and separating emotion from fact.

Some of the activities family law paralegals engage in are as follows:

- Preparing prenuptial agreements
- Obtaining background information from clients relating to income, assets, support, employment, and so forth to prepare for hearings relating to custody and support issues
- Drafting legal separation agreements and petitions for dissolution of marriage
- Preparing requests for temporary restraining orders
- Calculating support payments
- Assisting in enforcement of court orders relating to custody, visitation, and child and spousal support
- Assisting in preparing for and attending juvenile delinquency and dependency hearings

11. Immigration

An increasing number of paralegals now work in the immigration field in law firms, corporations, or legal clinics. The number of immigrants has increased in recent years and so has the need for services among immigrant groups. While we often think of port or border cities, such as New York, San Diego, Los Angeles, and Miami, as the only opportunities for employment in this area, immigrant groups are now flourishing in many midwestern and other centrally located cities. Legislation is now being considered that could have far reaching effects on the need for professionals in this area.

Some firms have immigration paralegals who work with in-house counsel in large international corporations. Their job is often to secure the proper paperwork to allow highly skilled professionals, such as scientists, doctors and educators, to enter the United States to work for short or extended periods of time. In other instances, firms specialize in or handle immigration issues as part of their services. Legal clinics are especially in need of those who are bilingual and understand cultural differences among various ethnic groups. This area of law also overlaps with administrative, family, international, criminal, employment, and labor law.

While there is much paperwork involved in this field, it is also a very people-oriented experience for interns who can expect to:

- Assist clients in filling out applications for visas or work permits
- Disseminate information on how to become a U.S. citizen
- Explain government and administrative agency benefits
- Prepare paperwork for deportation hearings
- Refer clients to foreign consulates or ethnic advocacy groups that can assist with government processes
- Translate documents

12. *Intellectual Property*

The field of intellectual property (IP) comprises four related fields: trademarks (protecting designs, logos, and slogans), copyrights (protecting original works of authorships such as books and music), patents (protecting new and useful inventions), and trade secrets (protecting confidential business information). Trained paralegals in this area are in great demand, especially in larger cities. Some paralegal and continuing education programs provide certificates for those who are interested in this field. According to a National Association of Legal Assistants (NALA) Survey, paralegals who spent more than 40 percent of their time working in the IP field earned approximately 36 percent more than the average annual compensation. Working on IP projects is interesting and creative and often provides an opportunity for close client contact while learning about a client's business goals and strategies.

Paralegals play a significant role in the IP practice areas and can expect to:

- Conduct trademark and patent searches
- File applications for trademark, copyright, and patent registrations and monitor those applications
- Work with foreign clients and attorneys to obtain U.S. protection of IP rights
- Prepare ancillary documents, such as IP license and assignment agreements

13. *Real Estate*

Because almost everyone in their lifetime encounters a real estate transaction—whether selling or purchasing a home, renting a home, or inheriting real property—you may find this area of law interesting from a personal perspective. The term *real property* (or real estate) refers to land and is distinguished from personal property, the area of the law dealing with tangible items (such as jewelry, cars, and rare coins), and intellectual property, the area of the law dealing with the fruits of creative endeavors, such as trademarks, copyrights, and patents.

Most real estate cases deal with one of the following issues: acquisition or sale of real property (whether for residential or commercial purposes), matters relating to financing of real property, cases relating to landlord-tenant relations, litigation in which real property is involved, or corporate transactions involving real property. Thus, there is some overlap with other areas of law. For example, a corporation that buys real estate will need to have a board of directors meeting to discuss and authorize the purchase, and minutes of the meeting will need to be prepared. Work in the real estate area of law can be intensive and challenging, as well as providing knowledge for your own personal transactions. It is a very document-intensive and deadline-driven field.

Paralegals play significant roles in real estate matters and are engaged in the following tasks:

Lien: A claim against property for settlement of a debt.

- Conducting searches of public records to verify the chain of title and to ensure property is not subject to **liens** and encumbrances
- Coordinating closings — preparing a checklist for real estate closings, attending closings, and preparing closing binders with all relevant documents
- Drafting and reviewing leases, subleases, and assignments of leases
- Preparing notices for landlords and tenants, such as default in rent, eviction notices for landlords, and breach of contracts for tenants
- Assisting in litigation by drafting complaints for unlawful detainer or breach of lease

14. *Other Internships and Opportunities for Paralegals*

a. Private Sector Jobs

Challenge yourself to think of a job where legal knowledge is *not* an asset. You will be hard-pressed to find one! Even those working in manual labor positions are responsible for contracts, quality work product, and honoring the terms of their employment. Individuals with legal or paralegal training have qualifications to work in jobs that may not be classified specifically as paralegal or legal assistant positions. One of the greatest things about the profession has been the expansion of job availability and possibilities for those who complete a paralegal program. Years ago, paralegals only worked in law firms. Now, the creativity of college curricula and acceptance of the profession by attorneys has afforded graduates opportunities in many more areas. Human resource departments hire paralegals to work on employment issues. Banks hire paralegals to be compliance officers, and title insurance companies hire paralegals to search for and maintain legal documents. Those with excellent computer skills may work for large corporations or companies that are required by law to preserve and catalog numerous documents. Companies hire contract specialists. After years of experience, paralegals may have an opportunity to be paralegal and law office managers. The list is virtually endless. Always remember the adage: "Wherever there is an attorney, there is the potential for a paralegal."

While paralegals may not give legal advice, they can contract their services to attorneys or companies on either a short-term or a long-term basis. Independent, or "freelance," paralegals often create a thriving business where they set their own hours and income according to their abilities and their clients' needs. Paralegals working in an independent capacity will always be under the supervision of an attorney because they will be given specific tasks to do and the attorney will always approve the work. Freelance opportunities are primarily available to very experienced paralegals who have years of experience in a specific field of law. Like attorneys, they build up their reputation and can find themselves turning down work because they are so busy. The ability to pick and choose when, where, and on what cases they work, and the ability to control workflow, is a bonus for those who seek a measure of independence.

b.   Public Sector Jobs

The government is one of the larger employers of paralegals, but it is difficult to quantify the number of paralegals working in government jobs due to inconsistent and varying job titles. As you are looking for jobs be sure to read job descriptions. Oftentimes, you will find titles such as legal analyst, investigative assistant, junior paralegal, contracts analyst, compliance assistant, or case assistant. Your paralegal training will qualify you for the majority of these jobs because they all require knowledge of legal terminology, the court system, legal research and writing skills, communication skills, and a procedural knowledge of certain areas of law.

Never forget that there are many levels of government even within your own geographic location. Many government offices have formalized internship programs and often coordinate them with local colleges. Checking into government internship programs early in your educational career is a must because government internships often require a longer commitment in terms of the specific number of hours. They may also require a certain number of credits completed, and usually require a lengthy background check.

The U.S. Attorney's Office handles federal issues such as immigration and illegal drugs cases; the Attorneys General's Office handles both civil and criminal matters for each specific state; the District Attorney's Office handles mostly criminal but some civil issues for the county; while the City Attorney's Office may handle less serious criminal matters and their attorneys represent the city in many legal matters. The names of these agencies vary from city to city and state to state. Look in the government section of your phone book for contact information, or call one of the government legal offices to get clarification on the particular structure in your geographic location.

E. Market Assessment

As in any career, it is best to take a step back and objectively evaluate the reality and potential for paralegal employment in your area. By doing this early in your paralegal program experience you will not only get an idea of what to consider when you graduate, but you will also become knowledgeable about the opportunities for internship placements. Start with your own paralegal program and professional associations in your area. Does your program have statistics on the number of students who are placed, the areas in which they work, and the number of jobs that are called into their career center? Have they done surveys to determine compensation, working conditions, and areas of law where the graduates are placed? Are they willing to share that information with you? Does the association have career or survey information?

Make a list of all the jobs that are advertised in local and legal newspapers and publications. What are the areas of law that most of the job ads mention? What experience do they want? Where are the jobs located? Some students have actually called firms that were advertising positions and volunteered to do an internship.

Contact any temporary legal placement agency. Ask the staff questions about the number of positions available, salaries, and areas of law most in demand. Many firms use agencies as a screening device for employees, as a way to "test out" an employee without making a commitment to permanency or benefits until they are sure it is a good fit. Ask what kind of organizational and legal skills are required and especially what kind of computer skills firms are looking for.

Network, network, network. There is a theory that only 10 percent of the jobs that are available are ever advertised. That leaves 90 percent waiting to be discovered. This is often referred to as the "hidden job market." Many positions are filled because of personal contacts. Faculty positions at paralegal schools are often filled by someone a faculty member knows who is interested in teaching a course. Anyone you know who works in the legal field — whether it is an attorney, legal secretary, paralegal, or human resource manager — is usually willing to spend some time talking with you or to give you contacts. Arrange for an informational interview. This involves calling the contact, indicating that you would like just 20 minutes of their time to discuss the legal field and to get their impressions of paralegal careers. Most people in the field remember a time when they too needed guidance and are very willing to help.

F. Determining Marketing Trends

Many of the strategies listed above will you help you assess local market trends. Keep lists and make notes as you pursue the above ideas. But, in order to understand marketing trends in a broader sense, you should also contact your local and state paralegal associations. Many of them do surveys of their members that will give you a broader view of the legal community in your area. On a national level, the National Association of Legal Assistants (NALA), the National Federation of Paralegal Associations (NFPA), the American Association for Paralegal Education (AAfPE), the International Paralegal Managers Association (IPMA), and the Association for Legal Professionals (NALS) all have publications and information available on trends in the paralegal field. *Legal Assistant Today* has articles that are of interest to paralegals and offers a student subscription rate.

G.   Some Strategies for Beginners

- In order to have a successful and satisfying internship, several things are important. You must have written and well thought out goals and objectives. Think about your own strengths and weakness, likes and dislikes, and particular personality traits. Explore and read about different areas of law and educate yourself about the possibilities in your own geographic location. Talk to as many people in the legal field as possible, starting with your own program administrators and practicing attorneys or paralegals. Do Internet research to help you find contacts in law firms, corporations, banks, companies, and government agencies. Once you have developed your lists and done your research, you will be ready for your internship and the beginning of your career. Explore the various areas of law and match up your personality, skills, and future plans with the different environments and settings.
- Assess the local market by interviewing those in the legal field and reading any literature that pertains to your geographic location.

NetWorks

www.nala.org	The National Association of Legal Assistants site provides general information about the paralegal profession and resources for those interested in pursuing a paralegal career.
www.paralegals.org	The National Federation of Paralegal Associations site has information about careers, employment, ethics, and other related paralegal information.
www.abanet.org/ careercounsel/home.html	The ABA site offers tips on finding jobs and information on legal internships. Articles related to career planning and success in the workplace are also provided.
www.careerpath.com	Careerpath.com offers self-assessment testing, career guidance resources, and other helpful tools to assist in making a career decision.

In addition to the above, each city or geographic region has legal newspapers and paralegal associations that have Web sites.

Chapter Summary

- Think about your internship pursuits and begin the process by clarifying your objectives and evaluating your personality and interests.
- Create a personal inventory of skills and possibilities.
- Decide what you like and dislike about your current situation and what you would like to continue or change.
- Concentrate on what you can do now to get ready for the experience.
- Make a list of all those who can help you reach your goals.

Key Terms

Sole practitioner: An attorney who practices by himself or herself.

Paralegal association: Professional organization for individual paralegals — may be local, regional, statewide, or national.

Bar association: Organization administered by a state; licenses attorneys and provides assistance to its member attorneys and to the public.

Copyright: The exclusive right for a limited amount of time to print, copy, or sell an original work.

Class action: A lawsuit in which a specific number of people sue on behalf of an entire group.

Statutes: Laws.

Rescission: The act of cancelling a contract.

Due diligence: A reasonable effort to carry out a duty or direction.

Will: A document that lays out the details of estate disposition.

Trust: A document that provides for the handling and disposition of property, either during a person's lifetime or after death.

Probate: The settlement of an estate.

Intellectual property: The fruits of creative endeavors, such as trademarks, copyrights, and patents.

Liens: A claim against property for settlement of a debt.

Bits and Bytes

- According the U.S. Department of Labor, Bureau of Labor Statistics, about seven out of ten paralegals and legal assistants work for law firms; others work for corporate legal departments and government agencies.

- Many nonprofit and community-based organizations have legal volunteer and internship positions available.

- Within the federal government, the Department of Justice is the largest employer, followed by the Social Security Administration and the Department of the Treasury.

Discussion Questions

1. You have decided to pursue a paralegal internship but are unsure of the area of law in which you are interested. What steps would you take to help decide what kind of law, and what kind of firm you should look at?

2. List all possible sources of internships and then discuss how you will pursue the people or items on your list.

3. What qualities have you acquired during your studies that will be applicable to your internship experience?

4. You are an intern working in a real estate office. In what ways could your basic knowledge of other areas of law be beneficial?

WebWork

1. Go to www.careerpath.com and complete the personal assessment.

   a. What are your interests and style results?
   b. Do you generally agree with these results?
   c. Which area of law do you think would most benefit your interests and style?

Internships:
Setting the Stage

*Sow a thought and reap an action. Sow an action and
reap a habit. Sow a habit and reap character.
Sow character and reap destiny.*
—William Thackeray

Chapter Overview

This chapter provides insight on how to structure your internship and put
in place a framework that will result in a successful experience. Just as an
astronaut does not launch into space without months and years of careful
training and preparation, neither should you launch your legal career
without carefully laying the foundation. Initially you should focus on
the purpose and scope of the internship. You will want to get advice
and ideas on how to accomplish this goal. Directors, faculty, and those
you know who have a connection to the legal field can all be sources of
information and guidance. We will discuss school-sponsored and self-
initiated internships, compensation options, and the various settings
available. Additionally, there are options outside the scope of a structured
internship, and you may find these opportunities quite valuable both
during and after you leave a formalized training program.

This is a good time to go back to review your self-assessment and the
inventory of your strengths and interests to determine what environment
is best for you. If you live in a larger city you will have more choices than if
you live in a rural setting. If you live in a rural setting, there are still many
possibilities. Stop to think and make an inventory of all the attorneys and
businesses that have law-related matters. Take a look at the yellow pages,
starting with attorney and then paging through headings such as real
estate, environmental, escrow, legal clinics, and the like. No matter
what your environment, opportunities are there if you do the research
and explore all avenues available to you.

A. Purpose and Scope of Internships

The internship experience is meant to give you exposure to the legal field — a taste of the possibilities. It is a chance to experience for yourself what the books are explaining or what teachers and other paralegals have described to you.

The internship experience will result in valuable contacts, concrete experiences to put on a résumé, and prepare you for interviews for paid positions in the future. You will have an opportunity to gain practical experience in an area of law you learned about in a class or possibly in another area that you touched upon in an introductory class or may later take as an elective or continuing education course. More importantly, it is a test to see how your personality meshes with those already in the legal field or to determine if your perception of the field is accurate. It is an opportunity to experience the legal setting as opposed to other professional fields or jobs that you may have worked in.

Within the last 20 years in the higher education field, internships have become more and more popular. There are many reasons for this. Job markets in specific areas are often flooded and any kind of experience gives you a foot in the door ahead of those who have no experience in the field. It gives you a preview of what you will actually be doing in the field prior to making a permanent commitment to a job.

Within several fields, including the legal field, there are many avenues to explore and these can expand or narrow your focus. Reading books, doing practical assignments, and taking exams and quizzes is a must in preparation for your degree or certificate but actually getting out into the world and putting that reading and knowledge to work is what will give you the experience so many employers are looking for. In a sense, this is your practice period. Some of the benefits of internships include:

- Allowing you to try different tasks without the worry of failure.
- Giving you contacts and something concrete to put on a résumé
- Enabling you to sound knowledgeable and to give concrete examples of specific tasks in a area of law when you are interviewing for a job
- Developing a relationship with a mentor in the field
- Giving you the chance to ask questions and practice what you will need to do in a job
- Providing an opportunity to network and to obtain contacts for future employment opportunities
- Letting you find out how your personality meshes with other types of personalities
- Performing in a real-world setting some of the things you may have only done as part of your class assignments or read about in a textbook
- Showcasing your skills, personality, and attitude

Most potential students are eager to participate in internships and may choose a particular program based on whether or not internships are available. There can be some disappointments when the actual internship starts. You may feel that you can't contribute much to the firm or company. Internship supervisors understand that you are starting out in the profession and they know there will be a lot of training involved. A good internship often provides more instruction than you provide work. Remember that your employer understands that you are a novice and that there will be a learning curve. Be patient with them and they will be patient with you. A good internship is a two-way street with give and take, and questions and answers. You should come away from an internship with a better understanding of how your classroom learning experience relates to the workplace but certainly not an understanding of all the possible applications. That is a lifelong experience.

B. School-Sponsored Internships

Internships vary in length so it is a good idea to understand the total number of hours you will be required to work and take into account your current work and school schedule. Some internships last for one semester while others can be completed over the course of several semesters. Remember that you will be putting in a lot more time for the credit you get than you would for a regular class. A three semester credit or unit class will require you to put in 42 to 45 hours of time in the classroom, but internships require three times the number of hours. So, for a three credit internship you are required to put in 135 hours. The rationale for this is that if you were taking a course you would have outside reading assignments and studying, all of which normally adds up to 135 hours. Check with your program director for specifics, as colleges' internship requirements vary.

It is a good idea to start thinking about your internship at the beginning of any program. This will give you time to see what you like, assess your personal preferences, where your interests lie, and start making plans for the end of the program. In most programs you do the internship toward the end of the program. You are better qualified through experience and knowledge and are closer to graduating. An internship can provide you with an opportunity to produce writing samples and a work product that you may share on an interview for a paralegal job.

Many institutions sponsor internships in one of two ways. One is to assign you to a specific internship site and the other is to offer you a list of potential internship sites, from which you choose after having a chance to explore each one. Let's first consider the assigned internship.

a. Assigned Internships

There are many good reasons for assigning internships. Assigned internships have already been evaluated by a program representative. This means that the intern supervisor understands the standards of the program, including the number of hours, working conditions, student schedules, expectations for job assignments, reporting procedures, and the assessment or evaluation process. Most likely, someone from the college has visited with the internship supervisor, seen the environment and work station, and discussed the types of duties that would be acceptable to the college for the student to receive credit. Your program representative will have explained the evaluation process deadlines and procedures, and the types of students in the program and will have listened to the firms' needs both in terms personality, skills, schedule, and academic standing. In other words, they are ready for you.

In the assigned internship, it is unlikely there will be surprises either for you or for the internship site. In many cases they will already have had student interns. That gives you the advantage of the firm understanding your program's curriculum and its students' potential. Either the program director or another administrator will be able to place you according to your background, academic ability, and interests. Many internships possibilities are the result of previous students getting a job at a firm or corporation and then volunteering to take an intern because they remember being a student who was searching for the "right fit" internship. These graduates also understand the apprehension students often experience and try to provide a comfort level that is conducive to a successful internship for all parties.

Be sure to consult with the internship coordinator or appropriate administrator prior to starting the internship to see if they have any suggestions and can tell you a little more about the environment, personality of the supervisor, and recent job duties. It is good to let the coordinator know if you have special interests or did particularly well in one of your classes. Remember they are choosing for you but you should try to assist in that process. Remind them if you have previous experience in the legal field or any other transferable skills that might help them choose the right internship placement for you. If you are an English major, perhaps there are internships that require drafting documents, writing memorandums, or doing legal research. You could be asked to write interrogatories (questions) that will be asked of a witness in a personal injury case. Perhaps you will research an issue in employment law on overtime laws and write a memo to your attorney about your findings. If you are a former social worker, a firm that handles cases involving contact with people, such as family law, could be a good fit. If you worked at a company that handles business matters, an internship where you may be reviewing contracts or drafting articles of incorporation would be appropriate.

b. Selecting an Internship

When it comes to finding your own internship, some colleges have a book of potential internships that students can review in order to select an internship for themselves. It may include sites that other students have enjoyed or firms, companies, government agencies, or other sites that have made contact with the college. Selecting an internship in this way can be a longer process and involve interviewing with people at several sites, so it is necessary to plan accordingly and get started early. Check with the program coordinator to see if you can talk to students who did an internship at a particular site or if they are familiar with the type of law the firm practices. In pursuing this type of internship, keep the following in mind:

- Start your calls early and arrange to meet with the supervisor.
- Be ready to ask good questions about the working environment, areas of law, supervision, expectations, dress code and hours.
- Clearly express your goals and relay your interests.
- Write down questions or follow up with a phone call so you have a clear understanding of what to expect.

You may also be required to set up and find your own internship. There are several strategies you can use to make this process easier:

- Check first with program director and find out if there are any sources you can use to get you started.
- Check the want ads for leads.
- Ask to speak to past graduates who are now working in legal settings to see if they might be willing to mentor you.
- Join a paralegal association as a student and start networking. Ask around to find out if any of the members know about a site or are willing to assist you by mentoring you at their own place of employment.
- Research firms or companies that are hiring or have part-time positions available and are willing to take on a volunteer.
- Call local paralegal associations and bar associations to find out if they can give you any leads on clinics, which are often in need of volunteers because of a lack of funding.
- Make a list of everyone and anyone you know who works in the legal field. Make some calls to find a site. You will find that law students, other paralegal students, friends, and neighbors often have at least one name they can give you.

In general, that first phone call can be awkward, but you will find that it rapidly gets easier, with one name leading to another, and so on. Keep track of your contacts and have a system for recording your conversations and email interactions.

C. Compensation Issues

Most internships during college result in credits. This means that you will be getting academic semester or quarter credit depending on the number of hours you work. This also means you do not get paid for doing the internship. The most important thing to remember is that you are getting experience, making contacts, and developing marketable skills outside the classroom, all of which will give you an edge when you pursue your career. The majority of programs have unpaid internships because you are getting an in-kind reward (credit). It is always helpful to have the credit on your transcript as a permanent acknowledgment of what you did as part of your academic career. Those who are diligent and work hard will be rewarded with a good grade, which will be figured into their grade point average. Because students have so much control over their work product during an internship and if they put in a good effort and have a positive attitude, the grades for internships tend to be higher than they are for other courses where students are tested or produce practical assignments. Internship supervisors are appreciative of the intern's efforts and usually want to reward them, if not with money, then with a good grade to acknowledge their efforts.

However, there are some situations where the firm requires that you be paid. Be sure to check ahead of time so you have a clear understanding of the policies of the firm or college. There are federal laws that govern credit or pay for internships. Check into the policies and culture or practices in your area before making a commitment to an internship site. Oftentimes, internships that are paid are in government agencies where

Work-study: Academic program that enables students to gain related work experience and get academic credit while continuing their studies.

more formal **work-study** programs exist. These programs generally require verification of attendance at a college and a commitment of longer than the total number of credits the college may require for course credit. Many internships continue over two semesters and can require up to 20 hours of student work per week. Depending on your situation, you may want to make the longer commitment of time than is required for the credit-only internships.

D.   Internship Settings

Law firm settings provide the majority of opportunities for students seeking internships. Go back to Chapter 1 and review the different areas of law practiced and you will understand why there are endless opportunities. As the paralegal profession develops, there are many more opportunities for paralegals because of the education of the public and legal professionals about the value of paralegal interns. Paralegals work any place there is an attorney, which includes banks, corporations, health care facilities, colleges, government agencies, clinics, nonprofit agencies and other nontraditional settings.

In law firms, there are structures that vary depending on the size and type of law practiced.

1. *Sole practitioners* often have limited support staff and practice in a variety of areas. You may be supervised by a legal secretary or the attorney. The setting is usually more informal and provides more

flexibility in hours and experiences. This can give you an opportunity to do a wider variety of tasks.

2. *Large firms* may be very compartmentalized and offer opportunities to go from one practice section to another. Or you may be assigned to just one area of law. You could work with several people including a wide variety of support staff, such as paralegals, legal secretaries, law students, or clerks, and many different attorneys.

3. *Corporate settings* include places such as a large corporation, your local community hospital, or a small technology company. Legal departments exist within the company and are a separate entity from the rest of the support staff. The work may vary from law firms because the primary focus is corporate matters.

4. *Government agencies* offer internship opportunities at several levels. In larger cities, there are usually city, county, state, and federal entities that employ attorneys and paralegals. For those interested in criminal law, these settings provide golden opportunities The one thing to remember is that most government offices and agencies require background checks and so the lead time to getting started at a government site is longer. Background checks include an investigation into criminal and financial issues. This can take as long as several months depending on the agency's workload. If this site interests you, plan on getting a good head start on the process.

Again, as with any search, do not underestimate the yellow pages. Go through the different categories listed alphabetically and try to imagine whether the businesses listed ever have legal issues or would deal with attorneys, government agencies, or legal professionals. Match the places to the legal substantive law areas listed in Chapter 1.

E. What to Do if Your Program Does Not Offer an Internship

If your college does not offer organized placement in internships or traditional internship opportunities, consider blazing your own trail into the legal field. Directors often tell students who do not have any legal experience and worry about competing with those who do, to start working in a law firm or legal setting as soon as they begin the program. There are always the stories of those in any field who started in the mail room and worked their way up to be CEO of a company. While that might not be your ultimate goal, the take-away message is the same: It is always advantageous to have some law-related work on a résumé, no matter what your overall career goal.

Remember that it is impossible to be in a setting and not absorb some of what is going on around you. Even if you are the copying clerk in a law firm, you will become familiar with documents, procedures, clients, and the workings of the firm. Take every opportunity offered to you and do not discount what you might consider to be menial tasks. Anyone who carries out menial tasks well generally has a good attitude and is often shown appreciation by then being given more substantial work and tasks. Look at it as the "means to an end." Firms recognize efficiency, good attitudes, a good work ethic, and a willingness to get the job done. More often than not, learning from the bottom up can be more valuable than any book learning or the ability to perform well on a test.

1. **Volunteering can give you an extra edge,** help you assess your capabilities, and put you on the road to employment. Call the local bar association and ask for the names of legal volunteer organizations in your area. There is always some organization looking for extra help and those places can often be the setting for valuable hands-on experience as they are often short-staffed and under-funded. Interns get to interview clients, experience varied areas of law, and do more substantive work because of the great need for help.

Shadowing:
The act of following another person around with the intent of gaining knowledge about his or her job or duties.

2. **Shadowing is a newer concept that means following someone else as he or she performs a job.** First, you need to find a person willing to let you do this. You might try the following to find a shadowing opportunity:

- Call local paralegal associations and ask for a mentor or someone you can talk to.
- Call local colleges or universities that have paralegal programs and ask if you can have the name of a graduate who would be willing to talk to you.
- Call anyone and everyone you know who works in the legal field and ask for an informational interview. This means that you will ask them to spend a short amount of time with you and talk to you about the field. After you meet with them, you can ask for just one contact to help you achieve your goal.
- Everyone knows someone in the legal field and most people are very willing to help because they have been in your position — just starting out in a field — or have a relative who has and needed someone to help them along the way.

F.   Preparing for the Internship

As you embark on the internship process there are some very practical things you need to consider:

- Do I have a copy of my résumé?
- Do I have directions to where I am going?
- Have I thought about parking?
- Who should I ask to see?
- Am I appropriately dressed?
- Do I have a positive attitude?

- Am I ready to begin my journey?
- Have I adequately prepared myself for the interview?

While all of the above are very obvious issues, it is sometimes the very basics that we forget. Take a little time to think about the obvious. While Chapter 3 will deal with preparing a résumé, always remember to bring extra copies with you to any interview. The interviewer may have misplaced it or perhaps several people will be interviewing you. You look organized and thoughtful if you have additional copies so no one has to make copies for other interviewers.

Just as you would for a permanent job, take the time to go down to the internship site and find your way around the area and the building. Observe what people are wearing. Check out the elevator situation and determine if different elevators get you to different floors. This will make you less nervous and anxious the day of the interview. Go to mapquest.com or another Web site to get directions to the internship site. You can also call and ask whoever answers the phone for directions. Allow for plenty of time to get there. Mapquest will give you an approximation of the time from your address to the site, but add on time for traffic or making wrong turns as you follow the directions.

Parking in larger metropolitan areas can be expensive and spaces fill up quickly. When you do your test run, look around for parking lots, find out the cost. If lots are full find alternative locations. If you will use parking meters, get the appropriate change and observe signs to determine how long parking is allowed. There is nothing worse than the stress of looking for parking, not having the money to redeem your car, or worrying about getting a ticket while you are trying to make a good impression and are already nervous about the first interview.

Be sure you have the correct spelling of the name of the person you will be seeing, as well as the exact location of the person's office. Large firms often have many floors in a single building, and going to the wrong floor wastes time and could make you late. Arrive a few minutes early but never late. Be polite to receptionists. Someone once noted that oftentimes the most powerful people in law firms, and sometimes the decision makers, are the support staff. A receptionist may later relay to the managing partner or supervisor your demeanor, whether it was positive or negative. If there are many candidates to choose from, it may be the receptionist who gives the final word on whom to hire or accept.

Remember that for every placement, the most important thing is not always grades or education but attitude. Those who hire and accept interns uniformly agree that if applicants have all of the desirable qualities on paper but cannot get along with people or are difficult to work with they will be of no value to the firm or company. If you come across as being negative or complain about the weather or your program, it is likely it will get worse once you are working there. Interviewers presume you are always at your best when you interview, so anything less than close to perfection will fall short.

Take a good look in the mirror and then have someone else give you an opinion. Are you dressed appropriately for the interview? Remember that you are entering a conservative profession where many workers follow dress codes provided by the establishment. Until you know differently, dress as though you were interviewing for the most formal firm or company that you can think of. Trendy clothes, shoes, and hairdos — as well as personal expressions of individuality, like tattoos and piercings — are better left for after business hours. While none of us likes to be criticized for our choice of clothes, it is good to remember that the workplace requires a certain standard that will only be in effect 40 hours per week. You still have your time to be expressive when it doesn't affect your career.

As you go out to start your career there are many things that you can no longer control. Your grades are forever recorded by the registrar's office, you will not get taller or change the color of your eyes, and you may not have lost those extra few pounds, but do remember to control the things that you can. Your manners, dress, and communication skills (both verbal and nonverbal) are under your control. Be positive! Dress appropriately. Treat everyone with respect, and honor the commitment you made to be on time and put your best self forward. Then, you can give yourself the best chance to get the internship and generally have a positive experience. Always look upon the internship as potential employment. Maybe the firm is hiring — you could be the next person listed on the firm letterhead or handing out a firm business card with your name on it.

NetWorks

www.mapquest.com	A Web site offering directions, maps, and other helpful tools to assist in finding the internship location.
www.craigslist.com or www.lawjobs.com	Web sites with employment listings also post listings for internships.
www.nationalparalegal.org	The National Paralegal Association (NPA) is an international organization offering benefits and services to individuals, independent paralegals, paralegal training schools and colleges, and offers a student membership.

Chapter Summary

- There are a variety of ways in which to satisfy your goal of securing an internship.
- Plan well in advance for this part of your education. Go back and reflect on your strengths and then tap into both your personal and your program's resources for possible internship placements.
- Find out whether you are on your own or if your program prescribes the parameters for the internship.
- Get some clear direction on procedures, and research the required number of hours and academic timing to sign up for credit internships.
- Explore all potential internship sites and choose one that is compatible with your goals. Be resourceful if it is up to you to find a site.
- Be ready for interviews with extra copies of your résumé, directions, quarters for the parking meters, and the appropriate attire to make a strong first impression.
- Research the places where internships can be completed. Then check your personal and college resources for opportunities. You are ready for your first internship experience and will soon be on your way to an exciting new career.

Key Terms

Shadowing: The act of following another person around with the intent of gaining knowledge about their job or duties.

Work-study: Academic programs that enable students to gain related work experience and get academic credit while continuing their studies.

Bits and Bytes

- Despite the growing diversity of the American workplace, conservative clothing still dominates industries such as law, accounting, and investment banking. Be sure that you understand the dress code for your internship before the first day. (Tip: Dress the way your supervisor or boss dresses, not the way your peers dress. Try to look like you are worth the amount you or your firm is charging.)

Discussion Questions

1. What are the personal traits that can be controlled when walking into an internship interview? What are those that cannot? What steps can be taken to ensure that you are making the best impression?

2. If your school or paralegal program does not offer an internship as a part of the curriculum, what steps can you take or what resources can you use to help gain that experience?

3. What questions will you ask to make sure you understand the expectations of your supervisor?

4. How will you know that the fit is right for you?

WebWork

1. Locate the 2004 National Utilization and Compensation Report, Section 1, named "The Participants Education and Experience" on the NALA Web site.

   a. From table 1.12 on the site, for someone with a High School Diploma, how many years of experience do they need to have in order to make the salary stated?
   b. From the same table, how many years of experience does someone with a CLA or CLAS credential need to have to make stated salary?
   c. How does this comparison speak to the importance of experience?
   d. How could an internship help increase a student's employability and salary potential?

2. Locate the National Association of Legal Assistants (NALA) and
   National Federation of Legal Assistants (NFPA) membership
   applications.

   a. What is the cost for a current paralegal student to become a member
      in each organization?
   b. What are the benefits to a current student becoming a member
      of a Paralegal or Legal Assistant association?

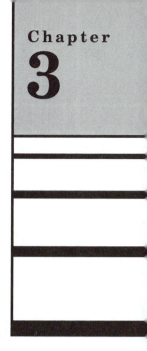

Building an Effective Résumé and Cover Letter

You never get a second chance to make a first impression.
—Anonymous

Chapter Overview

Your résumé is an essential professional document. It is you in a nutshell. A well-organized résumé piques the interest of a potential employer or internship supervisor and gives them a reason to want to meet you. By definition, a résumé is brief. It effectively and succinctly relays to the reader your goals, education, work experience, and skills. A good résumé will likely result in an interview because it gives the reader the feeling that your transferable skills and background will be a good fit for their needs. Keep in mind the essentials of a good résumé: organization, content, truthfulness, good grammar, professional appearance, and the effective communication of the skills you bring to the workplace. Once you have a good, solid working résumé you can always tailor it to specific jobs for which you are applying.

A. Creating an Effective Résumé

1. Introduction

While many students already have résumés, other students have never needed one, worked in a job that only required an application, or were just in the right place at the right time. Once you have a basic, well-organized résumé, looking for your next job and revising your résumé will be as simple as adding in your most recent experience and summarizing or consolidating past experiences. Remember too that résumés for the legal field are as specialized and focused as résumés for other fields, such as teaching, nursing, and social work. Each field has its own unique language and format.

Nothing could be more important when conducting a job search or internship search than the first impression you make with a potential employer. Your résumé will likely be your method of introduction. Consequently, you should devote a considerable amount of time to building, revising, and refining your résumé and the accompanying cover letter. Ideally, your résumé will be one printed page, organized to highlight your legal education and experience, and draw the reader's attention to your qualifications that meet the firm's or company's needs.

Résumés and cover letters must be printed on high-quality paper. Advances in technology allow you to circulate your résumé and cover letter not only by printed copy but by fax or email. Like a standard résumé, electronically transmitted résumés should be error free and designed in a format that is easily read and printed. The cover letter may be the text of the email or a separate attachment.

Larger places of employment sometimes use scanners to review résumés they receive, and so it is a good idea to follow some basic best practices. There are no absolute rules, but in general you should submit a very clean copy of your résumé and use common résumé headings. Use a standard, easy-to-read font of 10 or 12 point size and limit the use of italics and underlining. Bolding is fine. Use off-white paper with black ink, limit the information to one page, and make sure that all contact information is at the top of the résumé. Scanners search for key words so be sure to use legal terms and transferable skill words. As with traditional résumés, always proofread your work and use your word processor's spell check feature.

A word of caution: Stay away from trends and templates. Trends change quickly. More than one student has become frustrated because he or she could not make changes to or manipulate the margins and headings of the template.

The legal field is essentially conservative. Colored or textured paper, personal photos, quotes, and gimmicks are not as acceptable as they might be in a more creative field. You do not want to stand out in a negative way.

Many recently graduated college students include a summary of qualifications and skills paragraph that takes up space but does not give the reader an idea of actual skills and accomplishments. Healthy, nice, cooperative, outstanding, reliable, creative, and self-starting are not skills unless they are connected to specific tasks. Let the reader conclude that you have those qualities by your job descriptions. Many law office administrators refer to the above word list as "fluff."

2. *Résumé Content*

Before you begin writing your résumé, consider the most critical error in many résumés: poor organization. Reviewers often receive so many résumés that they have little time (20 seconds or less) to decide whether you will be put in the "pursue" or "do not pursue" pile. They do not have time for putting the puzzle together but want to quickly get a snapshot of your skills and potential fit. Once you have mastered some organizational tricks, you will more easily complete your résumé and increase your chances of finding yourself in the "pursue" pile.

While preparing a résumé seems like a relatively easy task (who knows *you* better than you do?) it can get confusing nearly as soon as you record your contact information at the top of the page. For most students pursuing internships, a chronological résumé will be best. That means relaying all of your information from most recent to longest ago. Keeping the time factor in mind (20 seconds), it becomes more evident that a one-page résumé is essential. Even students who are changing careers or have considerable work experience and education can put the information on one page by varying the format and mastering a "good use of space" philosophy. The more headings or categories you have on a résumé the more space you will use. While there are probably at least 20 possible headings, ranging from Vital Information to Skills categories, the essential headings usually include Personal Information, Internship or Job Objectives, Education, Work Experience, Skills and Affiliations, and References.

a. Personal Information

This section makes it as easy as possible for the reader to get in touch with you. Remember that a résumé is a formal document and should include your given name (the one used on your school records and driver's license). After you are working, or even if asked during an interview, you can indicate your preference for a nickname.

Include your address, spelling out "avenue," "road," and so forth. Be sure to include apartment number, city, state, and zip code. All states can be abbreviated by using two capital letters without periods, for example, CA, AR, NY, or TX. When using more than one phone number indicate in parentheses after the number whether it is a cell phone, home, or work number. The person calling you will appreciate the clarification and, depending on when they are calling, can decide which number to use. When using your home number, alert all family members and roommates that you are expecting professional calls and that they should carefully record phone numbers and times of calls.

Cell phones are becoming the preferred method for reaching people. Voicemail greetings should be short and professional. Intern supervisors or other hiring managers do not have the time to listen to your favorite Beatles or Madonna song or listen to your child recite the alphabet or say hello in two different languages. Likewise, repeat your phone number on your messages or indicate your name so callers know they dialed the correct number.

Email addresses are not required but can be a helpful way to communicate with many people. Your email address must be professional. What you or your friends considered a clever or cute email may not be well received in a different setting by a human resource manager. Your email address and phone greeting contribute to the positive or negative impression you make about your seriousness about the profession.

b. Internship or Job Objectives

Although this category or heading is not essential, you may want to consider it for your résumé. Job objectives take up space and are good if you do not have enough information to fill an entire page. They can also bring attention to specific skills that you have. For instance, "Bilingual college graduate with ABA Approved Paralegal Certificate seeks internship in family law" immediately interests a reader who is looking for those qualities. A job objective can mention language skills, related work experience, and education immediately without the reader having to scan the entire résumé. Consider this objective: "Current paralegal student with six years' experience in human resources seeks paralegal internship." This objective might interest a reader who wants a person who has been in the work force for a while or has experience working with a variety of people.

Job objectives (also called objectives, career objectives, career goals, etc.) can also be detrimental to your résumé. If you have extensive work experience that includes good transferable skills, the objective can take up valuable space. They can be too specific: "Paralegal graduate with experience in social work, computers, and retail positions seeks a position in family law in adoptions in the Orland Park suburb of Chicago" would exhaust the reader and be so specific that the job seeker would be eliminated from many excellent entry-level or internship possibilities. Try not to put a burden on the employer by mentioning in your objective what you expect the firm to do for you by asking for opportunities for growth. Likewise, do not mention that you want to work at an ethical or forward-thinking firm. Firms already presume these qualities are true.

c. Education

Education is one of the most important résumé categories and it is at this point on your résumé that you need to review the "tricks" of an organized résumé. Let's first cover the best way to organize your résumé entries.

For both education and the next category (work experience) you will have four categories each time you list an educational milestone or job. They are:

1. Name of educational institution or employer, including city and state.
2. Date graduated or attended or employment dates.
3. Name of your degree or program or job title. For example, your title could be administrative assistant or supervisor; your program or degree could be Litigation Certificate or A.A. in Computer Science or B.A. in Journalism.
4. A description of your educational or work experience starting with good past or present-tense verbs depending on whether you are currently at the job or left it a while ago. In the case of education, you would list courses you took, grade point averages, and minors, fields of concentration, or activities while in college.

The order of the above may turn out to be a matter of personal choice (although it would be unusual to start with description). What does matter and what is crucial is that you have the same order each time you list an education or work experience.

Now that we have the organization of the résumé entries planned, let's go back to the substance of what you should list in the education section. List your educational experiences backwards, starting with the most recent program, which is most likely your paralegal education program. Then, continue until you have listed all of your educational institutions. It is not necessary or advisable to list high schools. At this professional level, college work is more valuable and a high school diploma is assumed.

When describing paralegal programs that have specialties or degrees, it is good to explain them. For instance, a Business Specialty could include courses in corporations, contracts, real estate, legal research, and intellectual property. A degree may include numerous courses that would be of interest to the reader. While it is not necessary to list all courses, list those that correspond to the job for which you are applying. Or you can list practical assignments that you have completed as part of the course.

All education, whether academic, vocational, practical, or continuing, is important. Be proud of all of your educational experiences. If you attended several colleges you may want to consolidate them or just list colleges from which you were awarded degrees.

The person reviewing your résumé may have attended one of the same institutions. Listing one date after your program or degree presumes that you completed or graduated on that date. Listing inclusive years, especially if you were on the six-year plan can be detrimental. List minors if they include transferable skills, such as business, computers, communications, writing, or English. List activities and awards if they were recent and memorable. Finally, any grade point average above 3.2 is noteworthy.

If you did not complete a degree but compiled credits toward that goal, be sure to mention those accomplishments by indicating "successfully completed (number of credits) toward a degree" or "completed general education requirements" so you give the reader the impression that you have goals, ambition, and have made progress in your educational pursuits.

d. Work Experience

Prior Employment: Remember the trick for organizing your résumé. (Go back to Subsection c, above, and review the four numbered sequences.) List all of your jobs in the same order you listed your education. List each job: location (including city and state), title, dates, and description. List your most recent job first and go backwards from there. At this point, do not worry about going back too far. You can always edit after you determine the final length of the resume. You may need all of your jobs to fill up one page. Even part-time or seasonal college jobs (possibly high school, too) show the reader that you are industrious, can multi-task, can organize your time, honor commitments, and have developed good work habits. As interviewers review résumés they start to identify with your transferable skills. Don't underestimate any job you've held.

- If you worked with customers, you can relate to different age levels and had an opportunity to develop good communication skills, which will help you talk to clients and other staff in the firm
- If you organized work schedules and trained new employees, you will understand the necessity for legal training programs and will value your supervisors and their efforts to train you.
- If you were in the medical field, you will be familiar with insurance, forms, terminology, recordkeeping, and possibly, litigation.
- If you developed manuals or wrote policies for a corporation, you will be able to write good memos and analyze potential case issues.
- If you were a teacher, you learned how to communicate with all age levels, organize your time, develop long-term (lesson) plans, and cooperate with a variety of staff at different levels.
- If you were an administrative assistant or secretary, you can do word processing, use office machines, create documents, and understand office computer programs.

Be sure to list skills that communicate your understanding of standard office cultures, getting along well with people, working as a team, mentoring others, and having a positive attitude.

No matter where you have worked, you developed resourcefulness, ambition, and skills. Never underestimate legal issues that you may have observed or been exposed to. Insurance companies, human resource offices, educational institutions, manufacturers, government agencies, businesses, and pharmaceutical companies all deal with legal issues at some point and so you need to realize what you have to offer. Oftentimes, people who have had their own business do not understand the significance of the creativity, business sense, and perseverance that is involved in setting up a business. Firms are looking for:

- Writing skills
- Organizational skills
- Knowledge of legal terminology and procedures
- A good work ethic
- A positive attitude
- Professional demeanor and dress
- Computer skills
- Critical thinking skills

This section of your résumé will probably encompass the largest amount of information. Put it aside for a day or so. When you review it a few days later, look for similarities in job duties. If you've established your proficiency in accounts payable in one job, it may not be necessary to include similar or the same skills in the four previous jobs you held. Remember that the goal of your résumé is to highlight the talents you bring to the legal field and to highlight the duties that would interest the reader and make them want to talk to you about your experience.

When describing work experience, start with a good past-tense verb unless it is your current job, in which case you would use the present tense. Use action words such as "organized," "developed," "provided," and "created." (See Figure 3-1 for a list of action words.) Use short phrases to describe your work experience, always keeping in mind those skills that are transferable. Recent jobs should contain more descriptive information, while jobs held a while ago should have shorter descriptions. Don't go on too long, but be sure to include jobs that have a connection (as vague as it may be) to the legal field. If you have too many positions to fit on one page, first attempt to edit or shorten the description.

Figure 3-1
Action Verbs for Résumés

Abstracted	Brought about	Delegated	Extracted
Accomplished	Budgeted	Demonstrated	
Accounted		Designed	Facilitated
Achieved	Calculated	Determined	Filed
Acquired	Catalogued	Developed	Focused
Acted as	Chaired	Devised	Followed up
Adapted	Collected	Directed	Forecasted
Administered	Communicated	Disseminated	Formatted
Advanced	Compared	Distributed	Formed
Advised	Compiled	Documented	Formulated
Affected	Completed	Drafted	Founded
Analyzed	Composed		Fulfilled
Answered	Computed	Earned	Functioned
Approved	Conceived	Edited	
Arbitrated	Condensed	Eliminated	Gained
Arranged	Conducted	Employed	Gathered
Assembled	Consolidated	Enacted	Generated
Assigned	Constructed	Encouraged	Guided
Assisted	Consulted	Enhanced	
Assumed	Contributed	Ensured	Handled
Assured	Conveyed	Entered	Headed
Attained	Coordinated	Established	Hired
Attended	Counseled	Evaluated	
Audited	Corresponded	Examined	Identified
Authored	Created	Exceeded	Illustrated
Awarded	Cultivated	Executed	Implemented
		Expanded	Improved
Balanced	Dealt with	Expedited	Improvised
Bargained	Defined	Explained	Inaugurated

Figure 3-1
Continued

Increased	Offered	Referred	Stressed
Influenced	Operated	Refined	Structured
Informed	Optimized	Registered	Submitted
Initiated	Orchestrated	Regulated	Succeeded
Instilled	Ordered	Reinforced	Summarized
Instituted	Organized	Related	Supervised
Insured	Originated	Rendered	Supplied
Interacted	Oversaw	Reorganized	Supported
Interfaced		Reported	Surpassed
Integrated	Participated	Represented	Sustained
Interpreted	Performed	Reshaped	Systematized
Interviewed	Persuaded	Researched	
Introduced	Piloted	Resolved	Tailored
Invented	Pioneered	Responded	Taught
Investigated	Placed	Responsible for	Tested
	Planned	Restored	Took charge of
Judged	Predicted	Revamped	Traced
Justified	Prepared	Reviewed	Tracked
	Presented	Revised	Trained
Kept	Prevented	Revitalized	Transferred
	Presided	Revived	Transformed
Launched	Processed	Rewarded	Translated
Lectured	Procured	Routed	Treated
Led	Produced		Tripled
Located	Programmed	Scheduled	Turned around
Logged	Proposed	Screened	
	Provided	Secured	Uncovered
Maintained	Publicized	Selected	Unified
Managed		Served	United
Marketed	Quadrupled	Set up	Unraveled
Mastered	Quantified	Shaped	Updated
Mentored		Simplified	Utilized
Minimized	Raised	Solidified	
Modified	Realized	Solved	Validated
Monitored	Received	Sorted	Verified
Motivated	Rectified	Spearheaded	
Moved	Recognized	Spoke	Won
	Recommended	Staffed	Worked
Navigated	Reconciled	Standardized	Wrote
Negotiated	Recorded	Started	
Networked	Recruited	Stimulated	Yielded
	Redesigned	Strategized	
Observed	Reduced	Streamlined	
Obtained	Reevaluated	Strengthened	

If you already have a résumé drafted, one of the challenges can be to take an old, two- or three-page résumé and tailor it to your current legal internship or job search. To begin, you need to edit or cut down the résumé so that it fits on one page. If you have overly long job descriptions, try to refresh old résumé descriptions and start anew. Sit down and list 10 to 15 tasks you did on previous jobs, using good past-tense verbs. Do not repeat tasks. Then prioritize those descriptions by renumbering them. Now leave the list alone for a few hours or a day and go back and review the list again. Choose the most important tasks (usually four to five items) and list them on the résumé. It is important to leave some room for questions and answers during the interview and not bore the reader with too much verbiage or overly long descriptions.

Achievements can be listed under education or work experience but can also be dealt with in a separate category at the end of the résumé. Think carefully about how the reader will perceive your achievements. Refrain from self-promoting words unless you can connect them to specific tasks or accomplishments. List measurable skills, such as grade point average, academic achievements, top sales awards, marathon participant, **notary public**, real estate license, or scholarship recipient. Omit unmeasurable skills, for example, outstanding personality, successful, intelligent, likeable, excellent writing skills, and organized. Your résumé is a place to proudly state your wonderful achievements as they pertain to your potential future work in the legal field, but it is not a place to brag or boast about personality traits that are not connected to actual job responsibilities.

Notary public: A person licensed by the state to administer oaths and witness the signing of important documents.

If you are someone who is reentering the work force after years of retirement or handling family responsibilities, writing a résumé can be a challenge. If you were going to school, work gaps do not have a big impact. It is often understood that students concentrate on studies rather than work. It also frequently happens that students travel after graduation or take time to consider different career options. Or, there may just be times when you have been unemployed for various reasons. Small gaps are usually not an issue. Most likely you did something of value during the gap. If the gap is more than a year or so, you may want to simply state what you were doing during that time. Then there is little room for speculation on the part of a potential employer. Other, larger gaps can be explained under another category at the end of your résumé called Activities or Interests. Under this category list community or family activities such as soccer coach, Brownie leader, PTA President, Auxiliary Treasurer, travel to Europe, along with the dates. The reader will quickly understand that you were quite busy and did have a job of sorts, even if it did not fall under the category of paid employment.

e. Skills and Affiliations

Perhaps the most important skills you can highlight on your résumé are the computer programs with which you are familiar. You don't necessarily need to list every program, but you should list those that are the most common and any that are unique to the legal field. Additional helpful skills are those such as being a notary public, licensed real estate agent, or trust administrator. Always mention language skills. Many firms or companies highly value those employees who can converse in another language and communicate with diverse clients.

Listing your affiliation with a particular club or organization can often be a springboard for casual conversation at an interview. Well-known volunteer organizations such as Habitat for Humanity, Rotary Club, AmeriCorps, or PTA can portray your sense of civic responsibility. Be wary of listing affiliations that can be controversial such as particular religious activities or political parties. It is acceptable to refer to those activities in a generic way by mentioning "active in a political campaign" or "raised money for church library" without getting into specifics.

Membership in law-related professional groups indicates your level of commitment to the new career you have chosen. Consider joining both national and local paralegal associations or your college's paralegal alumni or student organization. Many county bar associations also have a student membership.

f. References

The references section is optional. If you are running out of room on your résumé, it is perfectly acceptable to eliminate the traditional "References Furnished Upon Request" line. It is assumed that you will provide references (and, in fact, you should have a printed copy of those references when you arrive at an interview and should have already contacted your references to make sure they're available for this purpose). Of course, if you would like to include that line at the bottom, you can use other phrases as well, such as "Personal and Professional References Available Upon Request" or "References and Writing Samples Available Upon Request."

B.   Some Sensitive Issues

We have addressed gaps in employment and, briefly, religion and politics, but there are additional dilemmas that come up when developing a résumé. Be sure that the only name on the résumé is your own. Do not include names of supervisors, coworkers, or clients. Do not mention salaries or the reason for leaving a job. This information is best left to an interview.

Be sure that any email you send is professional and does not leave the wrong impression. As mentioned earlier, what may have been a clever email address when you were a teenager or in college is no longer appropriate for the work force. Likewise, have professional answering machine messages that do not waste the listener's time or cause them to get images of you that are inaccurate.

Another sensitive issue can be your age or dates that might let the reader know your age. Oftentimes, people who are reentering the job market or starting a new career worry that they will be discriminated against because of their age. Although this is illegal, we all know it does exist. However, years of experience tell us that for every attorney or supervisor out there, some will want younger applicants and others will want more mature candidates. Here are the two sides: Younger applicants can be trained and do not come with preconceived notions and are usually less set in their ways. More mature applicants, however, usually offer a good work ethic, have experience, and better understand the work force. So, no matter where you are there are possibilities out there for you. If you do not put dates on a résumé, readers may presume you are much older than your actual age or get worried that you are trying to hide something like gaps in employment because you were in jail. It's best to include dates where appropriate.

C. Polishing Your Résumé

Now that you have developed your résumé and followed all the generally accepted rules, put it aside for a day or two. Then, go back and proofread it. Read one time forwards for content and another time backwards for spelling errors. Check for consistency. Have you described your education and work experience in the same four-item order as mentioned in Subsection c? Do you have the city and state listed for all jobs and educational institutions? Is there contrast so that some words or headings are bolded, italicized, underlined or in larger type? Résumés that have all the same type face and size look less appealing. Is the résumé pleasant to read without too much "white space"?

Now have another person who does not know you read your résumé. Ask them to check for typographical errors and consistency and to make sure the information you are trying to convey is clear. If they do not understand an entry, perhaps a potential employer will have the same problem. Remember that the résumé should want the reader to invite you in for an interview. If you don't get an interview, you can't get the internship. Proofread, proofread, and then proofread again. This process is crucial. Many interviewers report that résumés that have errors are automatically put in the "do not pursue" pile.

After your résumé has been scrutinized for readability, consistency, content, and errors, it is time to get it printed. With the sophistication of personal printers, most students can buy quality paper and print their résumé themselves provided they have a good laser printer. Otherwise, go to the local printing store or your college printing center and ask them for suggestions for résumé paper. They will show you variations in subtle colors and weights and be able to assist you in choosing appropriate paper. Remember that the legal field is fairly conservative, so do not choose colored paper, use graphics, or put your picture on your résumé. Err on the side of being overly conservative. You will have time later, after you get the internship, to find out if it is acceptable to be more casual.

D.   Résumé Falsification

Honesty is always the best policy. If you are not honest about your education or lead the reader to believe something that is not accurate, you run the risk of losing your reputation, your internship or job, and any future good reference from your internship supervisor. Even in large cities the legal community can be very tightly knit, and once you have lost your credibility it is difficult if not impossible to get back. Do not exaggerate your degree completion, completed number of credits, dates of employment, work responsibilities, skills or volunteer experience. Where appropriate, use words that give you leeway such as "familiar with" rather than "expert at."

E.   The Cover Letter

The cover letter introduces your résumé and is a chance to show your enthusiasm for the job. A well-written cover letter motivates the reader to want to read your résumé. Always accompany your résumé with a cover letter even if you are faxing it. Cover letters should be several paragraphs long but should not repeat too much of what is in your résumé. At least three paragraphs are required for a cover letter and should include the following information.

1.   Why You Are Writing and What You Are Applying For

The reader will be curious about how you happened to choose this particular firm and what position you are applying for. Mention whether the program, a neighbor, a professional acquaintance, or someone else referred you. Did you read an ad in the paper and presume that if there was a job available the firm would perhaps prefer an intern? Firms have positions available for mail room clerks all the way up to paralegal supervisors and unless you specify, they have no idea where you see yourself best fitting into the firm.

2.   What You Have to Offer

Consider the internship position you are seeking and then give the reader a reason for further review of your résumé and the possibility of an interview. List the specific courses you have completed and any practical assignments you have completed in an area of law that would benefit the firm. Explain how many hours you are willing to work and whether you expect pay or are looking for an internship for academic credit. Along with succinct details of your legal knowledge, explain any other skills you have to offer such as computer knowledge, writing and drafting experience, and general office experience. Be sure to tailor the description of your skills to the type of law the firm is practicing.

3. *What Action You Will Take*

Let the reader know your availability for an interview or what proactive steps you will take to get in touch. Offer to bring writing samples and references when you meet with him or her.

4. *Closing Your Cover Letter*

Thank the reader for the time he or she has taken to read your letter and résumé. Indicate that you look forward to a meeting at a mutually convenient time. Always be gracious.

F.   Pre-Internship Interviews

Essentially, when interviewing for your internship, follow the same guidelines and rules as when interviewing for a permanent position. The following checklist should help you prepare for this important part of the internship process:

- Get the correct spelling of the name of the person you will meet, along with the address and directions if necessary.
- Take a practice run before the actual day of the interview to plan for parking, parking meters, elevator systems, and the dress of building workers.
- Be on time for the appointment, but try not to be too early and never arrive late.
- Be polite and respectful to all receptionists but do not engage in small talk or make negative comments while waiting.
- Shake hands and make eye contact.
- Concentrate on the questions asked and be sure you understand the meaning of the question. Take time to think about your answer.
- Practice your interview ahead of time by reviewing potential questions that may be asked.
- Try to relate previous classroom and work experience to the current situation.
- Explain clearly and succinctly what you can do for the firm.
- Ask questions about anything that you do not understand. Prepare a list of basic questions before the interview; have it ready and refer to it when the time is right.

- Listen carefully to the interviewers' needs and then try to explain how you can fulfill those needs in your responses about your prior experience.
- Softly sell yourself and ask for the internship.
- Be gracious, thank them for their time, and send a thank you note as soon as possible.

G.   Confirming the Internship

Once you have received word that you are a good fit and have been offered the internship, write a follow-up letter expressing your enthusiasm for the position. Carefully indicate your understanding of the start date, number of hours you will work, hours/days you will work, pay (if appropriate), and general duties. Be gracious and thank the interviewer again for the opportunity to work in the position.

NetWorks

www.hotmail.com or www.gmail.com	If you need a new, more professional email address, consider theses sites. They are free of charge and accessible on any computer with internet access.
www.microsoft.com	If you would like to become familiar with a computer program, or perhaps simply become reacquainted with it before an interview, this site offers free trials, tutorials, and training on the Microsoft Office Suite.
http://www. chicagomanualofstyle.org/ tools_proof.html	The Chicago Manual of Style Web site lists the most commonly used proofreading marks. It is helpful when others proofread your résumé.
www.jobweb.com	Web site with job listings, résumé-writing tips, interviewing tips, and other helpful articles for students drafting their first résumé.

Chapter Summary

- Résumés are essential tools for the job or internship search.
- Résumés must be organized, concise, and informative.
- Education and work experience are the two main areas that potential internship supervisors will be interested in.
- How you portray yourself in a résumé will determine how many interviews you get and how many opportunities you will have.
- Use good résumé paper and make sure that the information is accurate, well written, and error free.
- The résumé represents *you* in a nutshell and gives the reader cause to want to work with you.
- Once you have a good, basic résumé, it can easily be updated each time you change positions.
- A cover letter must always accompany a résumé, whether it is faxed or sent by mail or email. It is also a chance to show your writing skills and convince the reader that an interview will be worth their time.
- Be careful of sensitive areas and always be honest.
- Prepare for the internship interview by scoping out the location, looking for parking facilities, and observing the dress of building occupants.
- Review the answers to potential questions that will be asked.
- Be gracious, polite, and always on time.
- Write a thank you letter and a letter of acceptance if you get the position.

Key Term

Notary public: A person licensed by the state to administer oaths and witness the signing of important documents.

Bits and Bytes

- Microsoft Word has more than 200 different fonts as part of the program. However, there is no need to use more that one on your résumé. Stick to a traditional font such as Times New Roman or Arial. Avoid playful fonts such as Joker or Wingdings.

- Don't include hobbies on a résumé unless it is specifically related to the position you are applying for. It doesn't matter if you are a surfer, horseback rider, or singer unless the law firm deals with environmental law, animal care, or entertainment law.

- Be cautious about faxing a résumé because it may lack the polished appearance of a résumé printed on résumé paper. Many times fax transmittals arrive blurred or smudged and difficult to read.

- Don't rely on spell checking alone! It will not catch a typo like "form" in place of "from."

Discussion Questions

1. Name and describe the essential and most commonly accepted headings for a résumé. What are the possible consequences to using an inappropriate heading?

2. What are the four parts of each educational experience or job experience? Describe the importance of having each one. What would be the consequence of omitting one?

3. Why is it important to list all jobs even if they were not directly related to the legal field? How could you use those opportunities to market yourself to a law firm?

WebWork

1. Under the "Résumés & Interviews" section of www.jobweb.com:
   a. Find the sample internship résumé.
      i. Note the wording of the objective. How would this differ from a résumé developed for other positions?
      ii. How could this student improve the experience description she has listed?
   b. Find the list of action words and list five words you could use to describe your experience.

Chapter 4

The Internship Experience

Men acquire a particular quality by constantly acting
a particular way . . . you become just by performing
just actions, temperate by performing temperate
actions, brave by performing brave actions.
—Aristotle

Chapter Overview

Once you have confirmed your internship arrangement, you must properly prepare to make the most of your experience. This is your chance to put into practice the skills you have acquired in the classroom. It's also an opportunity to see firsthand the day-to-day operation of a law firm or legal department. This may be your first experience working in the legal field, and it's important for you to know your ethical boundaries, the system of billing and accountability used by the firm to ensure a smooth operation, and the general culture of the particular office. Your success in the internship will provide a foundation for your network of future employment contacts, an impressive addition to your résumé, and an opportunity to obtain recommendations as you begin your job search.

A. What to Do Before Your First Day

Some student interns find it helpful to set up a pre-internship meeting. During this time you can discuss with your supervisor details of the job, become familiar with the computer systems and your work station, and get a general tour of the facilities. You can also find out where to park and confirm specific hours and times you will report to the internship. Many paralegal programs expect you to turn in a sheet signed by you and the supervisor with many of the above details, especially beginning and ending dates and specifics of expected duties.

After the preliminary contact has been made and you have confirmed your start date and time, you can prepare to report to your internship.

The way you present yourself indicates your respect for yourself and the legal profession. During your initial interview with the firm and at your pre-internship meeting you will have had an opportunity to observe the dress of staff people in the internship environment. If you asked questions about the dress code, review the responses you jotted down. Until you have been instructed otherwise, dress for work the way you would for an interview. Clients expect their legal team to be professional in both attitude and dress. Appearance *does* count. The legal profession is generally thought of as conservative, although area of the country, city size, and general culture of the setting dictate the norm. Thus, when in doubt, always err on the side of caution and dress and act more conservatively rather than less. You can always shed a jacket, blazer, or tie if everyone around you has dressed "down," but if you dress too casually for a meeting, there's nothing you can do to "dress up" in a hurry.

B.   Ethical Considerations in Internships

Like all other law office personnel, interns must be familiar with and abide by the rules of ethics and professional responsibility that govern attorneys' conduct. Specifics of rules may vary from state to state but are generally modeled to some extent after the American Bar Association (ABA) Model Rules of Professional Conduct. Attorneys are ultimately responsible for the actions of those who work under their supervision and may be sanctioned for the misconduct of subordinates. Clients may sue lawyers for negligence, breaches of confidentiality, and **conflicts of interest**. Paralegal interns and other staff members may be named in these lawsuits if they were involved in the alleged wrongdoing. And some ethics violations, like the **unauthorized practice of law** and the misuse of client funds, may lead to criminal prosecution. Always remember that even though attorneys are ultimately responsible for your work, you must still be familiar with relevant ethical rules. The ethics rules that govern attorney conduct and guide the conduct of those who work with lawyers cover a full array of matters. Some of the ethical issues most likely to be faced by interns are:

Conflicts of interest: A real or seeming incompatibility between the interests of a lawyer's clients, such that the lawyer is disqualified from representing both clients if the dual representation adversely affects either client or if the clients do not consent.

Unauthorized practice of law: The practice of law by a person, typically a nonlawyer, who has not been licensed or admitted to practice law in a given jurisdiction.

- Supervision and competence
- Unauthorized practice of law
- Confidentiality
- Conflicts of interest
- Fees and client funds

1.   Supervision and Competence

Lawyers are obligated to supervise the work of their subordinates, including interns, and to see that the conduct of their subordinates comports with the ethical guidelines. The level of supervision required and the nature of the work that may be properly delegated depends on the credentials, experience, and skills of the subordinate involved. As an intern, you are probably near the end of your paralegal education program but may not have extensive legal work experience. Therefore, you should be assigned basic paralegal tasks at first, duties that match your level of skill and knowledge. All of your work will be closely monitored and reviewed by your supervisor, usually a lawyer or an experienced paralegal. As you gain experience and confidence and prove your ability to handle basic tasks, you will likely be given increasingly sophisticated work. The level of supervision and review to which your work is subjected may be adjusted too. But all paralegal work must be reviewed to some degree, no matter how proficient or experienced you become.

If you believe that your supervisor is not reviewing your work carefully, you are obligated to change that. If necessary, remind your supervisor of your status as a nonlawyer and a novice and of your desire to do a good job for the client. The attorney should review your work and is responsible to the client for the work product. You both should be guided by the goal of producing top-quality legal work for the client. And you will improve your skills and knowledge only if your work is carefully examined and corrected. If the assignment you submit is inadequate and is not corrected before it leaves the office, it is the attorney who could be disciplined or sued, or who may lose the client. But you could also be blamed and, perhaps, named in any malpractice suit. So, while the attorney has an obligation to supervise you, you have an obligation to seek supervision if necessary.

2. *Unauthorized Practice of Law (UPL)*

Only attorneys, licensed by the state after meeting requirements of education, competence testing, and moral character, are authorized to practice law. Nonlawyers who engage in conduct that meets the legal definition of the "practice of law" violate statutes prohibiting such conduct and in most states subject themselves to criminal prosecution for a misdemeanor. In addition, attorneys who help nonlawyers to practice law may be prosecuted and/or disciplined for aiding in the unauthorized practice of law. While nonlawyers who provide legal services to the public are most at risk of violating unauthorized practice statutes, interns and paralegals who work under the supervision of lawyers may also break these rules.

The generally accepted limitations imposed on nonlawyers are:

- A nonlawyer may not represent a client in court. Exceptions to this are self-representation and appearances before certain administrative agencies, as allowed by state law.
- A nonlawyer may not take a deposition since deposition testimony is taken under oath and may be admitted in court.

- A nonlawyer may not establish the attorney-client relationship by accepting a case or setting the terms of representation, such as the fee.
- A nonlawyer may not give legal advice.

While interns may see ethical issues involving all four of these areas, the final prohibition is the most complicated and troublesome. The commonly accepted sense of what constitutes legal advice is unclear and is subject to change; a task that was classified as legal advice a decade ago may not be now in all jurisdictions. Situations come up unexpectedly in which clients and others ask questions that require the intern or paralegal to give legal advice in response. If you are not prepared for this situation, you may give someone legal advice without realizing that you are doing it. To lower the risk of being faced with one of these situations and to ensure that you handle them comfortably and correctly when they do arise, follow these simple practices:

a. Always identify your status as a nonlawyer by giving your title to clients and others outside the firm, for example, "I'm Jane Smith, the paralegal intern for attorney Marilyn Jones." Giving your title when you meet someone or make or receive a call should become second nature. Be sure to follow this practice with everyone you talk to, such as clients, court personnel, witnesses, and opposing counsel and their employees.

b. Whenever a client asks you a question, stop and evaluate before you blurt out an answer. Think about the following:
   - Does your answer require you to utilize your legal knowledge or judgment?
   - Will the client take some action as the result of your words?
   - Does your answer concern your client's rights or responsibilities?

c. If you answered yes to any of these questions, do not answer the client's question, even if you know the answer. Remind the client that you are not an attorney and cannot give them legal advice. Then, check with the attorney and either have the client speak directly with the attorney (especially if the matter is beyond your expertise or is complicated) or speak with the attorney yourself and relay to the client the advice that the attorney authorizes you to give the client.

d. Prepare a brief memorandum to the client's file, indicating the information that you relayed from the attorney to the client and the fact that the attorney was aware of the situation and authorized your actions.

e. Do not expand on, alter, or change in any way the advice or information that the attorney approved for you to relay.

f. Do not advise friends or family about their legal rights and responsibilities. You are helping them more if you provide them with a referral to a good attorney or direct them to appropriate self-help materials.

3. *Confidentiality*

Confidentiality is a critically important duty in the legal field and has two components: first, the ethical obligation to keep information about clients and their legal affairs confidential; and second, the evidentiary rules covering attorney-client privilege that form the foundation for the critically important duty of confidentiality. Clients have a nearly absolute right to expect that anything learned by their attorney in the course of representation will not be revealed either in court proceedings or in any other way.

Confidentiality is an extremely broad principle — even broader than the attorney-client privilege, which protects only attorney-client communications and the attorney's work product from discovery and from being admitted in court. In contrast, the ethical obligation of confidentiality covers *all* information and communications relating to a client, sometimes even the client's location and identity.

Often, confidential information is revealed inadvertently because of the absence of good procedures to protect confidentiality or the failure of personnel to follow those procedures. Many times these common violations seem innocent and inconsequential: Neither the client nor the opposing counsel learns of the breach and no negative consequences result. As an intern, the best practice for you to develop from the start is to refrain from talking about clients, except with your immediate, authorized colleagues at work, and to take a careful and protective attitude in dealing with confidential information.

Many firms now require all employees, including interns, to sign confidentiality agreements under which the signer agrees not to disclose any information about anything learned at work. Some firms have explicit and detailed policies that cover confidential information, client files, and the like, and include these rules in their handbooks and orientation programs.

Whether or not your internship site maintains good policies, follow the following simple rules to avoid engaging in any impropriety in this area.

a. Do not talk about clients and their legal matters to people outside your firm or even to those in your firm who are not working on the particular matter in question.

b. Do not discuss any confidential matters in a public place, such as an elevator, hallway, reception area, restaurant, or social gathering. You may be overheard, with the result that the confidential information is out and the attorney-client privilege is waived.

c. When people come into your office, be sure they cannot see the client files or other confidential material that you are working on, either in paper form or on your computer screen. This is referred to as a "clean desk, clean screen policy."

d. Be careful when discarding confidential material such as handwritten notes and drafts of documents. Most firms have paper shredders to ensure that sensitive material does not get into the wrong hands.

e. Always double check addresses, phone numbers, and email addresses when mailing, faxing, or messaging confidential material. There have been instances of people inadvertently faxing a confidential and highly sensitive document to the wrong person, which can be disastrous if it happens to be the opposing counsel. It is best not to fax a confidential document at all, but if you must, be certain that an authorized person is on the receiving end to pick it up immediately.

f. Do not take confidential documents out of your office unless absolutely necessary. If you do, be especially careful about their security, that is, do not leave them in your car unattended or on the seat of an airplane.

g. Do not discuss confidential matters on a cellular telephone. These conversations can and will be overheard.

h. Take special care when using an intercom or telephone, especially a speaker phone. Keep your office door closed when discussing confidential matters and be sure you cannot be heard through the door.

i. When working on document production, get guidance from the supervising paralegal and attorney about what documents and information to look for that may be privileged. Inadvertent disclosure is common in document production and legal assistants and paralegal interns are often the ones who prepare the documents to be sent to the opposing counsel. Mistakes can be serious: opposing counsel can learn potentially damaging, confidential information and a court may decide that the inadvertent disclosure constitutes a waiver of the privilege.

4. Conflicts of Interest

The duties of confidentiality and loyalty combine to create a special duty that lawyers and their employees owe to clients: the duty not to have any interests, either personal or professional, that conflict with the interests of the client.

    The general conflicts rule prohibits a lawyer from representing both sides in an ongoing matter. This rule covers all matters, whether or not they are in litigation—including transactional and regulatory work, negotiations, tax and estate planning, administrative matters, and so forth. It extends, through a doctrine called imputed or **vicarious disqualification**, from the person who has the conflict to all others working in the same law firm.

Vicarious disqualification: Disqualification of all the lawyers of a firm or in an office because one lawyer is ethically disqualified from representing the client at issue.

    In addition to conflicts concerning the representation of two clients, conflicts may involve the attorney's own personal interests. The rules on this kind of conflict generally prohibit attorneys and their subordinates from entering into business transactions with their clients, lending money to clients, and accepting gifts from clients. This group of conflicts rules covering personal and business relations with clients applies to paralegals and paralegal interns, although the taint from personal conflicts is not always extended to all personnel in a firm. The nature of each job dictates these policies.

The rules that prohibit representation where conflicts exist can usually be overcome with the consent of the client or clients involved. Courts will honor the consent only if it is clear that the representation will be adequate under the circumstances and that confidential information is not likely to be revealed or misused. And courts are also more likely to uphold a consent if it was given in writing with the advice of independent counsel.

Screens, sometimes called **Chinese walls** or **cones of silence**, are used to protect against breaches of confidentiality and loyalty when a conflict is present. The screen isolates the person with the conflict from any involvement in the matter by prohibiting discussion of the matter with that person, and ensuring that the conflicted person has no access through computers or files to information about the case. Lawyers who are screened must also be excluded from sharing in any fees from the matter. Screens are generally accepted where legal assistants and other nonlawyers have conflicts and in successive conflicts where the risk of harm to the former client is remote. Screens are always more effective and likely to be recognized by the courts if the affected client has consented.

> **Screen, Chinese wall,** or **cone of silence:** A screening mechanism that protects client confidences by preventing one or more lawyers within an organization from participating in any matter involving that client.

When a conflict is discovered in a litigated matter, the client who may be harmed may move to have the firm with the conflict disqualified from further representation in the case. Disqualification motions have become increasingly common in litigation and many involve nonlawyers, such as paralegals. If a firm is disqualified, it loses a client and the investment of time that it has put into a matter, usually forfeits fees, and may also be sanctioned by the court.

To prevent conflicts of interest, a firm should conduct a conflicts check when they are hiring personnel (whether lawyers or nonlawyers), paid or volunteer employees, or independent contractors, and when they take on a new client or case. These checks determine if anyone in the firm, or anyone the firm is considering hiring, has a conflict or potential conflict with a past or existing client.

As an intern, you must begin now to make a list of all the client matters on which you work. When you are seeking a position in a legal environment in the future, you must be able to provide this information so that the hiring firm can check for conflicts. To preserve confidentiality while still permitting an effective conflicts check, you should not reveal any information about clients or matters you have worked on until the firm is ready to make you an offer of employment. Then, you should reveal only the minimum amount of information necessary to determine if a conflict exists. Initially, this probably means only the names of clients. If a potential conflict is identified from this information, you may then need to provide more information about the nature of a specific matter in order for the firm to assess the situation. The hiring firm is not only obligated to conduct the check, but it is required under ethical principles not to misuse the information obtained in the process of conducting the check.

If a conflict is discovered, you may be able to get consent from the former client and/or to erect a proper screen. If the conflict cannot be remedied in this way, you may be prohibited from working at the firm. The determination of how to handle the conflict will be made by the hiring firm, taking into account the extent and seriousness of the conflict, whether or not an adequate screen can be put in place, and whether consent can be obtained.

5. *Financial Matters*

Legal assistants and paralegal interns often perform tasks that relate to financial matters of clients, from billing for their time to handling client trust accounts. Unethical conduct relating to money is one of the leading causes of disciplinary sanctions and of the poor public image of lawyers. Some misconduct relating to client funds is also illegal and could result in a criminal prosecution for fraud or embezzlement.

Oftentimes, legal assistants and paralegal interns, especially in small law firms, have responsibility for client trust accounts in matters like probate and real estate transactions and for the processing of settlement checks out of which legal fees will be paid. Here are a few things to keep in mind:

1. Client funds must be kept in a separate client trust account and may not be commingled with the attorney's funds.
2. When funds are to be divided between the client and the attorney, they must be deposited into the client trust account first.
3. Clients must be notified promptly when an attorney receives client property or funds.
4. Client funds and property that are given to a lawyer for a client must be delivered promptly to the client.
5. A full accounting of client funds and property must be provided to the client upon request.
6. Accurate and complete records of client funds and property must be kept.

The manner in which an attorney determines the fee for his or her services depends on the nature of the services, related statutory and ethical regulations, and local custom. Fees are set by statute for some kinds of legal work, such as probate and administrative matters. Hourly fees are charged for most other services. Attorneys and paralegals keep track of the time they spend on client matters and clients are billed, usually monthly, at a predetermined rate for each person working on a given matter. The rate varies, depending on the nature of the work done and the qualifications and experience of the person doing it.

Charging clients for the time spent or the work performed by unpaid volunteers like interns raises interesting ethical questions that have not been definitively addressed by the organized bar or the courts. On the one hand, some would argue that just because clients pay a lawyer to provide professional services, they should not determine the way in which those services are rendered. This view holds that it is good business practice, and ethically proper, for lawyers to utilize processes and personnel in the most efficient and profitable manner, so long as the work is done competently and the client is satisfied. This view is most persuasive when the services are not billed on an hourly basis, but rather as a contingency or flat fee.

On the other hand, some would argue that it exploits both the client and the intern for an attorney to realize substantial profit from an unpaid intern's work. Pure profit is virtually impossible because utilizing an intern carries its own costs, including the direct costs of overhead and the nonbillable time expended by lawyers and others for training and supervising the intern.

In a firm that charges by means of billable hours, the time spent by a paralegal intern on work that is not professional in nature and would not therefore customarily be charged to clients should clearly not be charged to a client. The time spent by an intern on tasks determined to be billable may be charged to the client, within some important parameters. Since firms must disclose to clients the basis on which they are being charged for professional services, disclosure of the intern's status should be made. The firm must also consider the following in establishing the billing policies for interns: billing rates must be set at an amount that reflects the credentials of the intern and the nature and level of the work being performed by the intern; the intern's rate must be reasonable, taking into account the costs associated with utilizing the intern and the amount of profit generated; and charges for an intern's time must be carefully reviewed to ensure that the client is not paying for excessive time caused by an inexperienced intern's slow pace or for time spent training the intern and correcting the intern's work.

C. Timekeeping and Billing During Internships

Most interns are required to keep track of their time so that their college or paralegal program can award the appropriate academic credit for the number of hours worked. Oftentimes, your program will have its own form for you to use, which indicates:

- Intern name
- Date
- Time spent on a particular task
- The nature of the task such as telephone call or client interview
- The name of the client or case number

In order for clients to be billed there must be a systemized form of timekeeping for all legal staff persons who are working on a particular case. Clients may be billed by the hour, on a contingency basis, or for a flat fee, depending on the agreement and the nature of the case. Attorneys, paralegals, case assistants, law clerks, and others working on a case must each carefully record their time. Attorneys are billed at a much higher fee than paralegals or interns because billing rates vary depending on the education and experience of the person doing the task. It is important that time is recorded as soon as possible after a task is completed, especially when working on more than one case. Be as specific as possible in your description. Clients often want an explanation for charges and it is much easier to justify the expense when the specific nature of a telephone call is recorded rather than just the words "telephone call."

Billing practices are usually determined by managing partners who will decide if an intern's time will even be billed. Students often question the fairness of billing a client for an unpaid intern but should keep in mind that there are always training and overhead costs for an intern. Fees may also be determined by law, such as in the case of probate and administrative matters.

The specifics of timekeeping are discussed in detail in Chapter 7, but it is important to understand the concept and to adhere to firm or company policies. At the start of your internship, be sure to ask your program director or intern supervisor whether you will be using the college's timekeeping forms or the firm's system. Most billing is now done using computer software and you may need some training to understand codes and format.

D.   Law Office Culture

From the very beginning of your internship, be alert to the culture in the office in which you are interning. Think of the culture of a law office as its personality. Just as cultures and personalities differ in society, cultures in law offices will vary greatly. What is acceptable to one law office culture would be frowned upon at another. To determine the culture at your internship site, you can examine the following criteria:

1. Observe the interaction of the coworkers when you are in the office. Do people call each other by first or last names? Are office doors open or closed? Are there scheduled social activities or is socializing outside of the office taboo?
2. Look at the types of clients the firm accepts. Are they high profile, politically connected, powerful, or wealthy? Are they average-sized corporations or companies? Are they simple individuals in need of advice? Do they take a lot of pro bono work (legal services provided to those in need for no charge)? The clientele of the firm will tell you a lot about the firm's philosophy and personality.
3. Consider the firm's structure or hierarchy. Are there well-defined distinctions between partners, associates, paralegals, and support staff, or is it just one big team?

The internship is your opportunity to observe the culture at a law office and determine if this is an environment that fits your personality. If you feel comfortable, you can use the cultural standards you observe as a benchmark for your job search. If you don't fit in, certainly do your best to meet the standards while you're an intern and use the experience to avoid this culture when you interview for permanent employment.

E. The Orientation Meeting

Now that you inderstand the ethical rules governing law firm billing practices, and the office culture you might encounter, you will be fully prepared for your orientation meeting and your internship experience. By now you are probably able to determine the some of the "culture" of the office where you will be doing your internship. Remembering the above guidelines, you should attend your orientation meeting and be ready to get started right away. Be prepared to take notes so that you clearly understand your responsibilities and can meet deadlines that are given. Confirm with your supervisor the mutual expectation of hours you will work and when you expect to complete your assignment. You should jot down the hierarchy of the firm and the name and phone number of your direct supervisor. Be open-minded to all responsibilities offered to you. Remember the first impression edict and present yourself as a confident and competent professional.

F. The Internship Experience

1. Getting Off on the Right Foot

Nothing can be worse than having things go awry on your first day. If your internship site is in an unfamiliar area, be sure to make a "dry run" before your first day to ensure you will be on time. Scope out (or ask in advance) the best places to park or nearest public transportation. Keep in mind the traffic patterns may be very different during the work week. An upbeat, positive personality will contribute to your experience. Expect the unexpected. You may arrive at the appointed time and the attorney or supervisor assigned to you is not immediately available. Remember, their clients are their priority. They are offering you an opportunity. Be patient and understanding if last-minute issues arise that delay them from getting to you right away.

2. Doing Your Homework

You may think of the internship as a class with no homework. Nothing could be further from the truth. While the internship will not require homework in the traditional sense, prior to beginning the internship assignment, you should prepare yourself with knowledge about the firm or company. Use the Internet or other resources to research the firm's history, employees, and clients. Consider your knowledge base from the classroom and your other experiences and be ready to discuss the tasks you feel equipped to tackle. Be organized. Come with a copy of your class, work and personal schedule so that you will know your availablity for work hours at the internship site.

3.   Making the Most of Your Internship Experience

Your internship is not personal—it is a professional work opportunity. While many firms have social events throughout the year for their employees, socializing is best reserved for those events. If possible, avoid personal involvement with your coworkers and supervisors. Personal relationships in the workplace, however, may be misconstrued by co-workers or other interns and may be detrimental to your experience. However, the work environment is a good place to establish *professional* relationships.

4.   Communications Etiquette

Office communication etiquette and habits should be established at the orientation meeting or shortly thereafter. Find out specifically how each person in the office prefers to communicate with you. Before you yell across the office, "Hey, Susie, could you tell me about John Q. Client?" be sure to find out if this type of communication is customary in this particular law office or legal department. Just because the senior partner leaves the door open doesn't mean he or she welcomes visitors to just "pop in." Similarly, some individuals may work behind closed doors but welcome a friendly knock if you have a question. Some office members will prefer telephone communication and some will prefer email, which allows them to prioritize incoming questions. It may seem silly to send electronic messages to someone within earshot, but the firm might encourage this type of communication for documentation purposes. If you are ever in doubt, check with your immediate supervisor and remember what they tell you!

5.   Being Proactive

a.   What to Do if You Are Underutilized

You know what your capabilities are, but the firm may not. You may want to mention that you have recently learned deposition summaries in class and would be willing to assist with one. If you find yourself with time on your hands, politely ask your supervisor if there is anything else available for you to do. If your immediate supervisor is unavailable, offer your time to someone else before you decide to play solitaire on your computer. Remember that office work isn't always glamorous. This is a learning opportunity for you. You may learn by observing the daily operations of the office. Sometimes photocopying, filing, and other mundane tasks simply must be done. Be open and willing to do all tasks, and your services will be greatly appreciated.

b. What to Do if You Are Overutilized

Conversely, you must be careful that the firm doesn't take advantage of your eagerness to learn. Before you begin an assignment that is "way over your head," be frank with your supervisor about your level of knowledge. Feel free to ask your supervisor how much time he or she expects the assignment to take. Refer back to your notes at the orientation meeting and cite them if necessary. Part of the learning experience at your internship is self-advocacy. Beyond the legal knowledge to be gained, you may find that this situation provides an opportunity to practice tactfully approaching your supervisor when your job duties don't match your original assignment.

6. Getting a Recommendation at the Conclusion of Your Internship

Prior to leaving your internship, approach your supervisor and any other staff with whom you have developed a comfortable rapport or for whom you have successfully completed assignments. Explain that you will be looking for paralegal job in the future and that you would appreciate their support of your goals by writing a letter of recommendation for you to put in your portfolio and use as you embark on your career. Gently remind them of projects or tasks that you completed for them and mention how much their direction with those tasks gave you a better understanding of your classroom instruction. Try to clarify whether they will send the letter to you or whether they would like to set a time for you to pick up the letter. If you have honored your internship commitment, worked hard, had a good attitude, and behaved professionally, you will most likely earn a glowing recommendation. All of those you worked with have been in your situation before and are usually happy to provide you with a letter of recommendation.

7. Recordkeeping for the Future

As much as we like to think we will remember details, people, and events, they tend to fade from our memory soon after our experience. Now is a good time to make a list of the people you worked for and with. Jot down phone numbers, addresses, and titles. Write down your impressions of those people and details of your relationship with them, including tasks you performed together or help they may have given you as you completed your internship. Make notes on specific tasks you completed and the nature of the cases in which you participated. Then, prior to interviewing for paralegal positions in the future, you can review your notes and refresh your memory, which will allow you to speak more precisely about the work you did during your internship. You will also be able to much more readily put together your reference list with accurate names, titles, and contact information. Always keep accurate information on cases on which you worked because that information will help speed up the process of conflicts checks as you begin any new paralegal position.

G. Being Realistic About the Internship Experience

An internship is not a permanent job, although it sometimes will lead to one. Your attitude going into the internship should be one of willingness to learn and an open mind about assigned tasks and responsibilities. While we would all like to start our first day by going to trial or researching a legal dilemma and finding the answer, it is likely that you will start with some very basic tasks such as organizing files and then work your way up to preparing exhibits for trial. Educate yourself about what paralegals actually do on a job. Talk to classmates who have already done an internship and ask them what they encountered. Remember that this is a chance for you to observe specific legal environments. Observing the interaction of people in the firm will be much more valuable to you than reading about it in a book.

The work of a paralegal is often administrative and computer related and many a student has come back to a paralegal program director and complained that they are not doing paralegal tasks because they were Bates stamping, calendaring court appearances or deadlines, or going through boxes of documents just to find one relevant piece of paper. If you do those assigned tasks in a thorough manner and with a good attitude you will undoubtedly be given tasks with more responsibility as time goes on. Remember, too, that no internship or job is going to necessarily meet all of your expectations. Take the time now while you are in "practice mode" to discern how you can make a contribution to this particular team effort and you will be better prepared when you make a decision about your permanent place of employment.

H. Internship Documentation and Notebooks

Your program may require you to submit a timesheet or some sort of documentation about your internship experience. Be sure to keep your supervisor apprised of grade deadlines and necessary paperwork. You should also keep a personal notebook or journal to help you later recall specific tasks you completed and details of those experiences. Set aside time at the end of each day of your internship to write a brief journal entry. Note the types of cases you worked on, the people you encountered and the computer programs you used. Note both positive and negative reflections to help you later assess which types of tasks you like best and which you prefer others handle.

I. Lessons Learned: Evaluating the Internship Experience

An honest evaluation of your internship will help you when you describe the internship experience on your résumé and will serve as a point of reference while you are looking for a job. Students often underestimate the value of their internship. They may feel they didn't have the skill set required to perform substantive legal work; they may feel they didn't contribute in a "big" way to the overall operation of the firm. However, you must keep in mind the true purpose of the internship: to reinforce the knowledge you have gained in the classroom and to provide an opportunity for you to observe the legal setting and gain legal experience. Often, a student realizes just how much they learned during their internship once they begin working in a paralegal position.

Here's how you can honestly evaluate your internship: Look back at the self-assessment and goals you developed in Chapter 1. Determine which goals you've met and which you still want to accomplish. Revise them if necessary. Using your worksheet, internship notebook, and perhaps your personal calendar, match your specific internship experiences to the goals you set. Consider these questions:

- Did you work independently on any projects or work better under strictly supervised conditions?
- Did you demonstrate flexibility and/or help the firm with any extra projects?
- What did you learn about the size of the firm where you worked? What personality types did you encounter and what personal skills did you develop to help you work with a wide variety of people?
- Did you learn more about a particular area of law that interests you?
- Did you discover a talent or interest that you never knew existed?
- Were you able to parlay skills from previous education and/or employment to your internship experience?

Consider the overall experience, but also consider specific details:

- What area(s) of law did you experience?
- How many people were in the office (attorneys, paralegals, and support staff)? How many people directly supervised you?

- What types of documents did you work on?
- What cases did the firm have while you were there?
- How many clients did you speak to?

After completing your internship and considering these questions, you should feel well equipped to document the internship experience on your résumé and begin thinking about how this experience will relate to your future job search and, ultimately, your place of employment in the legal field.

J.   Thank You Letters

Throughout the duration of your internship, your supervisors, and probably other personnel, have undoubtedly sacrificed their time to help you on your way. Hopefully you have provided a service to them as well. Always remember to be grateful and gracious. A thank you letter is an opportunity for you to acknowledge time spent on your behalf and maintain a positive connection with individuals in the legal field. If you have several letters to send, it is fine to use a template, but make each letter as unique as possible. In your letter, cite specifically a time when the person stopped to show you something or mention a project that you worked on together. If you are using a template, make sure you proofread each letter to be sure it corresponds to the addressee.

NetWorks

www.timeslips.com	Web site for timekeeping software commonly used by law firms. This site offers a free trial and demos. Use this to familiarize yourself with the software for your internship.
www.abanet.org	The ABA's Web site has information on ethical guidelines for paralegals, as well as discussions and articles on paralegal ethics.
www.abajournal.com	The ABA's Web site for legal news. News and information for attorneys, paralegals, and legal personnel.
www.legalassistanttoday .com	Publication and Web site covering legal news for the paralegal profession. Has discussion boards as well as a Listserv to subscribe to.

Chapter Summary

- Prepare for your internship by confirming times, dates, responsibilities and, based on observations, appropriate attire.
- All paralegal interns must be familiar with the ethical rules of confidentiality, unauthorized practice of law, conflicts of interest, and financial matters.
- The firm or college will expect that you keep track of your time by recording dates, legal matter worked on, and case numbers or names.
- Law firms have their own culture so be sure you understand the general rules of who does what, of how to address people, and the general norms of behavior and decorum.
- Be ready to speak with your supervisor in a respectful, professional way if you feel you are being underutilized or overutilized.
- Be sure to get a written recommendation from your supervisor before you complete your required hours.
- Make notes of your general impressions and the tasks completed for future reference.
- Be realistic about the experience by understanding that you are in a learning mode and will probably have much more responsibility once you complete your education and are ready for a permanent paralegal job.
- Evaluate your internship in terms of your personality and the interest inventory you completed prior to the start of the internship.
- Write a sincere thank you letter at the completion of your internship experience.

Key Terms

Conflict of interest: A real or seeming incompatibility between the interests of a lawyer's clients, such that the lawyer is disqualified from representing both clients if the dual representation adversely affects either client or if the clients do not consent.

Unauthorized practice of law (UPL): The practice of law by a person, typically a nonlawyer, who has not been licensed or admitted to practice law in a given jurisdiction.

Vicarious disqualification: Disqualification of all the lawyers of a firm or in an office because one of the lawyers is ethically disqualified from representing the client at issue.

Screen *or* **Chinese wall** *or* **cone of silence:** A screening mechanism that protects client confidences by preventing one or more lawyers within an organization from participating in any matter involving that client.

Bits and Bytes

- Sixty-two percent of the respondents to a National Association of Legal Assistants (NALA) Survey indicated that they receive their work assignments from one or more specific attorneys or from specific departments.

- Guideline 6 of the ABA guidelines for the Utilization of Paralegal Services: "A lawyer is responsible for taking reasonable measures to ensure that all client confidences are preserved by a paralegal."

- Research shows that 85 percent of companies use internships and similar experiential education programs to recruit for their full-time workforces.

Discussion Questions

1. In what ways could you protect yourself from the unauthorized practice of law when answering client questions?

2. As an intern, what can you do to help keep the confidentiality of the firm's clients? What if your family or loved ones want to know about the cases you are working on?

3. Discuss the issues surrounding a firm or lawyer charging a client for the time/work of a paralegal intern.

WebWork

1. Go to the ABA's Center for Professional Responsibility at http://www.abanet.org/cpr/e2k/home.html.

   Locate the ABA Model Rules of Professional Conduct.

   a. What are the most recent changes to the Model Rules?
   b. What states have adopted the Model Rules?

2. Go to the ABA's Center for Professional Responsibility at http://www.abanet.org/cpr/professionalism/home.html.

   Under the "Additional Resources" heading, click *Professionalism Code and Reports*.

   a. What code is listed under your state and/or county?
   b. Describe the ethical concerns and duties.

3. Visit FindLaw's legal software page at http://marketcenter.findlaw .com/software.html3.

   a. List and describe the software that is used for timekeeping and billing.
   b. Which software packages include electronic billing?

Finding the
Right Job

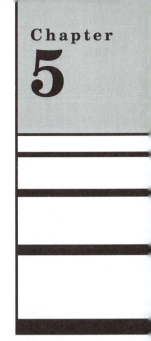

Revising Your Internship Résumé and Cover Letter for Permanent Employment

Each of us makes our own weather and determines the color
of the skies in the emotional universe that we inhabit.
—Fulton J. Sheen

Chapter Overview

As you near the completion of your paralegal education, it is time to revisit your initial self-assessment and update your goals. Most likely you will have solidified some of your career decisions and discovered opportunities you didn't know existed when you first considered a paralegal career. Now it is time to revise your résumé and decide on a format, draft a succinct cover letter, and line up references. Consider all of the various contacts and resources available to you. Get an organized plan and set up a file to keep track of your efforts. Make copies of writing samples that you plan to share with potential employers. You may find the task ahead of you more challenging than any of your classes or your internship, but it is one that will culminate in your reaching your goal of starting your professional career as a paralegal.

A. Revisiting Your Goals and the Marketplace

Now that you have the experience of working in a legal setting, go back to your self-assessment and review your lists of initial objectives, interests, and career goals. Without a doubt, some of your goals and impressions have changed. Consider your personal internship experience, including the size of the firm, the type of law, your duties, and the personalities involved. Now, redraft your lists. Also, make a list of things that you could have done differently to make the internship a perfect experience. What were you surprised about? How was the experience different than what you anticipated? Based on all of the above, challenge yourself to rethink your initial lists and create for yourself some new goals and objectives based on your real-life experience.

B.   Updating Your Résumé to Reflect Your Internship Experience

Go back to the initial résumé you prepared for your internship. It will be exciting to record and document your legal internship experience and see how different the résumé looks. For many paralegal students the only legal experience they have will be an internship. While some students might find it appropriate to have a new category titled "internships," others will just list the internship under "experience." Be sure to follow the same format that you did for your other paid experiences by indicating the complete name of the firm, city and state, your title (Intern or Paralegal Intern), dates, and a description of your duties. It is often helpful to ask your internship supervisor to help you with your description or to review a draft of your description. Be very specific when describing what you did and leave out generic phrases such as "did legal research" or "drafted documents." Rather, indicate what issues of law you researched and what specific document you drafted. Take into account the following phrases taken from actual graduates' résumés.

- Summarized depositions
- Provided litigation support
- Conducted court and online research
- Gathered, sorted, filed, classified, and copied documents
- Maintained and updated client records
- Indexed documents
- Drafted pleadings
- Handled administrative duties

Although the above tasks are legitimate paralegal duties, they leave the reader wondering what area of law, the exact nature of the assignment and whether the intern actually performed the tasks because they are so devoid of explanation or specificity. Rather, indicate exactly what issues of law you researched and what specific documents you drafted. These phrases are also taken from actual graduates' résumés.

- Conducted research on 1031 Tax-Deferred Exchanges
- Prepared draft elements of Environmental Impact Report for proposed desalinization facility

- Prepared client documents for visa and labor certifications
- Utilized Miller and Starr to research licensing for brokers and salespersons
- Wrote special interrogatories for personal injury case and retrieved medical and billing records from local hospitals
- Researched and prepared report on debt remedies for senior citizens
- Drafted memorandum in support of parole hearing
- Developed Excel spreadsheet for conservatorship
- Calculated spousal and child support using SupporTax software

The difference in the two lists is readily apparent. The reader can now identify with the tasks performed and has a clearer understanding of the specifics of the assignments. By providing detailed information, you can anticipate the needs of a potential employer and thereby win yourself an interview. The résumé becomes much more interesting and encourages the reader to continue reading as the details become more specific.

In describing jobs or internships stay away from vague and unquantifiable words such as "various," "extensive," "some," and "all." Review each line of your description and make sure every word counts. Surveys of employers reveal that good writing and computer skills are in high demand. Always mention writing tasks and any computer programs you used in your internship, regardless of whether they were firm-specific or generally available.

While every intern and paralegal is occasionally called upon to do basic administrative tasks, leave out as much as possible routine secretarial duties such as: answered phone, filed documents in alphabetical order, faxed documents, and photocopied letters because it is understood that at this level you can already perform those basic tasks.

Do not violate any ethical boundaries by mentioning names of specific people, companies, clients, or parties. Be general enough in your descriptions so that you do not violate any confidentiality rules.

C. Variations on a Theme: Different Résumés for Different Jobs

While it is fine to have one generic résumé, it is often necessary to slightly tailor the résumé toward specific job qualifications. Carefully read the job description or ad. Go back and adjust your résumé objective to include some of the wording in the ad. Reread your job descriptions and make sure they also emphasize what the writer of the ad is requesting. Encourage the reader to continue reading by writing a job objective that emphasizes your skills. If an ad asks for a real estate paralegal and you have no direct experience in that field of law but have worked in an administrative capacity in that environment, word your objective accordingly. The following illustrates how to gear an objective to a specific job.

> **Job Objective:** Paralegal graduate with four years of experience working with real estate brokers and salespersons seeks paralegal position.

In a separate section we will also talk about how to adjust cover letters to a specific job.

D.   Switching Career Tracks

Most paralegal programs have students who are changing careers, and those students have a lot to offer because of previous work experience and transferable skills. Over the years many professions have suffered a period of glut in staffing or, conversely, cycles where staff are getting "burned out" in the field. These trends are cyclical, and paralegal programs gladly accept and value students leaving other fields because of what they bring to the classroom: a variety of business, technical, and professional perspectives. As you embark on your search for a new career that best fits you, highlight on your résumé and verbalize in interviews what unique qualities you would bring to an organization. The following are some examples of acquired, transferable skills, depending on your background.

1. **Nurses** understand the medical field, including its terminology, staff structure, and hospital or medical office procedures. Firms that are involved in personal injury or medical malpractice welcome applicants who have experience in reading medical records and understanding the culture of hospitals and doctors' offices. Those candidates will know how to obtain relevant medical records and how to read charts and are often very knowledgeable about doctor notations.
2. **Accounting** experience can be valuable because familiarity with accounting processes can be applicable to corporate law, firms dealing with estate planning and probate, family law firms, and banks. An understanding of money issues and basic business principles can be a part of the procedural aspects of law suits and settlements. People who have worked in the accounting field often have accounting-specific computer skills and may be adept at reading and interpreting budgets, spreadsheets, or financial reports.
3. **Business owners** are knowledgeable with contracts, vendors, licenses, accounting procedures, personnel issues, compliance matters, and other legal procedures that can be applicable to any field of law. Anyone who has owned a business must have been highly organized, resourceful, and hard working.

4. **Computer** experience is one the most prized skills in any legal environment because discovery information, accountings, documents, depositions, and thousands of pieces of paper are sorted, copied, and recorded in sophisticated computer programs. More and more, firms use complex computer systems to mange their trials, clients' files, office business records, and settlements. Firms often look for candidates with previous experience creating Web sites and programming skills.

5. **Construction industry workers** may find a niche in construction defect firms because they understand the industry, know the terminology, and have worked on construction sites, which paralegals often visit to obtain evidence for litigation cases.

6. **Human resources personnel** will have knowledge of employment law, benefits, insurance, hiring and dismissal procedures, and the particular statutes and codes that apply to employment issues.

7. **Insurance** experience can be valuable for litigation firms that deal with compliance issues, personal injury claims and accidents, workers' compensation, or corporate issues that deal with insurance.

8. **Law enforcement personnel** have experience writing reports, have knowledge of statutes and codes, and are familiar with the court system. They may find employment with a District Attorney, public defender, or criminal law attorney.

9. **Marketing** experience may be helpful to firms and companies that want good writers, creative methods to solve marketing strategies, and employees with good public relations skills. The skills in this field could contribute to planning marketing campaigns; designing brochures, Web sites, and stationery; and dealing with clients and the public.

10. **Office workers** already have a sense of business, deadlines, and general office tasks. They are familiar with computer programs, office procedures and equipment, and working as part of a team. Their experience makes them valuable in all firms, companies, and legal settings because of the professionalism acquired in previous office jobs.

11. **Real estate agents** have negotiation and people skills, familiarity with lending practices and procedures, geographical information, and a legal background to give themselves a head start at firms.

12. **Retail sales** provides opportunities for developing people skills, business acumen, goal setting, and teamwork.

13. **Social workers** will have obtained medical knowledge, arbitration and mediation skills, people skills, and, oftentimes, experience working with the elderly, children, families at risk, or disadvantaged members of the community.

14. **Teachers** have experience working with varied age groups, organizing activities, writing lesson plans, and generally good communication and writing experience. They have an excellent understanding of teamwork and working with people with a variety of backgrounds and needs.

15. **Title searchers**, or **escrow officers**, can be valuable in firms or corporations that deal with real estate development, transactions, and property issues.

Never underestimate any paid, volunteer, internship, or other life experience you have had. In fact, volunteer and unpaid work can often be more challenging than a paid experience. Applicants sometimes forget about the organizational, people, writing, and business skills they developed as part of volunteer work. One student mentioned that the most difficult job she ever had was being Girl Scout cookie chairperson, for which she had to muster up all of her accounting, marketing, selling, psychology, and parenting skills.

E.   Job Search Strategies

1. Personal Contacts

If you have followed the previously offered advice, you should by now have some friends and contacts in the legal profession. Classmates, professors, and friends should be acquainted with your background skills and goals. Don't be afraid to let them know the specifics of your plans. If circumstances allow, extend the duration of your internship to gain more experience. Never feel that you are bothering someone when you ask them for a referral or ideas about how to go conduct your job search. Most people have been in the same situation and needed help, and most are more than willing to assist you because they understand your angst, eagerness, and need for assistance and encouragement. Remember that most jobs (80% to 90%) are never advertised. They are generally found through word of mouth.

2. Building Your Network

Beyond your personal contacts, begin building a network of people who can help you accomplish your goals. Look for mentors and study their career paths. Read professional publications and know what is happening in the job market in your area. Connect with as many positive role models as possible. Go on informational interviews which are described later in this chapter. Remember, this is a time when your positive attitude is critical. Follow up on all leads. One contact turns into two, two into four, and four into eight; the possibilities increase in proportion to your pursuing all of your leads. Classrooms are sometimes the best environment for networking. Many students are already working in the legal field and have firsthand knowledge of job openings before they are ever advertised. Faculty often make announcements for available positions, and they can also act as references for you when you do apply for a job. Finally, be sure you tell everyone you know about your career goals and objectives.

3. *Professional Associations*

There is nothing better than a sense of belonging. By pursuing your education you are entitled to membership in myriad professional associations, such as national or local paralegal associations, alumni associations, and other groups that can provide a secure network for you. By joining these groups you will discover opportunities for growth in your field and establish your credibility as a member of the legal community. One word of caution: Before paying a large membership fee to any group or organization, investigate the association online or through your education office to ensure its legitimacy and track record. Many groups also have student fees that are lower than a regular membership.

4. *Paralegal Program or College Employment Assistance*

Paralegal programs that are approved by the American Bar Association (ABA) are required to have an employment assistance plan in place. This service usually includes résumé and interviewing workshops, help with developing and refining résumés, a list of firms that have submitted jobs to the program placement office, and books and articles on paralegal placement. Even if a program is not ABA approved, accrediting agencies usually require the institution to provide some type of assistance after graduation and to keep track of where graduates are working. If your program has an alumni association, join it while you are still a student. It may be less expensive and will allow you to get started on your job search much earlier. Students often find a job prior to graduating. Career counselors at your college may be better able to assess your transferable skills and give you suggestions for nontraditional placement. Program personnel are always willing to help you because a happy, successful graduate is the best advertisement for future students.

5. *Print Advertisements*

Although the majority of paralegal positions are not advertised in local community papers, find out if there is a legal newspaper in your area. Call your county bar association and ask for the name of a paper or any other publication that will be useful. Most firms will advertise in specialized legal newspapers if one is available. Never be afraid to apply for a job if it states that you need to have one to three years of experience. That requirement could be waived if you can offer some transferable skills such as writing, organization, communication, and computer knowledge. Oftentimes, firms advertise for experienced paralegals but find that they do not have the budget to hire such a person. You will then be in the right place at the right time.

Be sure to look beyond titles on any job listing. Read the job description. Entry-level positions may be called "case assistant," "case clerk," "legal analyst," "compliance assistant," "human resources assistant," or other titles that do not use the word "paralegal" or "legal assistant." Government legal jobs are rarely advertised in any newspaper; we discuss them in Subsection 7, below.

6. *Placement Agencies (Legal and General)*

In the last 15 years, there has been a proliferation of legal placement agencies that place paralegals, attorneys, or other legal staff. The positions available may be either full- or part-time and may be permanent or temporary. In the current job market, the firm or company pays a fee if the placement agency successfully finds someone who is a good fit for the job. Companies and firms use placement agencies because they want to avoid the interviewing process, computer testing, background checks, and the chance that the person will not be a good fit. In other words, for a fee, a professional group will do the hiring. In that situation, try to find out about the agency by looking online and getting information about how long they have been in business, their success rate, and who they work with in the legal community. Agencies can be an excellent resource for temporary and part-time positions for entry-level graduates, as well as for more experienced graduates and workers. When you submit your résumé and are asked in for an interview, be ready to be tested on your computer skills. You will also need to provide additional copies of your résumé, a list of references, and, possibly, transcripts from your paralegal program or a copy of your paralegal certificate.

General placement agencies may be less familiar with legal positions and generally have more listings for clerical and other positions outside the legal arena. Be sure to ask for specifics about the job listings so that you do not waste either your time or their time. Inquire about their knowledge about paralegals and the general duties assigned to their listed legal positions.

7. *Web Sites*

Web sites can be a valuable resource for job leads, as well as information about companies and firms to which you are applying. They can be fee-based or free. Be a good consumer before spending money to join a site that promises to have jobs available. Oftentimes the listings are in a limited geographical location or there will be very few legitimate paralegal positions listed.

Monster.com and craigslist.com are examples of free Web sites from which numerous graduates have found positions. Employers pay a fee to list their job but applicants are not charged for searching the listings. Local and legal newspapers' Web sites often include a help wanted section with listings broken down by category, such as "legal" or "paralegal." Do some exploring on the Internet by going to a search engine and typing in "legal" and "jobs" and the name of the city where you're seeking employment. You'll likely get numerous leads and it's a good way to begin.

Most government jobs are not advertised in local or legal newspapers. Remember: The government is one of the larger employers of paralegals. Government agencies hire at the city, county, state, and federal levels. Online search engines (such as Google.com) will be your best friends in finding these addresses. Simply type in your city, county, or state name, along with the word "jobs" and you will be referred to the appropriate source. Read job descriptions rather than titles. Most government agencies have their own specific applications and do not accept résumés. Any phone book includes a list all of the government agencies and contact information.

The Internet and Web sites are an excellent way to research firms and to get information on attorneys before you go on interviews. They can also help you find out if a specific firm has any jobs available. Do a search on **Westlaw** or **LEXIS** to research firms in your city that practice a certain type of law. Then go to the firm Web site to learn more about available job opportunities. With the advent of Web sites there is a great deal more publicly available information than in the past. The advantage of doing research ahead of time is that it makes it easier to ask relevant questions, comment on specifics of the firm, sound intelligent, and find out if the firm's culture will be right for you.

Westlaw and **LEXIS:** Fee-based legal research computer services; computerized systems used for legal research.

F. References

Put together your reference list, including at least one person from your internship. You should have one piece of paper with information on the top that says: "References for: [Your Name]." Include your address, phone number, and email address in case this piece of paper gets separated from your résumé. Offer the references to the interviewer at the end of your interview and allow him or her to contact the people on the list. Having this and a writing sample available will show your organizational skills. But more importantly, it will demonstrate your preparedness for and seriousness about the job search.

Your references sheet should contain a minimum of three and a maximum of five references. For each entry include the person's name, the relationship to you (teacher, supervisor, coworker), and include a complete address, phone number and email address. Be sure you have asked permission to list references in advance of giving out the list and confirm with each person his or her preferred form of contact by a potential employer. It is rarely a good idea to list names of neighbors, friends, or relatives because the interviewer will want an objective assessment of your work ethic, habits, and skills. Letters of reference that you bring to the interview may not be acceptable as you have already seen them and most authors of a written reference may not be perceived as being candid. If you hand a reference to the interviewer, it will always be good or you would not have offered it. The majority of the time, an interviewer will want to talk directly to the reference in order to ask about specific skills or personality traits needed for the job.

Sharing writing samples of work you have done in class may be a good way of convincing an interviewer of your skills and knowledge. Make changes to corrected papers and assignments ahead of time if they were less than perfect, and bring any papers with positive teacher comments, such as "one of the best assignments I have ever read."

G. Getting the Inside Scoop: Informational Interviews

Informational interview: An interview set up by a prospective job seeker to obtain information about a practice field or job.

Informational interviews are an excellent way of networking. For an informational interview the student contacts someone associated with the legal field and asks for 20 or 30 minutes of the person's time to get advice about embarking on a paralegal career and gathering general information about the legal field. The interview could be with a faculty person, working paralegal, graduate of a program, attorney acquaintance, or business person who deals with attorneys. Clearly explain to interviewers that you understand they might not have a position available but that you would simply like to talk with them as a way to prepare for your job search and focus your career goals. Bring a copy of your résumé and cover letter and ask the interviewer to comment on them. The informational interview almost always results in the name of another person or two whom you can contact. Be sure to follow up on the leads quickly and *always* write a thank you letter to the people who gave you their time and ideas.

H. Job Search Myths

1. **There are no paralegal jobs**. No matter how glutted the market gets, there are always opportunities for good people with good attitudes.
2. **No one hires without experience**. Recent paralegal graduates get jobs all the time. You must sell yourself, articulate your transferable skills, be willing to start with whatever opportunity you are given, and communicate your "can do" attitude.
3. **My paralegal program will get me a job**. You are responsible for your success. Pretend your program does not exist, develop a reasoned, well-thought-out job plan, and then execute it. Your program can guide you and provide support, but it cannot get a job for you.
4. **I didn't learn enough in my paralegal program**. All programs give you the basics but you need to apply them. Hopefully you learned how to do some practical things in each class. Mention those to any interviewer. Indicate that you are a quick learner, a hard worker, and can be a success if someone gives you a chance.

5. **I don't want to compromise my standards.** Rarely is any job going to meet all of your standards. If the salary is not quite where you wanted it to be but you like the area of law and the people and will receive a performance review and possible raise in six months, then give it a try.

6. **They need to accept me the way I am.** Not really. It is a buyer's market and that means that employers have many applicants from which to choose. You need to stop and remember that all of the following will determine your success: being on time, shaking hands, making eye contact, researching the company or firm in advance, dressing professionally (according to firm standards), communicating clearly, listening, and, most importantly, having a positive attitude.

I. The Cover Letter

A cover letter is an introduction to your résumé and should be an example of your best writing skills. It should be brief, usually containing three paragraphs, and include the following: why you are writing, what position you are applying for, what skills you have to offer, the action you will take, and a thank you. Review samples of cover letters from your program office, career counselor, or paralegal or general career books. Be sure your cover letters use a professional business format, are addressed to a particular person, are grammatically correct, and are free of typographical errors. Be professional in your tone. Do not be chummy or gimmicky. Choose your words carefully: Be positive and avoid fluff or flowery descriptions of yourself. Your qualities should be apparent from the education and work experience sections of your résumé and not from the adjectives that you use to describe yourself personally. You may lose credibility with the reader if your cover letter includes such descriptions as self-starter, excellent writer, energetic, healthy, born leader, ethical, perfect candidate, enthusiastic, positive problem-solver, good at multitasking and decision making, organized and devoted, dedicated, hard-working, extremely focused and analytical, team player. The list goes on and on. These qualities should be apparent from your accomplishments, education, and experience described on your résumé or through the answers to questions during an interview. Unfortunately, you may never get to the interview without carefully developing your cover letter. Hype or fluff do not encourage the reader to either seriously consider your résumé or schedule you for an interview.

The first paragraph of the cover letter should include information about why you are writing and what position you are applying for. Although both points seem obvious, it is essential to let the reader know up front where you found out about the job and the specific job for which you would like to interview. Did your paralegal program office refer you? Did a friend give you the lead? Did you find an ad on a Web site or in a newspaper? The source gives readers a frame of reference or refreshes their memory if they have advertised through various sources. Many firms or companies have numerous jobs available and need to know exactly which job you want. A large firm may have positions available in the mail room all the way up to attorneys, and your identifying the specific job you are eligible for saves the reader from guessing.

The second paragraph should include information about why you believe you are qualified for the job. This is the most difficult paragraph to write because you have to engage the reader but do not want to repeat too many details that are already on the résumé. Think summary. For example, "As a recent paralegal graduate with experience as a medical records examiner I am especially interested in the paralegal position in your personal injury department" gives the reviewer good reason to call you in for an interview.

This part of the cover letter should be a general summary of your education along with any experience that would be of significant interest to the employer. For those who do not have related work experience, you can connect your practical training in the classroom and internship experience to the specifics of the job: "In civil litigation class, we completed complaints, interrogatories, and pleadings. That experience, coupled with my internship at a construction defect firm, has given me the background to begin a paralegal position at your firm." Sentences such as these pique the interest of the reader and encourage them to call you to find out more about your education and experience.

The third and final paragraph is where you thank the reader for taking time to review your résumé, indicate your enthusiasm for your new career, and suggest a next step. "I look forward to meeting with you to discuss the position."; "Please feel free to contact me at your convenience to set up a time to meet."; "I am available to interview at your convenience and look forward to meeting you." These statements, combined with a sincere "thank you," are a courteous way to end the correspondence.

J.   Common Blunders on Résumés and Cover Letters

1. Résumé Blunders

• **More than one page.** The majority of interviewers prefer one page because they have a limited amount of time to review your information. More is not better. Most applicants, if they present information in an organized fashion with a careful formatting, can relay the relevant information in one page.

• **Typographical errors.** This is one of the main reasons people do not get called for interviews. There is no excuse for typos, and carelessness and a lack of attention to detail will be an automatic mark against you.

• **Hype (a flowery description of yourself).** There is a trend toward paragraphs that are titled Qualifications or Summary of Skills.

Most of the time this is the adjective category and is not a list of actual skills. Self-starter, intelligent, honest are neither qualifications nor skills and can be seen as boastful or egotistical.

- **Dishonesty.** Honesty on your résumé is what creates a sense of your ethics. If you omit crucial information or mislead the reader, it can be cause for dismissal from a job. Hiding information or inflating it can be perceived as a character flaw.

- **Disorganization, poor formatting.** If a reader cannot find the relevant information they are seeking in about 15 seconds or if the information is presented in a confusing fashion, your résumé will quickly find its way to the "do not pursue" pile. No matter how qualified you are, the reader does not have time to reconstruct your life.

- **Listing religious or political affiliations.** Do not bring out latent prejudices in the reader. While we hope no one actively, illegally discriminates, certain affiliations bring out impressions that may not be accurate but that can eliminate you from consideration for a job.

- **Oddly colored or overly heavy paper.** Do not try to stand out from the crowd with unconventionally colored paper or extra-heavy stock paper. You may end up standing out in a negative way.

- **Complete sentences rather than phrases.** This is one time in your life when you do not have to write in complete sentences. Take advantage of it and start your phrases with active present- or past-tense verbs.

- **Using pronouns.** If you write your résumé using phrases, as noted just above, you should not have a problem with this.

- **Poor grammar.** This falls in the same category as typos. Any grammar mistakes will be perceived as carelessness or poor education and will ensure that your résumé lands in the "do not pursue" pile.

- **Listing any name other than you own.** Your résumé should never explicitly name supervisors or references. It is a document describing you and your skills.

2. *Cover Letter Blunders*

- **Using a "one size fits all" cover letter (too generic).** Tailor your cover letter to the specific job you are seeking. Do not ask for a job with "your firm" when it is a company or clinic or agency.

- **Starting too many sentences with "I."** Once you start, it is hard to stop. Vary your sentence structure and be creative with words so that the reader admires your writing style and creativity.

- **Too much repetition from résumé.** It is not necessary to bore the reader by completely duplicating the information on the next page (your résumé). Be considerate of the reader's time and succinctly summarize the portions of your skills or education that directly pertain to the job you're seeking.

- **Typographical errors.** As with résumés, this is a big problem. Using a word processor spell check will not catch incorrect word usage — for example, "abut" instead of "about" — and is the one blunder that is sure to sabotage your goals. While you may not be able to change your education and cannot add to your experience, you are in complete control of the image you give the reader. Proofread your cover letters as carefully as you did your résumé.

• **Poor grammar.** Your résumé will never be read if you have a grammar mistake in your cover letter. If grammar is a personal weakness, ask someone with good skills to review and correct your work. You should also consider investing in a solid grammar book and review it often. Writing will most certainly be part of your paralegal career, and it would be good to hone your grammar and writing skills.

• **Mixing verb tenses.** Be sure you use consistent verb tenses, following the rules of good grammar. Have someone else proofread your work if you are in doubt.

• **Listing high school information or activities.** Sadly those carefree days are gone forever. Employers want to know what you have accomplished in the way of education and experience that supports your application for the professional job they are trying to fill. Rarely would any high school activity or other awards be relevant to that goal.

• **Being too familiar.** Avoid being cute or overly friendly. The reader expects to be treated the same professional way in writing as in person.

• **Sounding too aggressive or pushy.** Do not annoy the reader or come across as pressuring the potential interviewer. You will have lost the job before you have begun.

• **Using Xerox or copy paper.** While you do not want to use overly heavy paper stock, you should use a quality paper that feels substantial in the reader's hands. Your career and future are well worth this small investment.

K.   Your Job-Hunting Notebook

Throughout the course of your job search, you should keep a notebook or journal of your thoughts and impressions. As soon as possible after an interview, jot down your thoughts and impressions about the position being offered, the interviewer, and the office environment. Your job-hunting notebook can be as sophisticated or simple as you choose. It can be done by hand or on a computer. What matters most is that you develop a process and then stick to it faithfully. After a while, or if you have numerous interviews in a single day, it is easy to mix up the names, places, and details of an interview or a lead. By having a system and entering the information while it is fresh in your mind, you will later be able to review your notes and refresh your memory.

The following is a list of items that could also be included in your notebook:

• **Résumés:** Always keep copies of your résumé available, remembering that you may need different résumés for different jobs.

Bring extra copies of your résumé to an interview. Have extra copies available in your car and always bring them to meetings or places where you will have contact with legal personnel. Update your résumé as necessary.

- **Sample Cover Letters:** Develop several templates so that you readily have the document available and can also tailor it to the particular job.
- **Reference Sheet:** Prepare your one-page sheet, update it as necessary, and have it available at interviews.
- **Writing Samples:** Bring to interviews copies of assignments you did in class or examples of work you did during your internship in case your specific skills are discussed in an interview. Be sure to delete or mask names of firms or people and make corrections on your class assignments.
- **Interview Reminders:** Make a checklist of interview "dos and don'ts" and review it the day prior to an interview. Make note of dress, eye contact, manners, directions, parking, names; check that you have extra résumés and references; develop any other reminders that work for you. Preparation is the key to calming nerves.
- **Question List:** This should include both questions that are often asked in an interview and possible questions that you will ask the interviewer. Review them before you go into the interview.
- **Contact Log:** Every time you go on a Web site, are given a name, or are referred to another person, you should record names, addresses, phone numbers, impressions, and the proactive step you took to utilize the resources of the contacts.
- **Interview Log:** Each time you are interviewed, record names, addresses, phone numbers, impressions, and any other information that will refresh your memory when you write a thank you letter. Also, make notes as to how you did in the interview, things you would do differently, and techniques that worked. Assess yourself.

L. What to Do if Nothing Works

You have combed the want ads, called everyone you know, checked out the job board at your paralegal program, looked on the Internet, joined the paralegal association, and, so far, no luck.

What then? If you did not get any interviews, perhaps it is time to have an outside, objective person review your résumé and cover letter for tone and content. If you do not get any interviews, the reason may be those two documents. Be ready to take the criticism constructively and refine and rewrite your résumé and cover letter to address the reviewer's suggestions.

If you have been interviewed but received no job offers, it may be time to get an objective person to do a mock interview with you. Have someone, perhaps a faculty person, program administrator, or working paralegal, sit down with you and conduct a practice interview for a paralegal position. Have them critique you on your appearance, eye contact, ability to answer questions succinctly, answer content, and general demeanor. While this can be a difficult exercise for both parties, it is often a learning experience. Constructive criticism is difficult to hear but it is sometimes the only way to improve your skills. Even if you do not agree with the critique, openly consider that if one person perceives you that way, others may too. The mock interviewer has your best interests in mind. You might even contact a previous interviewer and ask if they have any suggestions of things you need to work on for future interviews. You could include this request in your thank you letter. Or, call and leave a message that you would appreciate any feedback.

Finally, never give up. Discouragement can come across in an interview, so be sure to tackle every opportunity as though it were your first and with a positive attitude. While everyone wants a job immediately after graduation, for many graduates that process is protracted. (The norm for landing that first job after graduation is three to four months.) Keep busy networking, and every week go back to your list of search strategies and begin again.

1.   *Additional Internships*

You might consider going back to your internship site and volunteering to get more experience. If it cannot take you, ask for suggestions of other firms that might want an intern. Ask your program director if there are other internship opportunities available. Offer your services for free to one of the people who spent time with you on an informational interview. The more continuous experience you get, the better your chances of someone recognizing you and your persistence and dedication to your goal.

2.   *Pro Bono Opportunities*

Pro bono:
Legal services that are provided for the public or for those in need without charge.

Many legal clinics welcome help and your county bar association can be a good source of information about **pro bono** opportunities. Call the local paralegal association. Through their members you may find some leads to get involved in agencies and groups that need your expertise or are willing to take someone with little practical experience and lead them along. Within each of those groups there will be attorneys and paralegals who will be good contacts and could provide you with even more leads and additional references in the future.

3.   *Temporary Jobs*

Consider taking any job that is related to the legal field, even if it is not ideally suited to your skill level. It will afford you the chance to mingle with new contacts, give you additional information to include on your résumé, and possibly ensure that you are in the right place at the right time if other opportunities become available. Be sure to let placement agencies know that you are available for part-time or temporary work. Temporary employees who substitute for personnel on a leave of absence often end up getting hired for the job if the on-leave staff person decides not to come back to the job.

4. *Reconnect with Faculty*

Ask your paralegal faculty if they have any special projects you can work on for them or if they know of anyone who could use some volunteer help. As you go through your paralegal program, let faculty know about your availability and interests and ask them for ideas and advice.

NetWorks

www.roberthalflegal.com	National firm specializing in the temporary and permanent placement of attorneys, paralegals, and legal support personnel.
www.usajobs.opm.gov	The official job site for the U.S. government. Site highlights the hiring process, application requirements, and open positions in all branches of the government.
www.findlaw.com	Site that contains information about local lawyers and basic information about any firm; can be used to find firms that practice in a particular area of law. Can be used before an interview to research a firm or sole practitioner.
www.jobweb.com	Web site with job listings, résumé writing tips, interviewing tips, and other helpful articles for students drafting their first résumé.

Chapter Summary

- Embark on your goals with a positive attitude and determination to start your new career.
- Successful paralegals will tell you that the job search was far more difficult than the job was once they got it.
- There are almost always times of uncertainty and discouragement during a job search, but you should remember that you have all the tools you need to succeed.
- Thousands of paralegal graduates get jobs every year and there is no reason why you should not join the ranks.
- The odds are with you.
- With all the competition and all things being equal in education and experience, what separates out the winners is fairly simple.
- Those who succeed have good résumés and cover letters, develop a realistic job search plan, know where to look for jobs, follow through on every lead, and keep track of their progress.
- All of the education, experience, networking, and hard work will finally pay off if you are persistent and follow all of the above suggestions. It is guaranteed!

Key Terms

Westlaw: A fee-based legal research computer service; a computerized system used for legal research.

LEXIS: A fee-based legal research computer service; a computerized system used for legal research.

Informational interview: An interview set up by a prospective job seeker to obtain information about a practice field or job.

Pro bono: Legal Services that are provided for the public or for those in need without charge.

Bits and Bytes

- Paralegals and legal assistants held approximately 200,000 jobs in 2006.

- 84 percent of executives say it takes just one or two typographical errors in a résumé to remove a candidate from consideration; 47 percent said one typo is a deciding factor.

- 42.7 percent of résumés contained one or more significant inaccuracies.

Discussion Questions

1. List and describe the items that should be included in your Job-Hunting Notebook. How could missing one of these items be detrimental to your job search?

2. You have an interview at a law firm in your city. What are some questions that you should ask the hiring manager? What are some things you would like to find out about the position, firm, or office culture?

WebWork

1. Access the "Exercises (And Answer Keys)" section of the OWL Handouts, located at http://owl.english.purdue.edu/handouts/index2.html#exercises.

   a. Complete the following exercises:
      i. Exercises for Eliminating Wordiness
      ii. Adjective or Adverb?
      iii. Punctuation Exercise
   b. Also, under "Professional Writing," review:
      i. Résumé Design
      ii. Tailoring Employment Documents for a Specific Audience
      iii. Reference Sheet

Interviewing and Negotiating

Practice is the best of all instructors.
—Publicus Syrus

Chapter Overview

One of the most important tasks you will ever undertake is selling yourself during a job interview. This chapter introduces you to types of interviews and the interview process. Although there are a variety of different types of interviews, all require planning and preparation. You must research the potential employer, examine the market in your area, alert your references, and rehearse your answers to anticipated questions, especially the difficult ones about employment gaps, poor grades, and the like. After your interview, update your job notebook, and be sure to thank the interviewer. A thank you note showcases your communication skills and your professionalism. This chapter also discusses how to respond to an offer, provides some strategies for salary negotiations, and concludes by reminding you to contact your network and your paralegal program as soon as you accept an offer of employment. Because nearly three-fourths of all paralegals are employed by law firms, this chapter focuses primarily on interviewing and negotiating for law firm positions; however, the key steps in interviewing in other legal settings (for example, for in-house positions) are nearly identical.

A. Preparing for Interviews: Seven Key Steps

If your cover letter and résumé are polished and professional, you will likely be contacted for an interview, but don't wait until you are called for an interview to prepare for it. There are seven critical steps you must take now to be fully prepared for a future interview.

Mock interview:
A practice
interview held
with someone
familiar to help a
candidate pre-
pare for an actual
interview.

• **Participate in a mock interview.** One of the best ways to prepare for an actual interview is to participate in a practice or **mock interview**. Your paralegal program may offer interview workshops or mock interviews. If not, ask a friend or fellow student to role-play the part of an interviewer. Participating in a mock interview will give you valuable experience as you practice responding to tough questions. Ask your "interviewer" to ask you difficult questions about your grades, career expectations, and salary demands. Mock interviews make you more comfortable when the time comes for an actual interview because you will have already practiced answers to the common questions asked during interviews. Consider videotaping your practice interview, and review the tape carefully to determine whether you have any distracting mannerisms or are too fidgety. Don't practice during your actual interview — practice beforehand to gain experience and reduce jitters. Consider practicing how you will answer the telephone when contacted by potential employers, and alert those in your home or apartment how you would like the phone answered and messages taken while you conduct your job search. Children and teens should be reminded of proper telephone etiquette.

• **Gather your documents.** Make sure you have several folders or portfolios ready for any interview. Each folder should include additional copies of your résumé, your transcripts, a copy of your certificate from your paralegal program, your list of references, and writing samples. Consider including personal "kudo" letters or complimentary notes from those you have worked for. These letters provide specific evidence about your praiseworthy work on projects. Writing samples may consist of projects prepared for your research and writing class, such as letters, memoranda, and court documents. Copies of litigation documents (sample complaints or sample answers) and transactional documents (copies of agreements you drafted) should also be included. Make sure that all writing samples are "clean copies," and not the ones marked by your instructors. Similarly, you may include sample writings and projects from your internship (ensuring confidentiality). If your folder is voluminous, consider preparing an index for it and having the materials placed in a spiral binding. In every part of the job-seeking process, be professional. A professional portfolio creates a good first impression and showcases your organization skills.

• **Do your homework about the firm.** Before going to any interview, do some homework. Find out some information about the firm or company. "Google" or do an Internet search for the firm's name to determine if it has been the subject of any press releases or other media announcements. Check LEXIS and Westlaw for information about the firm and the attorneys who may be interviewing you (if you know who they are). Read the firm's entry in *Martindale-Hubbell* so you will know what type of law the firm practices, its representative clients, its size, and other pertinent information. Review the firm's Web site. Most larger firms post pictures and bios of their attorneys; if you know who will be interviewing you, find out some information about the interviewer. Many attorneys write articles that are posted on their firm Web site. Skim a few articles so you can mention them during the interview. Similarly, make a point of mentioning during the interview that you reviewed *Martindale-Hubbell*, even if you comment on something general such as, "I noted that the firm opened an office in Atlanta last year." This will demonstrate not only your familiarity with an important research tool but also your initiative. It will be embarrassing if you ask a question that you should have known the answer to by reviewing *Martindale-Hubbell* or the firm's Web site.

• **Do your homework about the law.** If the position for which you are interviewing is for a certain practice group, such as litigation or corporate law, review your books and notes and generally brush up on this area of law so that you can demonstrate your familiarity with important concepts. If possible, bring writing samples relevant to the position.

• **Do your homework about the market.** You must be prepared to discuss salary. Review available salary information—from your local paralegal association, the National Association of Legal Assistants (NALA), the National Federation of Paralegal Associations (NFPA), the International Paralegal Management Association (IPMA), or *Legal Assistant Today*—so your salary request will be appropriate to your locality and for your experience level.

• **Get your script ready.** At the interview, you will be asked if you have questions about the firm or the position. Be prepared to ask a few questions, such as whether there is a defined career track for paralegals, the nature of the work, or how the firm utilizes its paralegals. Consider preparing a short, written list of questions and bringing it with you to the interview. See Section B.5 below for some ideas on questions to ask. Similarly, be prepared to explain any problem areas in your résumé, such as a poor academic record or employment gaps, and to explain why you left a job (or are looking for a new position). Rehearse your answers to these questions. Be ready to respond to questions about your salary requirements.

• **Alert your references.** Make sure you call or email the individuals who have agreed to serve as references, and alert them that they may be called by the firm with which you are interviewing. Thank them again for serving as references. Don't wait until after the interview. It's possible that the paralegal manager may immediately contact your references as soon as you leave the interview, and it may be devastating if your references can't place you right away or remark, "I didn't even know Jane was interviewing. I wish she'd told me."

Practice Tips

Use the following interview checklist to make sure you're ready:

❑ Do you have the address, directions, phone number, and name of the interviewer or firm?
❑ Have you verified the time of the interview?
❑ Do you have extra copies of your résumé and writing samples?
❑ Have you alerted your references?
❑ Have you reviewed the job description one last time?
❑ Have you glanced in the mirror to make sure your appearance is polished and professional?

B.   The Interview

1.   *The Formalities*

Use the potential employer's Web site (or Mapquest, at www.mapquest .com) to obtain directions to the interview location. If you are not familiar with traffic patterns, consider making a practice run the day before the interview to make sure you know where the office is, where you may park, and so forth. On the actual day of the interview, allow plenty of time. If you arrive more than ten minutes early, wait in the lobby or get a cup of coffee nearby. Plan on arriving at the office ten minutes early. If you are late, you will in all likelihood not get the job (and you may not even get the interview). Bring at least ten extra copies of your résumé. Allow some time in your schedule so you do not need to rush to leave or so that if you are asked to lunch, you can attend.

Do not attend the interview with a chip on your shoulder or make demands of the receptionist. In many instances, law firms rely greatly on the impressions of the support staff, and an observation by the receptionist that you were rude to her or him will result in your disqualification. Be courteous to everyone you meet. Similarly, be respectful of the firm: Do not tear pages out of magazines or newspapers in the reception area.

Unless you have been specifically directed to wear business casual attire, wear conservative business attire, meaning a suit and tie for men and a suit for women. It is considered somewhat risky for women to wear pantsuits to an initial interview. When in doubt, dress up, not down. Do not call in advance to ask if you may wear business casual clothing. See Chapter 8 for additional information on appropriate dress in office settings.

Just before the interview, review the job posting or advertisement about the job. You want to show that you are qualified for this particular job. If the want ad indicates that the position is for a litigation paralegal, focus on tailoring your comments to demonstrate that you are the right candidate for that job. Remind the interviewer that you have taken a litigation class and have with you several sample litigation documents and writing samples.

You will likely be met in the reception area. Stand and greet the person with a firm handshake. Make eye contact. You may be interviewed by any number of people, including the paralegal manager, human resources director, and the paralegals and attorneys with whom you will work. Address the individuals you meet as "Mr." or "Ms." unless directed otherwise. Make sure your cell phone is turned off.

2.   *Types of Interviews*

There are a few different types of interviews, including the following:

a. Preliminary or Screening Interviews

In some instances, the interview may be a *screening* or **preliminary interview** and you will meet only with the paralegal manager. If the paralegal manager believes you to be a good candidate, another interview will be scheduled, at which time you will meet the attorneys and others with whom you would work. Don't underestimate the importance of a screening interview. Although it is short (usually less than one hour), it is designed to weed out unqualified candidates. You will have a very brief period of time to make a good impression. In fact, the telephone call made to you to schedule an interview may be a type of screening interview. You will be judged on your professional demeanor, enthusiasm, grammar, articulateness, and so forth during the telephone call or preliminary meeting.

Preliminary interview: A short interview designed to weed out unqualified candidates.

b. Panel Interviews

You may be interviewed by a panel or group of people, possibly the various people in a practice group with whom you would work. There is no special agenda underlying a **panel interview** (although some experts believe they are intended to see how you handle pressure as you respond to numerous questions "fired" at you from all directions). In law firms, however, a panel interview is done primarily to save time. Establish eye contact with the individual who asks you a question but be sure not to ignore the others in the room.

Panel interview: An interview conducted by a group of individuals.

c. Telephone Interviews

Telephone interviews, in which an interview is conducted entirely by telephone, are not particularly common for paralegals; however, if you will need to work with attorneys or paralegals in a firm's other offices, these individuals may call you to speak with you. Treat a telephone interview as you would an actual interview. Keep your résumé and other materials near you, avoid your computer (it is too much of a temptation to check email or other information and the "clicking" of your keyboard is a dead giveaway that you're not that interested in the interview). Some experts suggest dressing for the telephone interview as you would for an actual interview as a way to remind yourself that you're not merely having a casual conversation but are rather engaged in a formal job search. Turn off the radio, television, and your cell phone, avoid looking at your computer, and give all of your attention to the interview.

Telephone interview: An interview conducted exclusively by telephone.

d. Lunch Interviews

It is possible that you will be asked to go to lunch with your interviewers. It is also possible that your interview is simply lasting a bit longer than expected and a quick decision is made to go to lunch. Follow these suggestions for a **lunch interview** or an interview involving a meal:

Lunch interview: An interview conducted at a restaurant over lunch.

- Wait to be seated after your host. If you arrive first at the restaurant, wait in the lobby. Do not wait in the bar area.
- Do not order an alcoholic beverage (even if someone else does).

- Follow the lead of your host with regard to menu items, although if you must order first, order something from the middle of the menu price range.
- Do not order anything difficult or messy to eat.
- Order dessert only if your host does.
- Assume that your host will pay for the meal, and do not reach for your wallet or handbag.
- Thank your host for the meal and his or her time.
- Treat the waitstaff with courtesy and respect.
- Remember that this is a job interview, not a social occasion.

e. One-on-One Interviews

One-on-one interview:
Interview in which candidate meets with interviewer(s) individually rather than as a group.

A **one-on-one interview** (meeting with one individual at a time) is the most common type of interview. In a law firm, however, you will generally meet with several people sequentially during the same day. Some firms (usually the larger ones) will greet you with a brochure about the firm and your interview schedule, indicating whom you will meet with and when. No decision will be made until everyone has interviewed you and all have had the opportunity to discuss whether you are the right candidate.

f. Informational Interviews

Informational Interview:
Interview set up by prospective job seeker to obtain information about a practice field or job.

Informational interviews are conducted by the job seeker of others already working in the field to find out information from insiders about a selected field or job. The interview is a type of fact-finding mission by a potential job seeker to gain insight into what a job or profession is really like. Typically, the prospective job searcher sets up the interview and desires only to obtain information at this point. Because law firms are very busy, they are often less inclined to grant informational interviews than some other businesses. Use your contacts within your paralegal association to locate paralegals who might be willing to participate in an informational interview and give you the inside information on what it's like to be a paralegal in a law firm. Occasionally, an informational interview will lead to a job offer, but this is not the goal. Prepare for and treat an informational interview as you would any type of interview, and write a thank you note to those you interviewed.

3.   *The Actual Interview*

There are as many interview styles as there are individuals. Some individuals will have experience conducting interviews and others may be inexperienced, in which case, the first question asked of you may be "What can we tell you about us?" or "Tell me about yourself," forcing you to take the lead during the meeting. Some may ask you very pointed questions, testing your knowledge about an area of law or the role of a paralegal. For example, you may be asked, "How would you go about obtaining medical records from a doctor in a personal injury case?"

Generally, however, interviews follow a fairly predictable pattern. They typically begin with some "warm up" conversation about the weather, traffic, and so forth. These preliminaries are intended to break the ice for both parties and allow the interviewer to judge your professional demeanor, attitude, dress, and so forth. The middle part of an interview generally focuses on substantive questions (such as "where do you see yourself in five years?" or "describe your greatest job challenge"). The interview is beginning to wind down when you are asked, "Do you have any questions?"

There are several "standard" questions that are asked during interviews. If your interview begins with the conventional statement, "Tell me about yourself," give a little bit of background about yourself and your education and then tell the interviewer the three most important things you want the interviewer to know about you. For example, you might indicate that you are organized, conscientious, and hard working. You will also probably be asked to identify your strengths and weaknesses. Give some thought before the interview to how you will answer this question. For strengths, consider your organization and communication skills and your ability to work as an effective team member. Try to turn any weaknesses into positive attributes. For example, indicate that you may have a tendency to be so interested in your work that you lose track of time or that you sometimes continually review a project until you are sure it's right. Perhaps you could say that sometimes your expectations are too high. Do not say that you have no weaknesses. Consider indicating that you are currently working on improving your proofreading or computer or other skills. See Figure 6-1 for a list of some of the most common interview questions and Figure 6-2 for NFPA's guide to answering difficult interview questions.

Listen carefully to the questions asked of you and do not interrupt the interviewer. If you do not understand a question, say so, or ask if the interviewer can give you an example. Deal with problem areas such as numerous job changes or poor academic performance honestly but briefly. Don't be defensive and don't overexplain. For example, you might say, "When I first started college, it was a big adjustment for me, and I didn't study as hard as I should have. It was a really valuable lesson to me that it's very important to begin school or work as seriously as possible."

If you are asked if you can draft a complaint or summarize a deposition, but have never done so, respond by saying, "I have not had the opportunity to do that yet, but I am eager to learn and would be willing to study this or take a class on my own time. I am a quick-learner and think I would be able to get up to speed on this very quickly." Do not indicate that you can do a task if you cannot. Simply state the truth and indicate your willingness to learn.

In many instances, what you say is not as important has how you say it and how you react to questions. Most firms believe they can readily train paralegals to do the specific tasks required. What they are interested in is someone who has core values of diligence and persistence and who can "fit in" with their office environment.

Figure 6-1
Common Interview Questions

Some of the most common interview questions include the following:

- Tell me something about yourself.
- Describe your qualifications for this job.
- Identify your major strengths.
- Identify your weaknesses.
- What do you know about this firm?
- Where do you see yourself in five years? What are your long-term career plans?
- Describe your ideal job situation.
- Describe some of your most significant contributions and accomplishments.
- Describe a challenge you have had in your previous job and how you handled it.
- Why do you think you would be the best person for this position?
- Why should we hire you?
- How do you work with other people?
- Describe your work style. Are you an independent worker? Do you prefer to work alone or in a team?
- How do you handle stress?
- Describe the best job you have had and why you liked it.
- What are your salary requirements?
- Is there anything else you'd like to tell me about yourself?
- Is there anything we can tell you about us?

Be scrupulously honest. If you are asked whether you can travel as part of the job, but family commitments preclude this, you must say so. You may wish to leave the door open a bit and say, "At present, I am not able to travel, but I would like to do so in the future." Similarly, if the firm asks about your availability to work overtime in the evenings, and you are taking classes two nights each week, disclose this. Do not indicate you can travel or work overtime when you cannot. If you try to fudge these issues, they will come back to haunt you—usually during the first week on the job. If the fit between the employer and you is not right, it's better to determine that now rather than later.

4. *Illegal Questions*

Some questions are illegal, namely, those relating to your national origin, religion, race, age, political or other affiliations, marital and family status, disabilities or health conditions, and arrest record. Handling these types of questions calls for tact and diplomacy. The interviewer may be inexperienced and has no intent to discriminate against you but is rather trying to be friendly. Thus, questions such as, "Are you married?" or "How does

Figure 6-2
NFPA's Guide to Answering Difficult Interview Questions

Q: How much money do you want?

A: Only indicate what you are presently earning and that salary is one of several factors you are considering. Emphasize that the opportunity is the most important consideration.

Q: Tell me about yourself.

A: Placing emphasis on your recent experience is most important; however, briefly covering previous experiences and education can also be useful.

Q: What are some situations in which your work was criticized?

A: Give only one or two examples and emphasize how you addressed the criticism and how it is now not a problem. Be sure to show that you are open to constructive criticism.

Q: What do you think of your boss?

A: Create a positive image, even if this is not the case.

Q: How long would it take you to make a meaningful contribution to our company?

A: Realistically speaking, experience and requirements of the job will influence your making a meaningful contribution.

Q: Why haven't you found a new position before now?

A: Explain that finding the right job is more important than finding just any job. Also, indicate the difficulty of this task if the current economy could be considered a factor.

Q: Why were you laid off?

A: Be as positive as possible. Do not discuss interpersonal conflicts, regardless of how sympathetic the interviewer may seem. Discuss economic conditions. Do not go into much detail unless asked.

Q: Why should we hire you? or Are you interested in this job?

A: Explain why this is a logical position for you, sum up your work history and reemphasize your strongest qualities and achievements. Above all, let the interviewer know that you will be an asset to the company.

From www.paralegals.org (Web site of NFPA)

your spouse feel about your commuting into the city to work?" may be asked in all innocence but are still inappropriate.

There are really only two ways to handle such questions. If you point out that the question is a violation of federal law or offends you, you will probably not get the job. Even a tactful reminder that the question is objectionable may embarrass the interviewer and doom your chances of getting the job. Thus, consider trying to finesse your answer. Perhaps you could offer, "Everyone I know is excited that I might work in the city. I have many friends who work here and they really enjoy it." If the question relates to whether you plan to have a family, consider responding, "Right now I'm really focused on my career and that is where my priorities lie at present." On the other hand, if the questions reveal blatant discrimination, you may want to end the interview; you would not want to work for such an employer.

5.   *Your Role in an Interview*

As mentioned earlier, during the course of an interview you will undoubtedly be asked what questions you have about the job or the firm. You need only ask two or three questions. Asking a long list of questions conveys the impression that you are doing the interviewing. The following are some possible questions you could ask:

- Are paralegals assigned to individual attorneys or practice groups?
- What specific types of responsibilities do paralegals have in this organization?
- What attributes or skills are required to be successful in this position?
- What is the most pressing case or project that I would be working on?
- Does the firm focus on any particular specialties or practice areas?
- How are paralegals in the firm evaluated and reviewed?
- Has there been, or do you anticipate, growth in the paralegal ranks?
- What reference sources does the firm have? A law librarian? LEXIS? Westlaw?
- What computer technology and software programs does the firm use?
- Do paralegals have client contact?
- Is there opportunity for continuing legal education? Is there in-house training for paralegals?
- Is there a minimum number of hours paralegals are required to bill?
- Is there opportunity to do pro bono work?
- What support assistance is available to paralegals? Is there a secretarial pool or are secretaries assigned to attorneys, paralegals, and practice groups?

Be cautious when asking questions about billable hours and overtime. You want to ensure your questions convey your honest attempt to understand the firm and its policies rather than convey the subtle message that you are not interested in working hard. Similarly, avoid questions about vacation policies and firm benefits that might imply you are more interested in what the firm can do for you than what you can do for the firm.

Do not discuss salary unless and until the interviewer raises the issue. If you are asked about your salary requirements, give a range (based upon your research of the market and the average salary paid to paralegals in your field). Additional information on salary negotiations is provided in Section D, below.

If you meet with several people, you may ask the same questions of different individuals. In fact, this may well help you obtain an accurate view of the employment environment.

Don't forget that you are interviewing the firm as well. You not only need to find a job, you need to find the right job. Try to learn as much as you can about the firm. Notice the interaction between people. Observe the layout of the office. Are people working in teams and group settings, or is everyone sequestered in offices behind closed doors? Are workers permitted to display personal items on their desks? All of these visual cues offer information about the work environment.

6. *Interview Dos and Don'ts*

Following is a list of some of the best and worst approaches you can take during interviews.

Interview Dos	Interview Don'ts
Do practice interviewing with a friend, and do your research about the firm.	Don't sit until a chair is offered to you. Stand and shake hands with anyone else who enters the interview.
Do dress conservatively, and arrive about ten minutes early.	Don't fidget, chew gum, or engage in any other unprofessional behavior.
Do bring extra copies of your résumé, list of references, and writing samples.	Don't badmouth any former employer or your paralegal program or classes.
Do make eye contact with each person with whom you meet.	Don't make jokes or bring up personal issues.
Do convey some enthusiasm so that it is apparent you want the job.	Don't merely reply "yes" or "no" to a question. Explain your answers. Don't bring up anything about salary unless you are asked.
Do turn off your cell phone.	Don't glance at your cell phone or PDA.
Do have a list of a few questions that you can ask the interviewer.	Don't interrupt the interviewer. Listen carefully before you answer any question.

Interview Dos	Interview Don'ts
Do be honest in every part of the interview.	Don't brag or exaggerate your accomplishments. Don't continuously name-drop if you know someone very senior in the firm (although a brief mention of this person's name and relationship to you is acceptable).
Do thank the interviewer for his or her time and write thank you notes to each interviewer right away.	Don't ask what benefits are available, how much vacation time there is, and so forth. These are topics that would be discussed when the firm extends a job offer.

7. Full Disclosure: Should You Disclose Special Needs, Pregnancy, or Health Issues?

It is unlawful for employers to inquire about the existence, nature, or extent of a disability. Similarly, it is unlawful for employers to ask whether a candidate is pregnant or plans to have children. It is, however, lawful for employers to ask if candidates have the ability to perform the job for which they are interviewing. Although it is unlawful for employers to discriminate on the basis of disability and pregnancy, it can and does happen. The difficult question for candidates is when to disclose a disability (especially one that is not obvious). There is no perfect answer to this question. It's up to you.

If you have an obvious disability (e.g., you are in a wheelchair) you may want to contact someone before your interview to alert the firm to your situation (especially if you might need some accommodation). Some employers have stated that they're not concerned about the disability, but simply don't want to be taken by surprise.

If your disability is not obvious (e.g., you are hearing impaired or have a chronic illness), the issue is more delicate. You are not under a legal obligation to disclose your disability. However, many experts believe that full disclosure is the best policy, especially if you will need some reasonable accommodation (e.g., some time for routine medical appointments). Don't be defensive about your situation or automatically assume you're going to be the victim of discrimination. If you disclose the disability and do not get an offer, you will never know whether it was because of your disability or because you weren't the right candidate. Use the opportunity to demonstrate that your disability actually shows how hard a worker you are because you have had to overcome difficulties that others have not. For example, note that you finished college on schedule even though you had a hospitalization. Reassure the interviewer that your disability has not affected your ability to perform in the past. Then move on to the next topic.

One difficult issue that may arise for women in the workplace is interviewing while pregnant, especially in the early stages of pregnancy when the pregnancy is not obvious. The dilemma is whether the applicant should disclose the pregnancy (and risk losing a job offer) or wait to reveal it until after an offer has been made or the job has commenced (and risk having the employer think the employee hid something during the interview process). If the applicant discloses the pregnancy and is rejected for the job, she may never know if she was not hired because of the pregnancy or for some other reason. Under the Family and Medical Leave Act, an employee who has been with an employer (that has 50 or more employees) for at least one year may have 12 weeks of unpaid leave. Some states and employers have more generous policies, and in those states, the employer may be required to extend leave to the applicant whether or not the pregnancy is disclosed.

Some pregnant job applicants wait until an offer is extended, accept it, and then disclose the pregnancy and indicate their maternity leave needs. Keep in mind that many employers may feel misled by this approach and may view this as a reflection on the way you meet difficult challenges. You may want to try a compromise: Wait to disclose your pregnancy until you know the firm is interested in you but before an offer is extended. Disclosure of your pregnancy at this time demonstrates your honesty. Find a way to mention that you thought this was the best thing to do for the firm. Your ethical approach will be appreciated.

If you have a disability or pregnancy, you may want to work with a placement agency, which can act as your advocate and disclose the disability or pregnancy for you. You can also try a creative approach: Offer to work as an independent contractor for 30 or 60 days. Tell the prospective employer that if you haven't performed satisfactorily, they need not extend an offer of permanent employment to you. This approach shows that you are perfectly willing to take a risk because you have the confidence of knowing you will perform so well the firm will undoubtedly extend a permanent offer to you.

There is no perfect way to handle the delicate situations of whether and when to disclose a disability or a pregnancy, but job applicants should keep in mind that an organization that punishes an applicant for having a disability or for being pregnant is probably not a good organization to work for anyway.

In a related disclosure issue, consider that the potential employer may well conduct a background check on you. Even a simple Internet search (e.g., on Google, FaceBook, or YouTube) may show you in a less-than-flattering light. Purge Web sites of any pictures or comments that could reflect poorly on you. Employers are increasingly sophisticated about searching the Internet, and the pictures that you thought showed your fun beach week might be seen in quite a different light by a potential employer. Review any of your blogs and postings to ensure that there are no embarrassing entries. Be scrupulous about how you present yourself to the public.

8. *Concluding the Interview*

At the end of the interview, indicate that you are very interested in the job. Show some enthusiasm. For example, say, "I'm impressed with the firm and everyone I met. I would really appreciate the opportunity to work here." If you want the job, go ahead and say so. Mention something positive, for example, that you enjoyed meeting the other paralegals. If you misstated something earlier, use this opportunity to correct or clarify a previous answer. Make sure you receive a business card from each person you spoke with so you can write the appropriate follow-up thank you notes. If you have not yet been asked for them, offer your transcript, writing samples, and list of references. Ask if any additional copies of your résumé are needed.

You will probably be escorted back to the reception area by the paralegal manager who will then tell you what the next step will be (usually, either another round of interviews or a telephone contact after the firm has completed its interviews). If you do not receive this information, ask the firm's expected timeframe for making a decision. Thank the individual for allowing you to interview with the firm, express your interest in the position once again, and firmly shake hands.

Practice Tip

Continue your job search even if you feel you have had a positive and successful interview. When an interview has gone particularly well, it is common for some job applicants to stop looking for a job, believing it's a "sure thing" that they'll be hired. This is a recipe for disaster and depression. You can never predict what might happen after an interview. For example, you might have had a spectacular interview but before the firm can extend you an offer, it loses a significant client, forcing it to cut down on its staffing.

---

9. *The Second Round of Interviews*

In many instances, law firms bring candidates back for a second interview. This could be to have the candidate meet with someone who wasn't available during the first interview. On other occasions, the second-round interview is to help the firm decide between two or three "finalists." Don't become complacent and think that you are the likely hire. Treat each interview as if it were your first interview and your only chance to make a good impression and "close the sale."

10. *Improving Your Odds of Being Hired*

According to a number of experts, the following are some common reasons that candidates are not hired (even if they are qualified for the positions for which they interviewed):

- Candidate was late to the interview.
- Candidate appeared unenthusiastic and disinterested in the employer and did not ask any questions about the job.
- Candidate failed to perform research about the prospective employer and was thus unprepared for the interview.
- Candidate was arrogant and acted as if he or she would be doing the employer a favor if hired. Candidate did not understand that less experienced workers need to start at the bottom of the ladder.
- Candidate was unprofessional in appearance or attitude.
- Candidate was inarticulate or evasive in answering difficult questions.

If you can avoid some of these common interview pitfalls, you will greatly increase your chances of getting a job offer.

Practice Tip

If you really want the job you interviewed for, consider asking one of your references to call the firm or attorney and put in a good word for you. This is especially helpful if your reference knows someone at the firm. You need to save this "silver bullet," however, because your references will only be willing to make this effort for you once or twice. Don't overlook the impact of having your reference affirmatively call the firm rather than waiting to be called.

C. Post-Interview Activities

1. *Maintaining Your Job-Hunting Notebook*

After the interview, enter the name of the firm, date of the interview, and identities of the interviewers in your job-hunting notebook. Indicate what salary discussions took place (if any) and note any critical information you gained (e.g., that the job requires overtime or that employment will begin on the first of the next month). When you attend several interviews in a short amount of time, these facts tend to "run together," so unless you take good notes you may forget which details are from which firm. Write down your overall impressions of the firm and the people, whether they seemed friendly, stressed, and the like. See Figure 6-3 for a sample page from

Figure 6-3
Sample Page from Job-Hunting Notebook

Date of Action	Law Firm or Company	Date of Contact	Date of Interview	Contact Persons	Interview Impressions	Topics to Note	Thank You Note	Follow-Up Activity
Jan. 15	Cover letter and résumé sent to Taylor & Allen in Los Angeles (response to ad)	Receptionist called on Jan. 20 to set up interview	Jan. 25	Hillary Metzger, paralegal co-ordinator (213) 478-3300	Screening interview only; will not meet attorneys until next set of interviews	Benefits and salary are average; overtime is required; travel may be required	Note sent by mail on Jan. 26	Called Hillary on Feb. 10 to check status; left message on voice mail
Jan. 17	Cover letter and résumé sent to Adams & Bailey in Los Angeles (response to ad for entry-level paralegal)	H.R. manager called on Jan. 22 to set up interview	Jan. 30	Susan Pryor, Paralegal Manager (213) 445-2345; Stan Connell, Litigation Attorney (213) 445-2346	Firm is friendly; well-organized; 5 paralegals in litigation department; casual atmosphere	Benefits are good; parking is expensive; good 401(k) plan; billable hour requirements; Start date is Feb. 15; no salary discussed	Notes sent by mail on Jan. 30	None yet

| Jan. 18 | Cover letter and résumé sent by email to Gorman Law Group in Los Angeles (response to networking tip from Lynn Carr) | Tim Hardy called on Jan. 19 to set up interview | Jan. 21 | Tim Hardy, paralegal manager (213) 552-1990; Ann Mason, attorney (213) 552-1990 | Firm is fairly formal; Ann Mason allows paralegals to have much responsibility | Start date is Feb. 10. Good benefits; great vacation; some flex time for senior paralegals; salary is in range of $35,000-40,000 | Notes sent by mail on Jan. 21 | None yet |

a job-hunting notebook. Tape the business cards you obtained into your job-hunting notebook so they will be accessible later. Consider assessing your own performance (e.g., noting whether you were nervous, under-dressed, and so forth) so that if you are called for a second interview, you can correct any problems or misimpressions.

2.   *Thank You Notes*

On the day of the interview, write and mail your thank you notes. If you met several people, you may either write a separate thank you note to each of them (this is the better approach) or you may address your letter to the paralegal manager, indicating that you enjoyed meeting the other staff members and listing their names. A combination approach is to write thank you notes to the paralegal manager and the attorney with whom you will be working. This puts your name in front of the people who will make the hiring decision.

Make sure the spelling of the firm name and each person's name is correct. Check the business cards or the Web site to verify correct names and titles. Some individuals have emailed thank you notes, but this is an unconventional approach; the traditional approach is to send a formal note by regular mail. Thank you notes serve several purposes: They are the polite and respectful thing to do, they showcase your writing skills, they distinguish you from candidates who didn't write thank you notes, and they allow you to inquire about the next step in the interview process or to add something you may have forgotten during the interview.

Thank you notes may be either handwritten or typed (using station-ery and envelopes that match those you used for your résumé and cover letter). If you type your thank you note, type the address on the envelope. Many experts advise taking the extra step of handwriting a thank you note so that it stands out from regular office mail. However, if your hand-writing is not legible, type your note or letter. Enter the date you mailed your thank you note in your job-hunting notebook.

Your thank you note should include three components: Thank the individual for meeting with you, reiterate your interest in the job, and indicate where you can be contacted. Try to mention something that was discussed in the interview. See Figure 6-4 for a sample basic thank you note. Additional samples can be found in Appendix E.

3.   *Following Up After an Interview*

If you do not hear from the firm right away, do not assume that you have been rejected. Law firms, especially large ones, have several levels of man-agement. The hiring partner may be on vacation. A crisis may have arisen in a case. Wait seven to ten days, and then telephone the paralegal man-ager or the person who interviewed you to determine the status of your application. Ask if the firm has made a decision, and ask whether there is anything you can provide to help the firm make its decision. Enter the date of your follow-up call in your job-hunting notebook.

Figure 6-4
Sample Thank You Note

Your Name
Your Street Address
Your City and State
Your Zip Code
Your Telephone Number
Your Email Address

Date

Interviewer Name
Interviewer Title
Firm Name
Firm Street Address
Firm City and State

Dear Ms. Lowell:

Thank you for taking the time to meet with me on Tuesday regarding the opening for a litigation paralegal at Smith & Jones, L.L.P. I enjoyed the opportunity to meet with you and have a brief tour of your offices. I was particularly impressed with the law library and the firm's commitment to technology.

I am very interested in the litigation paralegal position. Please let me know if you have any questions or comments or if you need any additional information. I look forward to hearing from you.

Sincerely,
Your Name

If you hear nothing within two weeks after your interview and your phone calls to the paralegal manager or human resources director are not returned, you can probably assume that you are no longer in the running for the position. The firm, however, should communicate to you in some manner that it has rejected your candidacy. If it does not, this is a sign that the firm is either disorganized or lacking in compassion. Tell yourself you wouldn't want to work there anyway and move on.

If you are informed that the firm has hired another candidate, thank the individual and move on to the next opportunity. If you believed the interview went well and that you were qualified for the job, consider asking whether there was anything you could have done or said that would have made a difference. Try to learn from the experience. Consider the following true story:

Cheryl, a legal professional, went on a job interview. She felt she was perfect for the job and loved everything about the employer. Both of her interviews were very successful, and Cheryl was certain she would be hired. When the employer called to say that another candidate had been hired, she was crestfallen. After worrying over the matter for two weeks, she telephoned the hiring manager and simply stated how disappointed she was that she didn't get the job, and, to help her learn from the experience, asked how she could have handled things better or differently. The manager indicated that the candidate who had been offered the job had just rejected it, and the firm offered the job to Cheryl on the spot. Cheryl was a little disappointed to be "second choice," but she still believed her instincts were right about the firm. She took the job and worked there happily for several years.

If you have gone on several interviews and are in the enviable position of having an offer "on the table" from Firm A but prefer to work for Firm B, consider the following strategy: Ask Firm A for a few days (three to five) to respond to its offer. Call Firm B, and without being dramatic, indicate that you have an offer from another firm and ask when Firm B might be ready to make a decision. Do not give up a sure thing for a speculative opportunity. Moreover, be careful that your attitude does not seem arrogant or convey a threat to Firm B that it better hire you or you'll go elsewhere. This is a definite way to lose out on an offer.

4.   *What to Do if Nothing Works*

If your interviews produce no offers, start all over again. Redouble your efforts. Start with your personal contacts and let them know you are still looking. Review your job-hunting notebook, and contact anyone with whom you interviewed to see if there are other job openings. Contact your school placement office or program director and ask for suggestions. Rewrite your résumé so it has a fresh appearance. Continue your review of want ads published both in conventional print newspapers, including legal newspapers, and on the Internet. Finally, there are three approaches that may yield results:

- Ask your school to place you in a short internship with a firm, or ask someone who has a job if you can "shadow" him or her for a few days. Although an internship is usually unpaid, it will widen your circle of contacts, could lead to a job offer, and may give you sufficient additional experience so that a placement agency will now work with you. If your school does not provide such services, contact a placement agency or send résumés to large law firms in your area asking to do a two- or three-week unpaid internship.
- Do volunteer legal work. Work in a legal clinic. Contact your local bar association to find out what pro bono activities are available. You will learn a great deal, and you may well meet individuals who can help you find a permanent job or serve as references for you. You will be able to add this work experience to your résumé.
- Use the services of a temp agency and find a temporary legal job. You will have the opportunity to learn about various law firm environments and different practice fields. More important, in many cases,

if you prove to be a diligent and competent worker, the employer may try to find a position for you as a permanent employee.

If none of these approaches yields the desired results, consider jobs outside of law firms, for example, in a corporation or working for a government agency or trade association. Apply to work in a courthouse as a court clerk or research assistant. Apply to legal aid societies, the public defender's office, or the public prosecutor's office. Consider writing an article and submitting it to a paralegal publication to enhance your résumé. Look for jobs in law-related fields. Apply for jobs in law libraries or with banks, title companies, or trust companies. (See Chapter 11 for information on alternative career paths.)

D. The Offer and Salary Negotiations

1. *Evaluating an Offer: Considering Employment Terms*

Generally, when an offer is made to a job applicant, it will include all of the terms of employment. Smaller firms may make the offer to you by phone (and typically follow it up with a written letter), but larger firms will almost always provide you with a written offer. At a minimum, an offer should include job title, starting date, salary, and an outline of benefits, such as types of insurance, vacation time, and the like. If an offer does not include these elements, don't be afraid to ask. You need not accept an offer on the spot. It is customary and reasonable to ask for a few days to evaluate the offer.

You may need a job right away and almost any job will do, so long as the salary and benefits are adequate. On the other hand, if you are in an employee-favorable market or have some time before you must make a decision, remember that salary is only one part of a job (although it is usually the most important factor for most workers). You should also consider the following when you are evaluating any offer:

• **Compensation issues.** Are wages paid every two weeks or once per month? How frequently are raises given? Are salary decisions made by the firm as a whole or by your particular supervisor? Are bonuses awarded? Are bonuses based on hours billed?

• **Benefits.** What benefits are provided? What are the details of the health insurance offered? What portion of the premiums do employees pay? Are life and disability insurance provided? Maternity and parenting coverage? Dental and vision insurance? Are there "flex" or "cafeteria" plans? Are there employee retirement, pension, or 401(k) plans? If so, what contributions, if any, does the employer make to these plans? What is the vacation policy? Is parking provided? Tuition assistance? Continuing education? Will the firm pay paralegal association dues? How and when are expenses reimbursed?

- **Career advancement.** Is the work in a field you will enjoy? Will your work be interesting and challenging? Will there be opportunities for advancement? Does the firm have a performance review program? Is there training? Will you have client contact? Will you learn important skills so that if you need to find another job, this job will prepare you?
- **Work environment.** Will you be happy working in this environment? Is the employer located in a nice area? How will you commute to work? Is the location convenient for you? What have you heard about turnover at this firm? Is the firm stable? Does the job offer some flexibility so that if you have a doctor's appointment one day you can simply work a bit longer the next day rather than having to take a vacation day? Do any professionals work part-time? Do any professionals telecommute on occasion? Will you be required to travel? Will you be required to work overtime? Is the firm nationally known? If so, it may be easier for you to obtain another job if you relocate because the firm is prominent in legal circles.
- **Legal market.** If the competition for jobs in your area is intense, you may not have the luxury of considering the above factors. If you don't take the job, there may be many other individuals ready to do so. Thus, temper your desire for the "perfect" job with the realities of the market in your locality. If you reject a job because the salary is $500 less than you wanted, and you then spend two months looking for another job, have you gained anything?

Consider making a checklist, like the one shown in Figure 6-5, to help you evaluate and review the various terms and benefits of any employment offer. Review it carefully to determine if this is the best job for you.

2.   *Salary Negotiations*

In many cases, the stated salary will be listed in the job advertisement. If so, there may be very little room for negotiation. If no salary is stated, the issue may arise during the interview or during the offer stage. Be prepared by carefully studying all of the national and local survey information that is available. In addition to being prepared, you must also be realistic. If the average annual salary for starting paralegals in your community is $34,000, and you demand $40,000, you will price yourself out of the job. On the other hand, if you have unique talents that the firm needs, such as language skills, you should ask for more than the average. Be realistic both about the job market in your area and about your experience. Remember, if you are new to the paralegal field, you must be prepared to start at the bottom of the salary scale.

If you are asked for your salary demands before an offer is extended, avoid undervaluing yourself by saying that you will consider "any reasonable offer." If you are already employed, you can merely provide current salary information. It is implicit that you want a salary higher than your current one. If pressed, respond with a range (for example, $32,000 to $36,000). Understand that you may well be offered a job at the low end of the range, so the amount you set at the low end should be one you are prepared to accept.

Figure 6-5
Job Offer Checklist

The following is a list of elements you should consider when you receive a job offer. If the offer does not provide any information about some of these items, you should call the paralegal manager or human resources director to obtain the needed information. Note that not all employers offer all of these benefits.

Topic	Information
Title	
Salary	
Starting date	
Bonus	
Working environment; type of people	
Challenging work	
Opportunity for advancement; future prospects	
Training	
Location; costs of commuting	
Résumé enhancement value	
Travel required	
Health coverage	
Dental coverage	
Vision coverage	
Vacation	
Holidays	
Sick days	
Tuition reimbursement	
Payment of professional dues	
Payment for professional seminars and conferences	
Schedule for salary and performance reviews	
Other benefits (health club, etc.)	
Laptop	
Cell phone	
Personal digital assistant	

If the salary is a bit lower than you would like, but everything else about the job is right, consider saying so and then ask whether your salary could be reviewed after three or six months. If your work is acceptable, you may then be awarded a raise within that shortened period of time. (Salary reviews are usually conducted every 12 months.) Such an approach displays confidence in your skills because it conveys the message to the employer that you know you will be such a good worker, you will undoubtedly get a raise.

One of the advantages of working with a recruiter is that he or she will often participate in salary discussions and serve as both a liaison and an advocate for you. The recruiter will have experience in evaluating applicant skills, the overall market, and employers' needs and will be able to advise you on setting and accepting a reasonable salary.

If you decide to reject an offer, do so right away so the employer can proceed to the next candidate. Consider using a written letter of rejection. It demonstrates your professionalism. Do not be specific about why you rejected the offer; you never want to burn any bridges, and it is possible the employer will make a counteroffer that might change your mind.

3. *Offer Contingencies*

It is becoming increasingly common for law firms to ask paralegal candidates to make a commitment to stay with the firm for at least two years, primarily because it is expensive for an employer to go through the hiring process and train a paralegal, only to have the paralegal leave for another job opportunity. The offer of employment, then, would be contingent on an oral promise to stay with the firm for at least two years. Such a request is unfair, however, because the firm will probably not make a corresponding two-year commitment to the candidate.

Responding to a request for such a commitment calls for a great deal of tact and diplomacy. You may be considering a move, starting a family, continuing your education, or some other goals that would preclude you from working for two full years. If asked to give such a commitment, try to sidestep the question. Consider the following response to such requests: "At present, I have no definite plans that would interfere with my ability to work for the firm for two years." This statement is true unless you have already been accepted to school or have made some similar commitment. In truth, none of us ever knows with certainty what we will be doing next year or in two years. Thus, if you can make such a statement in good faith, do so. Just as the firm's position is likely that you will be employed so long as you are a productive worker and the firm has adequate business, it is only fair that your position is that you will remain in the job so long as you are treated fairly and professionally and unforeseen circumstances do not arise.

In some firms, an offer will be extended to you contingent upon verifying your transcripts and checking your references. If it has been a few weeks since you alerted your references, make another quick phone call or send a short email to let them know that you have received an offer and that they will likely be called to serve as a reference.

4. *Reneging on an Offer*

Carefully consider any job offer because once you accept it, you may not renege on it (unless unforeseen circumstances arise, such as a family crisis or geographic relocation). Reneging on an acceptance is considered highly unprofessional, and the decision will come back to haunt you. Even in a large city, the legal community is insular, and word of your conduct will spread and will certainly impair your ability to get a job later. Moreover, because you represent yourself and your paralegal program, reneging on an offer will hurt other students from your program and your program itself. Finally, not only will the first employer be upset with you, any future employers may question your loyalty and integrity as well.

In some rare instances, employers have reneged after making offers to legal professionals. Sometimes called "blow-up offers," these situations happen far more often to newly hired attorneys than paralegals. If an offer extended to you is revoked, you will simply have to move forward. You may, however, ask if the firm or employer has any leads on other jobs or any outplacement services that it can provide you.

5. *Handling Multiple Offers*

If you are lucky enough to have received multiple offers and are having difficulty making a decision, write out the pros and cons of each job. Review your list. Brainstorm with friends and family. If possible, try to meet with a couple of the current paralegals in each firm to get the inside story about the working conditions at the firm. Be sure that each offer is solid. You should have a written offer from each prospective employer. You do not want to reject one offer only to find out that the second offer was not definite.

You can ask to meet with each firm again, but this approach is risky because it conveys the impression that you are the one interviewing the firm. Identify the three most important factors to you about a job. Select the offer that best responds to your listed needs. Don't give the salary too much weight (especially if the two salaries are close). If you hate your job, the salary won't be enough to compensate for poor working conditions or a lack of challenging work. Use the job offer checklist shown in Figure 6-5 to compare the specifics of each offer.

When you make your decision, promptly notify each firm. Handle the rejection diplomatically. Do not leave a message on an answering machine. You must personally speak with someone and indicate that you have accepted another offer. Send a thank you note to the firm you rejected, thanking it for its interest, expressing your regret, and wishing it success. Don't burn any bridges. See Figure 6-6 for a sample job acceptance letter, which should be sent in response to a written offer of employment.

Practice Tip

Stay in touch with your friends who are interviewing. If you find out that one of your friends received multiple job offers and rejected one or more, give your best wishes to your friend, and then immediately contact the rejected firms. You now know that these firms could have openings they want to fill. Don't be concerned that you're accepting "leftovers." Timing is everything, and you could very well be a better fit at the firm than your friend would have been.

Figure 6-6
Job Acceptance Letter

Your Name
Your Street Address
Your City and State
Your Zip Code
Your Telephone Number
Your Email Address

Date

Interviewer Name
Interviewer Title
Firm Name
Firm Street Address
Firm City and State

Dear Mr. [or Ms.] _____:

    I am very happy to accept the offer of family law paralegal with _____, with a starting date of July 1, _____. The position sounds interesting and challenging, and I look forward to being a part of the _____ legal team.

    As you requested, I am enclosing a copy of my signed and dated offer letter, which confirms the terms of my employment. Please feel free to contact me if you need additional information prior to my starting date. I look forward to a long and successful career with _____.

Sincerely,
Your Name

Encl.

E. Post-Acceptance Tasks

After you receive and accept a job offer, take the time to do two things:

- **Contact your network.** Make sure you call or email all your personal contacts, letting them know that you got a job, where you'll be working, and when you start. The people you asked for help will want to know the results of your job search. Make sure to let your references know that you accepted an offer. Thank anyone who gave you advice or job leads. Send a formal thank you note expressing your appreciation for their help. This is not only the courteous thing to do, but it will also serve you well if you need help in the future.

- **Contact your paralegal program.** Let your school know of your new position. If your program is ABA approved, it must conduct periodic surveys of former students. In that case, it will need to know how to contact you to obtain basic information about your tasks, salary, and other work-related information. Moreover, if your school has current information about your job situation, it can pass that on to new students to help them with their job-hunting activities. Finally, your program director and instructors will want to know how you fared and share in your success.

NetWorks

www.paralegals.org	NFPA's Web site offers an excellent "Career Center" with tips and advice for paralegal job seekers.
http://law.slu.edu/ careersvcs/student/ information.html	Saint Louis University School of Law's Career Services Web site offers excellent information about interviewing at law firms, responding to rejections, questions to ask, and more.
www.quintcareers.com	Quintessential Careers offers invaluable career advice and information related to interviewing, thank you letters, and salary negotiations.
www.jobweb.com	JobWeb's "Career Library" offers numerous articles offering practical advice about job search strategies and interviewing.
http://office.microsoft.com (select "Templates")	Microsoft offers excellent templates and forms for résumés, interview thank you letters, and other useful templates and forms.

Case Illustration

In Absence of Discrimination, Courts Will Not Question Hiring Decisions

Case: *Twilley v. Burlington Northern & Santa Fe Railway Co.*, 351 F. Supp. 2d 1299 (N.D. Ala. 2004)

Facts: The plaintiff, a female, interviewed for a position as a conductor-trainee with the defendant. The defendant hired several males for the position, and the female plaintiff sued for sexual discrimination.

Holding: No sexual discrimination existed in this case. The males were selected because they had experience with heavy equipment and safety training. An employer may make a decision regarding hiring an employee for a good reason, a bad reason, or no reason at all, as long as it is not based on discrimination. Federal courts do not act as super-personnel departments that will scrutinize a company's business or hiring decisions unless they are discriminatory. The Civil Rights Act does not mandate that employers make smart or even fair choices in their personnel decisions. Only where the merits of the employer's choice and proffered reasons for said choice are so utterly dubious that no remotely reasonable employer would make the same selection in the absence of illegal considerations will courts begin to question an employer's poor decision making.

Chapter Summary

- You must plan for your interview. Participate in mock or practice interviews, do your homework about the firms with which you will be interviewing, research salaries in your area, alert your references, and be prepared to discuss any sensitive issues in your résumé relating to your grades or job history.
- The most common type of interview is a one-on-one interview. Be on time, bring all appropriate documents with you, and listen before you answer any questions. Be prepared with a list of questions to ask about the firm and its policies.
- After your interview, send thank you notes to demonstrate your courteousness and professionalism.
- When you receive an offer, give it careful consideration. Remember that salary is not always the most important component of an offer. Once you accept an offer, you cannot renege on it.
- After you begin your work, alert your network and your paralegal program.

Key Terms

Mock interview: A practice interview held with someone familiar to help a candidate prepare for an actual interview.

Preliminary interview: A short interview designed to weed out unqualified candidates; also called a *screening interview*.

Panel interview: An interview conducted by a group of individuals.

Telephone interview: An interview conducted exclusively by telephone.

Lunch interview: An interview conducted at a restaurant over lunch.

One-on-one interview: An interview in which candidate meets with interviewer(s) individually rather than as a group.

Informational interview: An interview set up by prospective job seeker to obtain information about a practice field or job.

Bits and Bytes

- First impressions are formed within four to six minutes after someone meets you.

- Impressions made at job interviews are formed within one minute, and more than 50 percent of an impression is based on nonverbal signals, such as body language, eye contact, and the like.

- Although 72 percent of employers expect a thank you note after an interview, only 38 percent of college seniors send a thank you note.

- About 17 percent of hiring managers say they would not hire someone who failed to send a thank you note.

Discussion Questions

1. During an interview, the interviewer comments that your name is interesting and asks if you are foreign. How should you respond?

2. During the very early stages of your interview, the interviewer asks what salary you need. How should you respond?

3. You have received a job offer from a law firm that you love, but the salary is $3,000 lower than you would like. What should you do?

4. You have received an offer from the Smith law firm but prefer to work for the Jones law firm, where you just interviewed. What should you do? Are there any risks in contacting the Jones law firm and indicating that you have an offer from the Smith law firm? Discuss.

WebWork

1. Access the Web site for *Legal Assistant Today*, the paralegal magazine. Review the March/April 2001 article entitled "Negotiating Raises and Salary." What are the three variables you need to know when conducting salary research?

2. Access "Quintessential Careers" at www.quintcareers.com. Select "Career Portal Page."

   c. Select "Interviewing Resources." Review the *Interviewing Question Collection,* specifically the *Traditional Employment Interview Questions.* What is the first question that employers are likely to ask candidates?
   d. Select "Salary Negotiation" and review the article on salary negotiation do's and don'ts. What is the first "don't" of salary negotiation?

3. You will be interviewing next week with attorney J. Patrick Berry in the Washington, D.C., office of Baker Botts LLP. Do some "homework" and find out where and when Mr. Berry went to law school and the fields of law in which he practices.

The
Workplace

The Law Firm Environment

Remember that time is money.
—Benjamin Franklin

Chapter Overview

This chapter introduces you to the ways in which law firms operate, for example, whether as a partnership or a professional corporation. The features and characteristics of small, medium, and large law firms are reviewed, and law firm personnel are identified. Two of the most important aspects of a law firm, timekeeping and billing, are described. Finally, a variety of law office procedures in which paralegals are involved are reviewed, from conflicts checking to file maintenance. Careers outside traditional law firm settings are discussed in Chapter 11.

A. Law Firm Structures and Organization

1. *Introduction*

According to both the Bureau of Labor Statistics and the National Federation of Paralegal Associations (NFPA), about 70 percent of the nation's paralegals are employed in private law firms. These law firms, however, can vary widely in size (from a sole practitioner to Chicago-based megafirm Baker & McKenzie, with nearly 3,600 attorneys in 38 countries), culture (from casual and relaxed atmospheres to those in which the professional staff address each other as "Ms." and "Mr." rather than by first name), and in benefits offered (from very few perks to paid sabbaticals).

　　Although there is a great deal of variety in these firms and office settings, some general observations can be made about private law firms. Attorneys and law firms generally operate as one of five business entities: sole practitioners, general partnerships, limited liability partnerships, limited liability companies, or professional corporations.

Understanding the differences among these structures will help you understand the terminology employed by these firms and the way law firm personnel are identified.

2. *Sole Practitioners*

Sole practitioner: An attorney who practices by himself or herself.

A **sole practitioner** is an attorney who practices by himself or herself. The sole practitioner makes all business decisions, retains all profits (and must bear all losses), and owns all of the business assets of the practice, from the pens and pencils to the client list. Typically, a sole practitioner is a "jack of all trades" and handles a variety of different types of cases, from estate planning, to family law, to general business matters (such as forming corporations), and even some minor criminal matters. The sole practitioner usually employs one or two secretaries or clerical assistants and may employ a paralegal.

3. *General Partnerships*

General partnership: A business structure with shared decision making and personal liability for its partners.

Personal liability: Liability extending beyond what one invests in a business to one's personal assets.

Joint and several liability: Liability for an entire obligation.

Partner: The owner of a firm or business operating as a partnership.

Associate: A junior attorney.

Equity partner: A partner who owns business assets.

For well over a century, law firms of two or more attorneys operated as traditional **general partnerships**, in which all partners shared decision-making responsibility as well as all firm profits, but were also personally liable for all debts and obligations of the firm and for malpractice claims made against any attorney of the partnership. **Personal liability** is liability that extends beyond what one has invested in a business to one's personal assets. For example, if one attorney in a partnership of four commits an act of malpractice, the other three are liable for the obligation, and their personal savings accounts, jewelry, and other personal assets can be seized to satisfy the debt (assuming it exceeds the firm's assets). Under a concept known as **joint and several liability**, each partner is entirely responsible for all debts. Thus, in the example just given, a creditor may satisfy a judgment of $100,000 from one partner, two, or any combination of the four. Although this discussion focuses on liability, keep in mind that most law firms have significant malpractice insurance to cover potential losses, and so if a malpractice claim were to arise, the insurance could be sufficient to pay the claim, and the issue of a partner's personal liability would never arise.

In a traditional partnership, the **partners** are the owners of the firm and its assets. Newly licensed attorneys who work for the firm are called **associates** and after a period of time (usually seven to ten years) are elected to partnership status. Associates are employees of the firm and are paid a stated salary; partners, the owners of the firm, share in the profits of the firm, and these may vary significantly from one year to the next. The owner-partners are usually called **equity partners**. Not every partner is equal. Some may own a 5 percent interest in the firm while others own a 7.2 percent interest in the firm, and so forth. Ownership interests and profit calculations may be based on complicated formulas that factor in such elements as seniority and business generated.

Management and decision making is usually based on ownership interests, so that a partner with a 5 percent interest will have 5 percent of the voting power and will receive 5 percent of the firm's profits; however, firms operating as general partnerships are free to make other distribution and management arrangements. Larger firms usually elect a **managing partner** to run the day-to-day business operations of the firm and may also establish various committees, such as an ethics committee, training committee, and recruitment committee.

Managing partner: A partner who directs or manages a partnership.

Until a few years ago, associates who were not elected to partnership status at the appropriate time were usually asked or encouraged to leave the firm. Now, in recognition of the various career paths of attorneys, many firms understand that there may be **permanent associates**, attorneys who are employed by the firm and will never achieve equity partnership status (having ownership rights in the firm), but who are valued members of the firm and will continue to keep their jobs as long as the firm is profitable. Some firms call these individuals *senior attorneys, staff attorneys,* or *nonequity partners.* The term **of counsel** may be used, but it is usually reserved for older, semiretired partners or possibly experienced partners who are hired by the firm after they have been employed by another firm for several years. These **lateral hires** are then given one or two years to prove themselves; if they do, they will be offered a partnership at the new firm.

Permanent associate: An attorney who will remain an employee of a firm rather than an owner; also called *senior attorney, staff attorney, nonequity partner,* or *of counsel.*

Of counsel: Term usually assigned to older or semi-retired attorneys, although it might refer to senior attorneys joining the firm in a lateral position.

4. *Limited Liability Partnerships*

While law firms traditionally operated as partnerships and enjoyed the freedom and flexibility partnerships offered in terms of decision making, shared profits, and so forth, partnerships suffered one significant disadvantage: unlimited, personal, joint and several liability. When a new business structure, the **limited liability partnership**, was created in 1991 to eliminate such liability, law firms immediately recognized its advantages and began to convert from traditional partnerships to these new limited liability partnerships. A limited liability partnership (LLP) alters one principle of partnership law: It eliminates personal liability for the wrongful acts of another. Using our previous example, in a firm organized as an LLP, if one partner commits an act of malpractice, the other three partners have no personal liability for that act (unless they participated in it or supervised the malfeasing partner). LLPs are recognized in all jurisdictions.

Lateral hire: Attorney hired by one firm from another.

Limited liability partnership: Type of partnership that protects partners from liability for each other's wrongful acts.

To convert from a traditional partnership to the LLP form, a firm must complete and file an application with the state in which it maintains its principal office (and any other state in which it does business). You will always know that a firm has elected to operate as an LLP, because its letterhead, business cards, Web site, and the like must include the designation "LLP" or a similar designation.

The LLP is managed much like a traditional partnership, and its professionals are also called partners and associates. Because of the tremendous advantage of conducting business as an LLP, almost all of the nation's large law firms have converted from general partnerships to

LLPs. Electing to operate as an LLP allows a firm to manage its affairs with the flexibility of a general partnership but insulates partners from liability for each other's wrongful acts.

5. *Limited Liability Companies*

Limited liability company: Business structure that protects its members from unlimited personal liability; a new form of business organization that combines features of partnerships and corporations.

Like LLPs, **limited liability companies** (LLCs) are new business structures that are recognized in all jurisdictions. LLCs, however, are not based on partnership law; they are an entirely new form of business structure that combines the best features of both partnerships and corporations. Like LLPs, LLCs also protect their participants (who are called "members" rather than "partners") from unlimited personal liability.

Because the LLC is an entirely new form of business entity, law firms have been slow to adopt this form. Most prefer to operate as LLPs (because they are based on the traditional partnership model, which attorneys find familiar and comfortable). In fact, in some states (including California), professionals such as attorneys are statutorily prohibited from operating as LLCs.

LLCs are formed much like LLPs: A document is filed with the state in which the firm maintains its principal office (and in other states in which it conducts business). Law firms operating as LLCs must include the designation "LLC" in their names and on all written materials. In an LLC, the attorneys who own the firm are called "members" and the newer attorneys are typically called "associates."

6. *Professional Corporations*

Professional corporation: A corporation organized to provide professional services, such as legal services.

Shareholder: The owner of a corporation.

Director: The manager of a corporation.

Law firms and sole practitioners may also conduct business as **professional corporations**, in which case they are governed by corporate law rather than partnership law. The corporation is formed by filing various documents with the state. Like any corporation, a professional corporation is owned by its **shareholders** who elect its managers, called **directors**. Share ownership and management is usually restricted to the licensed attorneys. Attorneys operating as professional corporations retain liability for their own wrongful acts and the acts of those they supervise. A law firm or attorney operating as a professional corporation must use the designation "PC" (or a similar designation).

7. *Office Sharing*

Some sole practitioners opt to share office space and support staff with each other. In outward appearance, the arrangement may appear to be a single law firm, but it is really a collection of sole proprietors gathered under one roof who share the reception area, conference rooms, law library, and so forth. Such an arrangement allows sole practitioners low-cost access to nicer offices and amenities and the advantages of learning from close-by colleagues without sacrificing their ability to make all decisions (and retain all profits) for themselves.

B. Law Firm Environments

1. Introduction

The ways in which law firms function on a daily basis are as varied as are the number of law firms themselves. Each firm has its own distinct culture and methods of doing business. There are, however, some generalizations that can be made about working for smaller firms versus larger firms. First, however, it should be noted that the designations "small" and "large" could be misleading. For example, in New York City, a small firm might be 40 attorneys, while in Billings, Montana, such a firm would be considered extremely large. There is no concrete measure of what constitutes a small, medium, or large law firm. Nevertheless, Altman Weil, Inc., a prominent legal consulting firm, classifies a small law firm as having fewer than 15 attorneys. For the purpose of this discussion, assume then that a small law firm is 1 to 15 attorneys, a medium-sized firm is 16 to 40 attorneys, and a large law firm is more than 40 attorneys.

2. Working for a Sole Practitioner or Small Firm

A paralegal employed by a sole practitioner or small firm tends to be a jack-of-all-trades, much like the attorney. Many paralegals report great job satisfaction working for a sole practitioner or small firm. Paralegals in smaller settings often have a great deal of responsibility and significant client contact. There is little, if any, bureaucracy; the rigid hierarchies often seen in large law firms are nonexistent. The work is varied and challenging, affording paralegals the opportunity to work in several practice areas (rather than getting pigeonholed in one practice group, as may happen in large firms). Close relationships in the office and with clients are the norm. In small firms, secretaries sometimes assume basic paralegal duties, such as drafting documents and correspondence.

According to the 2004 National Utilization and Compensation Survey Report prepared by the National Association of Legal Assistants (NALA Survey), 15 percent of the respondents worked for sole practitioners, and 63 percent worked for ten or fewer attorneys.

Although there are several advantages of working for a sole practitioner or in a small firm, there are some disadvantages as well. In many instances, the compensation is lower than for paralegals working for larger firms. The equipment and technology may not be as modern, and the surroundings may not be as deluxe. Access to computer-assisted research services, such as LEXIS, Westlaw, and Loislaw, however, has evened the playing field, and the small-firm paralegal's ability to perform necessary legal research should be the same as those in larger firms.

In a small law firm, everyone is expected to pitch in, including making copies, buying supplies, or putting on the coffee pot. There might not be another paralegal to share the workload; if an emergency arises, there is no one else to ask for help. Thus, paralegals in small firms need the support of their local paralegal associations, so they have someone to call and ask advice, brainstorm, and share ideas. Additionally, a paralegal's work life in a small firm is greatly affected by the other staff in the office. If any of the individuals in the office are difficult to get along with, there is no place to hide, and no other department to transfer into, as is usually the case in a larger firm. Many of these perceived disadvantages, however, are outweighed by the close relationships that often develop with clients who are eager to express their gratitude for a job well done and the relaxed and informal atmosphere found in many small firms.

Practice Tip

Working in smaller law firms can be isolating; you may be the only paralegal in the office. Thus, joining your local paralegal association is critical. It will give you the opportunity to network, meet new colleagues whom you can call for advice, and provide you access to the latest local news, including salary and compensation surveys, which are important when you need to negotiate for a raise or additional benefits.

---

3. *Working in Medium-Sized Law Firms*

NALA's Survey reported that 15 percent of its respondents were employed by firms ranging from 16 to 40 attorneys. At the lower end of this range, these firms strongly resemble small firms; at the upper end of the range, they start sharing characteristics of larger law firms. These firms often employ a paralegal manager or coordinator to supervise the workflow and to hire, manage, and train paralegals. Because there will likely be other paralegals (in fact, NALA's Survey reports that in firms with 11 to 30 attorneys, there are usually 2 or 3 attorneys per paralegal), it is common to find paralegals working collaboratively, sharing ideas, and getting help. Medium-sized firms can offer the "best of both worlds," in that there is significant opportunity for client contact, a relatively relaxed work environment, and sufficient structure so that paralegals can rely on other paralegals and paralegal managers to help with workflow.

4. *Working in Large Law Firms*

The nation's large, elite firms often dominate the legal landscape, including media reports about law practice management, mergers, salaries, and revenues. The NALA Survey reported that only 4 percent of responding paralegals work for law firms with 100 or more attorneys. These large law firms often offer a generous starting salary, numerous other employment benefits and perks, training programs, bonus plans, and, sometimes, the opportunity to work with the nation's best-known companies and individuals. Everything is the best: The reception and conference facilities are beautifully appointed and include every technological update; the supply rooms resemble a large office supply store with innumerable choices as to types of pens, paper, and sticky notes; all legal professionals have desktop access to both LEXIS and Westlaw; photocopy assistants and messengers await instructions; holiday parties are lavish; and health club memberships may be provided.

So why wouldn't everyone want to work in a large law firm? Paralegals who work for some of the nation's largest law firms often complain of the mind-numbing and repetitive tasks involved in labeling and indexing hundreds of thousands of documents. They seldom, if ever, meet or even see a client. They may be assigned to one practice group with no opportunity for variety in their work. They may routinely work until midnight for clients who can and will insist on having their work done immediately. For some paralegals, all of this results in feeling like an anonymous laborer whose work and efforts are not truly appreciated in an environment in which there is always another crisis around the corner. Numerous committees and layers of management may frustrate career opportunities for advancement. For example, if a sole practitioner wants to reward a paralegal for a job well done, he or she can give an immediate raise or bonus. In a large firm, this must be approved by the compensation committee, which will be reluctant to bestow on one paralegal a benefit that others do not share.

There is, of course, a certain amount of prestige and status in working for one of the nationally known megafirms. Moreover, because of their strong name recognition, there is often greater job mobility for paralegals who work at these firms; other potential employers will immediately recognize the firm name and may be eager to hire paralegals trained at these large firms. Similarly, because many of these firms have numerous branch offices (both in the United States and in foreign countries), there is often the opportunity to transfer to another branch of the firm.

5. *The Bottom Line*

Resist the temptation to categorically decide, "I'd never work in a large firm" or "I'd never work for a sole practitioner." Some of life's most rewarding experiences are unexpected. One legal professional spent a great deal of her first year in law school disliking her real property class and decided she'd never do real property law, yet the only job she was offered after graduation was in a firm specializing in real property law. She reluctantly took the job and, much to her surprise, discovered that the cases and clients were interesting and fun. The lesson: Don't let your preconceived notions or biases turn you away from what might be a dream job!

6. *Organization Within Law Firms*

Although a sole practitioner or small firm might handle a variety of different cases (often called a **general practice**), many other firms specialize in one area of law. Some small firms (sometimes called **boutique firms**) may be devoted to one practice area or niche, such as labor law or appellate work. Firms that engage in personal injury work usually represent plaintiffs or defendants or insurers.

Larger law firms are often divided into two primary groups: litigation (the process of resolving disputes through lawsuits) and **transactional work** (nearly anything that is not litigation, such as corporate work or tax work). Review the Web sites of larger firms, and note the practice areas in which they are engaged. These may include bankruptcy, environmental law, intellectual property law, land use, mergers and acquisitions, and securities regulation. Paralegals and new associates are often assigned to a group depending on the firm's needs rather than their interests, and it could be difficult to move to another group within the firm.

General practice: Law firm practice that handles a wide variety of cases.

Boutique firm: Law firm that handles only limited types of cases.

Transactional work: Work that is not related to litigation.

C. Law Firm Personnel: Who Are These People?

Although the names can vary, the following is a brief description of law firm personnel.

- **Support staff.** *Support staff* is the term used to describe the non-professional staff in a law firm — namely, any individual who is not a paralegal or an attorney. This could include receptionists, file clerks, copy and mailroom staff, accounting clerks, and secretaries. Until a few years ago, most law firms employed one secretary for each attorney or paralegal. As attorneys and paralegals have become more proficient at producing their own documents, the ratio has changed, and many law firms employ one secretary for every three attorneys or paralegals. The NALA Survey reported that 28 percent of all responding paralegals shared a secretary with one or more attorneys.
- **Paralegals.** As you know, a paralegal is usually defined as a person who, by training, experience, or both, performs substantive legal work under the supervision of an attorney. Although paralegals may need to perform some clerical duties (such as copying or faxing) in small firms, attorneys in small firms also share in these tasks. Some larger firms have tiers of paralegals, each with its own name and salary level. For example, a firm may employ Senior Paralegals, Paralegal Specialists, and Paralegal Assistants, with each title having its own job description and set of responsibilities.
- **Paralegal managers.** Paralegal managers or coordinators are generally found in larger firms that have several paralegals. These managers hire, fire, train, supervise, evaluate, and mentor

the firm's paralegals. They may have nearly complete responsibility for the paralegal staff and sometimes have a significant budget for training and bonuses. These managers are experts in coordinating workflow to ensure that work is evenly distributed within the paralegal ranks. The importance of paralegal managers cannot be overstated. Many new paralegals are surprised to discover that attorneys are often poor managers. This is often the case because they are trained to be advocates, not businesspeople. On the other hand, paralegal managers are experts in developing the skills of their paralegal teams and assisting in overall professional development.

- **Law clerks.** Larger firms may employ first- or second-year law students to perform research. These law clerks may be on "probation"; if they perform well during their summer employment, the firm may extend them an offer to join the firm as associates after graduation. Law clerks often perform much the same work as paralegals (although they might conduct more legal research than paralegals).

- **Law librarians.** Larger law firms employ professional law librarians, who usually possess both a law degree and a degree in library science. These law librarians are experts in understanding how to use both conventional print books and new technology resources to get the answers attorneys and paralegals need.

- **Associates.** As discussed earlier, associates are the newer attorneys in a firm who often do the "grunt" work. In large law firms, associates can be compensated extraordinarily well (often more than $140,000) per year and, as a result, are expected to devote an extraordinary amount of time to the firm's work. In small firms, associates are expected to jump in on the first day and immediately assume responsibility for cases, business development, and client relations. In contrast, in large law firms, new associates are often given little responsibility and may even compete with paralegals for interesting work. Some law firms hire **contract attorneys** to work on a case-by-case or project basis. When a case or transaction is complete, the contract attorney's relationship with the firm ends. After seven to ten years, firms usually extend a partnership offer (or member or shareholder offer, if the firm operates as an LLC or professional corporation) to the associate. Associates who elect to work part-time or take some time off to raise children are often said to have departed from the **partnership track**, the firm's established course for becoming a partner.

- **Partners and shareholders.** As discussed, partners and shareholders are the senior attorneys in a firm who own the firm's assets. Rather than receiving a fixed salary (as do all other firm employees), partners and shareholders are paid from the profits of the firm, which usually vary from year to year. These attorneys manage the firm and implement all policies. The partners or shareholders usually elect a manager from their ranks, and partners or shareholders are usually expected to serve on firm committees to

Contract attorney: Nonemployee attorney who works for a firm on a project basis.

Partnership track: A firm's preestablished path to becoming a partner or owner.

Rainmaking:
Attracting new
business and
clients.

ensure that the firm operates smoothly. Generally, raising revenue by attracting new clients and business, called **rainmaking**, is required for success.

D.   Money Matters: It's About Time

1.   Introduction and Types of Fee Arrangements

Retainer: Initial
fee paid to
attorney or firm to
engage legal
services.

According to ethics rules and codes, only attorneys may establish fee arrangements with clients. In many cases, clients pay an initial or advance fee, called a **retainer**, to the firm to represent them. Attorneys also have ethical obligations to segregate clients' funds from the law firm's operating accounts. Commingling of these funds is a serious ethical lapse that can lead to disbarment. Law firms only make money by charging clients for the services performed for them. Generally, there are three common types of fee arrangements that attorneys and firms enter into with clients:

Contingency fee:
Fee paid to law
firm by client
only if firm is
successful in
recovering money
for a client.

- **Contingency fees.** In a **contingency fee** arrangement, the attorney does not receive any fee unless he or she is successful in recovering money for the client. Contingency fee arrangements are most common in personal injury, medical malpractice, and collections cases. For example, it would be nearly impossible for a poor person to pay an attorney for several years of representation in a complex medical malpractice case. Instead, the firm and the client agree to an arrangement that will pay the firm a stated percentage of any money recovered for the plaintiff in the action. The fee is contingent on the firm's success in the case. If there is no recovery, the firm receives nothing. Generally, the client will be expected to pay for the firm's out-of-pocket costs, such as court filing fees, fees for mailing and photocopying, and the like. The amount the firm will retain may vary with the stage of the case. For example, if a case is settled out of court, the firm may receive one-third of that recovery. If the case goes to trial, the firm may receive 40 percent of any damages awarded at trial. Firms that accept contingency arrangements must conduct careful analysis of a case prior to accepting it because the firm cannot be profitable if it works for free for several years on cases. To maximize recovery, firms may

Flat fee: Fee paid
to law firm by
client for a certain
legal task or
matter, regardless
of the time it takes.
Also called a *fixed
fee.*

delegate significant parts of a case to junior attorneys and paralegals. Contingent fee arrangements are usually prohibited in criminal and divorce cases.
- **Flat or fixed fees.** A **flat** or **fixed fee** is a specific sum agreed on in advance by the client and the firm for the work to be performed. For example, a firm may charge a flat fee of $1,000 for an uncontested

divorce or for preparing a trademark application or a will. Flat fees are common in cases in which the attorney is so experienced in a field that he or she can easily predict how much time the matter will require. Flat fees are advantageous for clients because they know in advance how much money their matter will cost. As with contingency cases, clients are required to pay the costs and expenses incurred by the firm in connection with the representation. Although clients often wonder why law firms cannot set fixed fees in more cases, remember that in lawsuits, many matters are outside the firm's control, such as the court's docket and the responsiveness of other parties. As is the case with contingency matters, it is more advantageous for the firm to allow junior attorneys and paralegals to perform as much of the work as possible in a fixed fee case, so as to maximize profits.

- **Hourly fees.** Since the late 1960s, most law firms have charged **hourly fees**, or a certain amount for each hour of time spent on the client's case. Hourly fees are the norm because it is nearly impossible for a firm to predict how much work a case will involve. Hourly rates vary depending on market conditions, the reputation of the firm, the nature of the case, and, most important, the level of experience of the legal professional working on the case. According to 2007 surveys by Altman Weil, Inc., the following are standard average hourly billing rates in the United States for various legal professionals:

Hourly fee: Fee paid to law firm by client for each hour expended on a client's matter.

Experienced equity partner	$305
Associate	$200
Paralegal	$160

Note that these are average rates. Large firms in major cities routinely charge in excess of $400 per hour for senior attorneys and more than $175 per hour for paralegals.

2. *Concerns About Billable Hours*

The obvious advantages of billing on an hourly basis are that it allows a firm to determine easily the productivity of attorneys and paralegals and allows clients to pay for the actual services rendered to them. The great disadvantage of **billable hours** (the time that can be charged to a client) is that it places tremendous pressure on legal professionals to bill more and more time in order to generate profit for the firm.

Billable hours: Time that can be charged to a client for work performed.

The problem is compounded by the fact that many firms require attorneys and paralegals to bill a minimum number of hours each year. For example, a paralegal might be required to bill 1,400 hours each year. In fact, the NALA Survey reported that nearly one-third of all paralegals are expected to bill between 31 and 35 hours per week. Because legal professionals attend training sessions, mentor new professionals, meet friends for lunch, and so forth, not every minute of the day can be billed. Thus, there is significant pressure to meet the stated quotas in order to remain employed, receive a bonus, or be viewed as a productive team member.

In recognition of the problems inherent in hourly billing, the American Bar Association (ABA) established a Commission on Billable Hours. It found that billing on an hourly basis decreases collegiality in firms, encourages skipping steps, and puts the client's interests in conflict with the attorney's interests. Moreover, it causes a reduction in *pro bono* work (literally, **pro bono publico**, or work done for the public good, for free by legal professionals). To encourage pro bono work, many law firms allow attorneys and paralegals to devote a certain number of hours each year (for example, 50 hours) to pro bono cases and count that time toward any minimum billable hour requirements.

Note that the emphasis on billable time is not nearly as great (and may be nonexistent) in public interest law firms, nonprofit legal clinics, government law departments, and in-house corporate law departments, because these entities do not bill time to a paying client.

Pro bono publico: Legal services that are provided for the public or for those in need without charge.

3. *Timekeeping Practices*

a. **Introduction**

Timekeeping: Method of tracking and entering time spent on client and other work.

Because most firms use hourly billing as the method by which they charge clients for legal services, **timekeeping**, which is the detailed and accurate recording of the time spent and tasks performed on client matters, is critical. Even firms that take cases on contingency fees or that assess flat fees require accurate timekeeping so they can evaluate the overall profitability of a case. Additionally, in cases in which a court orders payment of attorneys' and paralegals' fees, the firm will need to be able to document the time spent on a case.

b. **How Time Is Calculated**

Generally, law firms that engage in hourly billing divide the hour into tenths or into quarters as units of measurement. For example, if your firm bills your time to the client at a rate of $100 per hour, and it takes you half an hour to write a letter, the client will be billed $50 for the task. Usually time is rounded up to the next nearest fraction of an hour.

If a firm bills in tenths of an hour, each six minutes represents a billable entry. Consider the following example (again assuming the rate is $100 per hour):

Task	Time Spent	Entry on Bill	Charge to Client
Phone call	5 mins.	.1	$10
Note to file	10 mins.	.2	$20
Draft lease	45 mins.	.8	$80

Although it may seem unusual to divide an hour into six-minute segments, this method allows an easy calculation of fees based on the decimal system, and so it is a very common timekeeping approach.

When firms divide the hour into quarters, no task can be billed for less than one-quarter of an hour. If a phone call takes you ten minutes, you will record .25 for the time spent on the task.

c. How Time Is Recorded

For well over a century, legal professionals simply recorded their time on looseleaf sheets of paper and then handed these to billing clerks in the firm to prepare bills. The entry identified the client name, the task performed, and the time spent on the task. Standard abbreviations were often used. For example, "t/c" might indicate a telephone call. (See Figure 7-1.) Over time, firms began to use perforated, tear-off sheets or slips of paper with carbon copies. The slips were sorted into appropriate piles, and bills were prepared based on these slips.

Figure 7-1
Hand-Prepared Timekeeping Record

Timekeeper: Alan Lopez   Date: 5/08/08

Client Name	Client and Matter Number	Description of Task	Time Spent
Sanders Co.	00654.0012	Review franchise agreement	1.5
Sandra Cruz	00798.0001	Prepare will and trust documents	3.25
MJK Inc.	00349.0006	Review non-compete agreement	1.0
MetroTech, Inc.	00567.0154	Prepare summary of deposition transcript for defendant Taylor	1.75

Now, nearly all firms use specialized software programs that maintain time and prepare bills. The computerized systems merge the timekeeping and billing functions, so that once time is entered, a bill is automatically prepared (and then added to if additional time is spent on that client's file). In some cases, bills are sent electronically (rather than

Figure 7-2
Sample Page from Timeslips®

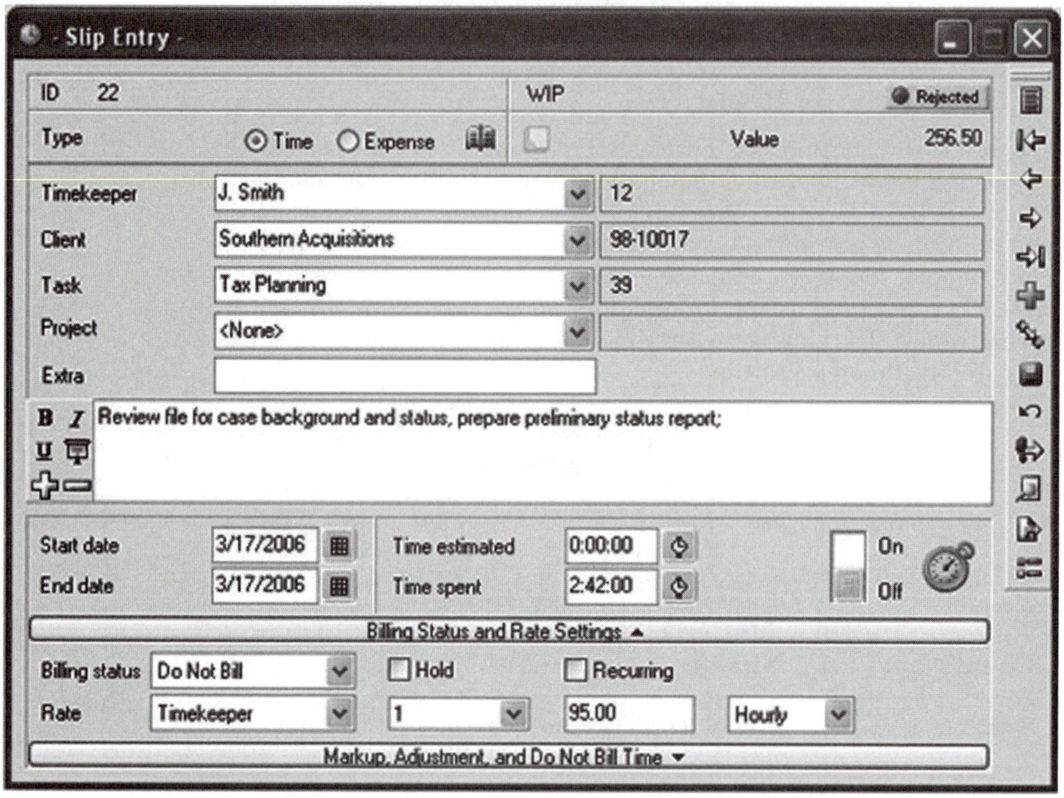

by "snail mail") to clients. As soon as you complete a task on a file or matter, you will access the system, input your time, and move on to your next task. Some systems include a stopwatch function to allow you to accurately track your time. Spell check programs and custom abbreviations make time entry efficient and accurate. See Figure 7-2 for a sample page from Timeslips®, a well-known software package for tracking time.

Legal professionals also track expenses so that these can be billed to the client. Most law firms use sophisticated computer systems so that making even one copy of a one-page document for a client requires entry onto a keypad of the user's employee number and the client's billing number. Similarly, long-distance telephone calls, court filing fees, LEXIS and Westlaw research fees, and travel expenses are tracked. At the end of the month, these expenses are exported from the tracking system to the billing system and are added to the client's bill.

Once a law firm is engaged, it will assign a **client number** to the client for billing purposes. Because the law firm may be representing the client in a variety of cases, each particular matter for which the firm does work is assigned a **matter number**. Thus, the client number may be

Client number:
Number assigned to a client by a law firm.

Matter number:
Number assigned to each individual matter handled by a firm for a client.

00942. When the firm works on that client's will, the matter is called matter number 001; when the firm drafts an employment contract for that client, it is assigned matter number 002; and so forth. The client receives an itemized bill for each matter so it knows exactly what it is being charged for each of its separate matters or tasks.

d. Best Timekeeping Practices

Although there are several ways of keeping time and law firm methods do vary slightly, there are a few basic principles that all paralegals and attorneys must follow in timekeeping:

- **Contemporaneously enter the time.** As you perform a task, immediately enter the appropriate client name or number, matter number, and a description of the work performed. You may be tempted to think you can "catch up" at the end of the day and recall all the work you did. Don't fool yourself; it's surprisingly difficult to capture time if you don't record your work contemporaneously with the task, generally because you will work on several different matters during a given day and will be interrupted by telephone calls, meetings, and the like.
- **Accurately enter your time.** Charging a client for work not performed or "padding" your time is unethical and is a clear violation of ABA Formal Opinion 93-379, which provides that "it goes without saying that a lawyer who has undertaken to bill on an hourly basis is never justified in charging a client for hours not actually expended." The ABA gives the following other examples of unethical billing practices:
  - Billing more than once for documents prepared only once but sent to several parties;
  - Billing for "form" or standard law firm documents as if they were originally created rather than merely recycled;
  - Double-billing by charging each client the full amount for time shared by more than one case. For example, if a paralegal must attend a court hearing for client Smith, the hearing is delayed, and the paralegal works on client Taylor's file while waiting in the courtroom, each client may not be billed for that time; generally, the time must be split between matters.

    The ABA position is that clients, not law firms, should benefit from economies of scale and other cost efficiencies that arise in the practice of law.
- **Describe tasks in detail.** Clients do not appreciate receiving a $300 bill for such vague tasks as "reviewing file" or "research." Thoroughly describe the work you perform, such as "Review deposition transcript of Martha Allen regarding conditions at time of accident" or "Telephone call to Mr. Davidson regarding discovery schedule."
- **Don't "fudge" your time.** As a beginning paralegal, you may be tempted to "write down" your time, entering one hour for a task that actually took you two hours to perform, thinking that as a

beginner you may be inefficient. Do not write down your own time. The firm pays its new paralegals lower salaries and bills out its inexperienced paralegals at a lower billing rate for exactly this reason and understands that it takes some time for new paralegals to become efficient. All bills will be reviewed by attorneys who will reduce the client's bill if they believe it is too high.

E.   Law Office Procedures

1. Introduction

Because the expression "time is money" is a guiding principle at law firms, law firms consistently strive to streamline office procedures and eliminate waste so that as much productive time as possible can be spent on client work, thus increasing the firm's revenue. The efficient administration of law offices is a frequent topic of seminars, courses, books, an ABA practice section, and a critical focus of the International Paralegal Management Association (IPMA). In fact, the NFPA offers a Paralegal Advanced Competency Examination (PACE), which specifically tests paralegals on the following procedures: conflicts checks, file maintenance, calendar systems, database systems, timekeeping and billing, law office technology, and other related topics.

2. Policy Manuals

Many firms (and almost all large firms) use office procedure manuals that describe general employment-related issues (such as sick leave and holiday schedules) and procedures for various office practices, such as how to ensure that a conflict of interest doesn't exist between one client and another, how to "open" a new file, how time should be recorded, and so forth. These policies may be maintained in a looseleaf binder or may be online. Generally, the larger the firm, the more detailed its policies and procedures. For example, a large firm will want to make sure all of its documents have a uniform appearance and so will have policies on preparing letters, including information on spacing, margins, and the like. You will be expected to follow all of the firm's policies, so review any manuals carefully.

3. Conflicts Checks

Conflicts check: Review of firm files to ensure a conflict of interest does not exist.

Before an attorney or firm agrees to represent a client, a **conflicts check** will be performed to ensure that representing a client will not create a conflict of interest. Paralegals are frequently involved in conflicts checking. Small firms may conduct their conflicts checks manually, by reviewing files and client master lists. Most firms, however, purchase sophisticated software packages that electronically check whether there is a conflict of interest between a firm's former or existing clients and a new client or new matter. Generally, attorneys complete a conflict of interest document that identifies all information about a potential client. If the potential client is a corporation or other business entity, information about its directors, officers, key principals, and subsidiaries is also obtained. The information gathered is then entered into the firm's database to determine if a match is found with any existing or former clients. If a preliminary match is found by a paralegal, an attorney will usually review the matter to determine if an actual conflict exists. If a conflict exists, the firm may attempt to obtain a waiver of the conflict from the existing or former client or might decline representation (if the conflict is one that cannot be waived).

4. *File Maintenance*

Most firms have procedures relating to the organization of client files so that any attorney or paralegal in the firm can readily locate pleadings, correspondence, and other important documents. Avoid the temptation to view file maintenance as meaningless activity or merely placing papers in a file. Poor file maintenance results in lost productivity while legal professionals aimlessly search through piles of paper. Maintaining orderly files is important so that information is readily available and deadlines are met.

Some firms maintain their files in alphabetical order. Most, however, use a numerical system, consisting of the client number, matter number, and perhaps other identifying information. For example, a file may be labeled "05-ET-1036.004," which would indicate that the file relates to client number 1036, matter number 004, and is an estates and trusts file opened in 2005.

Most law firms maintain one large file comprising several subfiles. There may be separate subfiles for correspondence, pleadings, research, and so on. Each subfile is typically kept in chronological order, with the most recent item placed on top. For pleadings, the file usually includes "tabbed" documents (for easy retrieval), and the top document in the file is an index to the pleadings file, for example:

Document / Tab	Description	Filed / Prepared by	Date Filed
1.	Complaint	Plaintiff Kirchner	10/1/07
2.	Answer to Complaint	Defendant Koch	10/29/07
3.	Interrogatories	Plaintiff Kirchner	11/15/07

Files may be kept in a separate file room or in cabinets near the supervising attorney's desk. When files are removed from cabinets or shelves, some law firms use a "check-out card" system that requires any-one who removes a file to sign for the file and indicate the date it was removed. Anyone looking for the file will then easily be able to determine its location. A new trend to facilitate finding files in large firms is bar coding. Each file has a label with a bar code. At the end of each day, a firm employee will use an implement (similar to a grocery store scanner) to scan all of the files on each attorney's and paralegal's desk. When someone needs to know the location of a file, the bar code system easily identifies the file's location. Some large firms use radio frequency identification to track and locate files. Sensors placed in office ceilings will locate files within a ten-foot distance.

When a matter is concluded, the file will be reviewed to determine whether any documents or pleadings can be used as forms in the future. These may be copied and maintained in form files or banks. The file will then be closed and, usually, sent to a commercial storage site. After several years (and after reviewing codes of ethics to determine the rules relating to periods of time that files must be kept), the firm will usually destroy the file, typically by shredding it to preserve confidentiality.

5. *Form Banks*

Efficient paralegals and attorneys maintain their own form files of useful documents that may serve as models or guides in the future. For example, it is far more efficient to draft a trust based on a previous model than to start from scratch. While some firms maintain centralized form files with indexes to the documents on file, the current trend is to maintain such files electronically in the firm's computer system so that others in the firm can readily access pertinent forms. It is also common for legal professionals to email their colleagues and simply inquire whether someone else has a form or document that has proven useful in the past. Collect and maintain your own form files so that you can efficiently prepare needed documents.

6. *Copying, Mailing, and Faxing*

Every law office, no matter what its size, produces masses of paperwork. Multiple copies are often made of nearly every document. In large firms, employees are hired solely to staff the copy room. In these firms, attorneys and paralegals do not copy documents themselves; they instruct the copy room employees as to the number of copies, desired binding, collating, and the like. These firms use automated copy systems so that before any copy-ing can be done, the client number, matter number, and employee number must be entered in the system using a keypad. The system then tracks the number of copies and a charge automatically appears on the client's bill at the end of the month. Smaller firms may use paper logs placed on the copy machine. Users manually record the client name or number and the number of copies made so that billing clerks can charge the clients for these expenses at the end of the month. Outgoing mail is handled in the same way as copying.

Procedures for sending communications by facsimile are identical to those used for copying, except that a *facsimile cover sheet* is used to describe the document being transmitted, the number of pages included, and other similar information. A confidentiality notice is placed on the fax cover sheet so that if the communication is inadvertently sent to the wrong number, the recipient is instructed to return the document. Email communications include similar confidentiality notices.

Ethics Alert

According to the ABA, legal professionals who receive faxes sent to them in error must refrain from reading them, must notify the sender, and must follow the sender's instructions as to the disposition of the document. Not all jurisdictions agree. For example, in the District of Columbia, the receiving attorney may use the inadvertently produced documents if they have been read before the reader determines that he or she was not the intended recipient. Thus, because confidential communications may lose their privileged status if they are sent to the wrong person, use extreme caution when sending faxes. Double-check the fax number, and use automated dialing features if your office has them. Similarly, do not send a confidential fax until you confirm that it will be received in a secure location. Call the client and alert him or her to the incoming transmission so that it doesn't sit in the open for all to see. Follow the same precautions when sending email.

---

7. *Calendaring and Docket Control*

All attorneys and paralegals live with the pressure of deadlines. Statutes of limitations require that lawsuits be filed within a certain time. Litigation professionals know that requests for admissions must be responded to within 30 days. Transactional professionals understand that the closing of a merger must occur on a scheduled date. Failure to observe these deadlines constitutes legal malpractice. Thus, all firms use some form of calendar to track important deadlines. This calendar is often referred to as the **docket**. A 1998 ABA survey entitled "Utilization of Legal Assistants Among Private Practitioners" reported that approximately 70 percent of the responding firms and attorneys used paralegals to monitor deadlines and calendars. Similarly, the NALA Survey reported that 63 percent of the responding paralegals calendared deadlines on a daily basis.

As with nearly all systems, the type of calendar or docket the firm maintains will vary based on the size of the firm and the nature of the practice. Small firms may use a large whiteboard calendar posted in a central location with dates and tasks entered in the appropriate calendar

Docket: Law firm's calendar of its pending matters and related deadlines (also refers to court's schedule of its cases).

square. Some firms and individuals use an index card system; a separate $3'' \times 5''$ index card is prepared for each deadline date (with information relating to the client name, the client and matter number, the task to be completed, and so forth), and then each card is placed behind tabbed dividers for the appropriate month and day. The cards are then reviewed on a periodic basis, and reminders are sent to the responsible paralegal and attorney. These index card reminder systems are often called **tickler systems**.

Tickler system:
A method of providing reminders to individuals of tasks that need to be completed or that have pending deadlines.

While these manual systems worked well for many years, today's megafirms, with their significant caseloads, require more sophisticated systems, usually electronic docket systems maintained by a professional docket clerk. After the appropriate data are entered, the system generates daily or weekly written reports and electronic reminders of tasks. Some programs are customized to the firm's areas of practice so that once a certain task or date is entered, other related dates are automatically calendared. These systems can also send reminders of recurring events, such as weekly office meetings.

8. *Complex Case Management and Technology*

In recent years, the number of large-scale litigation cases has increased significantly. Many are class actions against drug companies, tobacco companies, or companies making dangerous products. The cases involving asbestos claims involve more than 500,000 claimants who have sued more than 6,000 defendants. Cases such as these involve millions of pages of documents that must be organized and accessible to the legal professionals involved in the case. Even smaller cases generate reams of paper.

Bates® stamp:
An implement that assigns sequential numbers to pages and documents; may be done manually or electronically.

As documents are received by law firms, they must be organized. Many law firms continue to use a **Bates® stamp**, a device that places sequential numbers on documents. The documents are then indexed, a process by which the numbered document is described in a separate document. For example, document number 13,325 might be described by its author, its recipient, date, topic, key terms, and so forth. Later, if someone wants to see all documents written by a certain author or all documents relating to a certain topic, the index will identify which numbered documents should be reviewed. Paralegals frequently Bates stamp and index documents. Although Bates stamping was previously done manually by using an actual stamping machine, it is now commonly done by using peel-and-stick labels or by various electronic methods of assigning sequential numbers to each page in a document or case. Alternatively, bar codes may be assigned to each document and then a portable scanner is used to track and locate the documents.

Documents are then scanned into the firm's computer system, facilitating later retrieval by key terms, party names, dates, and so forth. The maintenance of paper documents in electronic format on disk or CD-ROM makes document review, storage, and production far easier than in the past when documents were housed in boxes in room after room at a law firm. Sophisticated software packages can manage all aspects of a case, from performing conflicts checks, to maintaining calendars and dockets, to tracking time, to allowing paperless files to enhance trial preparation.

These automated case management tools level the legal playing field so that smaller firms are not "papered over" by larger ones, and they also provide a streamlined way to find and review documents quickly, search testimony, collaborate with colleagues, and manage every aspect of a case. Because these software packages are commonly used, it is important for you to be familiar with them (see Chapter 10).

NetWorks

www.nala.org; www.paralegals.org; www.paralegalmanagement.org	The Web sites of the National Association of Legal Assistants, the National Federation of Paralegal Associations, and the International Paralegal Management Association offer excellent information on issues of interest to paralegals, including law firm billing practices and practice management strategies.
www.abanet.org	The ABA Web site section, *Law Practice Management,* provides information on law firm and law practice management.
www.abanet.org/genpractice/home.html	The ABA Web site's section on general practice is specifically oriented to sole practitioners, general practitioners, and small firms.
www.law.com	LawCom offers annual lists of the nation's largest law firms with information about size and revenues.
www.greedyassociates.com	Greedy Associates is a site designed to allow new associates to share inside information about their law firm employers, billing requirements, salary structures, and other related information.

Case Illustration

Necessity for Detailed Billing Information

Case:	*Certain v. Potter*, 330 F. Supp. 2d 576 (M.D.N.C. 2004)
Facts:	After prevailing on her claims of retaliation and hostile work environment against her employer, the plaintiff employee moved for an award of attorneys' fees and costs under a statute that allowed for an award of reasonable attorneys fees to the prevailing party.
Holding:	Reasonable attorneys fees may be awarded by a court. To establish the number of hours reasonably expended, counsel should submit evidence supporting the number of hours worked, reduced to exclude excessive, redundant, or otherwise unnecessary time. The applicant must make every effort to submit time records that specifically indicate the time spent on each claim, and those records should attempt to specifically describe the work. In such cases, reasonable fees may be awarded.

Chapter Summary

- Law firms vary widely in their sizes and structures. Lawyers may practice by themselves or with others. A newer trend is for law firms to organize as limited liability partnerships, a business structure that is governed by traditional partnership law but that limits liability so that individual attorneys are liable only for their own acts of malpractice and those they supervise.
- Working in a smaller firm affords a great deal of client contact and interesting and varied work for paralegals, but salaries may be lower and the amenities are not as luxurious as those offered by larger firms.
- Medium-sized law firms often offer the best of both worlds: small-firm practice (including client contact and varied work) and large-firm practice (with plenty of "perks" and a structured career path for paralegals).
- Larger law firms offer higher pay and opulent surroundings, but the work may lack variety and there may be little opportunity for client contact.
- The personnel in a law firm include support staff, paralegals, paralegal managers, associates, and partners or shareholders.
- Law firms enter into a variety of fee arrangements with their clients, including contingency fees (in which no fee is paid unless the firm is successful), flat fees (in which a set fee is charged for a task), or hourly fees.
- Nearly all paralegals are required to track the time spent on client matters. Paralegals must be scrupulously honest in recording their time.
- Paralegals are involved in a variety of law office procedures, including conflict checking, file maintenance, copying, calendaring and docket control, and case management. Firms handling large-scale and complex cases often rely on sophisticated software systems to manage nearly every aspect of a case, from conflict checking to tracking documents to timekeeping.

Key Terms

Sole practitioner: An attorney who practices by himself or herself.

General partnership: A business structure with shared decision making and personal liability for its partners.

Personal liability: Liability extending beyond what one invests in a business to one's personal assets.

Joint and several liability: Liability for an entire obligation.

Partner: The owner of a firm or business operating as a partnership.

Associate: A junior attorney.

Equity partner: A partner who owns business assets.

Managing partner: A partner who directs or manages a partnership.

Permanent associate: An attorney who will remain an employee of a firm rather than an owner; also called *senior attorney*, *staff attorney*, *nonequity partner*, or *of counsel*.

Of counsel: Term usually assigned to older or semi-retired attorneys, although it might refer to senior attorneys joining the firm in a lateral position.

Lateral hire: Attorney hired by one firm from another.

Limited liability partnership (LLP): Type of partnership that protects partners from liability for each other's wrongful acts.

Limited liability company (LLC): Business structure that protects its members from unlimited personal liability; a new form of business organization that combines features of partnerships and corporations.

Professional corporation (PC): A corporation organized to provide professional services, such as legal services.

Shareholder: The owner of a corporation.

Director: The manager of a corporation.

General practice: Law firm practice that handles a wide variety of cases.

Boutique firm: Law firm that handles only limited types of cases.

Transactional work: Work that is not related to litigation.

Contract attorney: Nonemployee attorney who works for a firm on a project basis.

Partnership track: A firm's preestablished path to become a partner or owner.

Rainmaking: Attracting new business and clients.

Retainer: Initial fee paid to attorney or firm to engage legal services.

Contingency fee: Fee paid to law firm by client only if firm is successful in recovering money for a client.

Flat fee: Fee paid to law firm by client for a certain legal task or matter, regardless of the time it takes.

Hourly fee: Fee paid to law firm by client for each hour expended on a client's matter.

Billable hours: Time that can be charged to a client for work performed.

Pro bono or **pro bono publico:** Legal services that are provided for the public or for those in need without charge.

Timekeeping: Method of tracking and entering time spent on client and other work.

Client number: Number assigned to a client by a law firm.

Matter number: Number assigned to each individual matter handled by a firm for a client.

Conflicts check: Review of firm files to ensure a conflict of interest does not exist.

Docket: Law firm's calendar of its pending matters and related deadlines (also refers to court's schedule of its cases).

Tickler system: A method of providing reminders to individuals of tasks that need to be completed or that have pending deadlines.

Bates® stamp: An implement that assigns sequential numbers to pages and documents; may be done manually or electronically.

Bits and Bytes

- A 2003 survey by NFPA disclosed that the average billing rate by paralegals was $81 to $90 per hour. A 2007 survey by *Legal Assistant Today* reported similar results.

- The ABA Commission on Billable Hours reported that of 570 firms that responded to its survey, only 22 did *not* have a minimum requirement of billable hours for their legal professionals.

- A 2005 survey by IPMA disclosed that 34 percent of the respondents reported that paralegals were required to bill between 1,600 and 1,799 hours per year. Moreover, half of the firms reported that, at least in part, bonuses were based on meeting or exceeding these billable requirements.

- NALA's 2004 survey reported that 63 percent of paralegals engage in calendaring and docketing on a daily basis.

- Ninety percent of the respondents to NALA's survey reported an increase in the level of sophistication of their work, primarily in the area of more complex cases.

Discussion Questions

1. Larger law firms nearly always pay higher salaries than smaller law firms. Why wouldn't everyone want to work in a larger law firm?

2. The law firm Jacobs and Pruitt operates as a general partnership. It has offices in six cities. One of the attorneys in the firm's Los Angeles

office recently committed an act of legal malpractice. Describe the liability of the attorneys in the Cleveland office for this act. Describe the liability of the attorneys in the Cleveland office for this act if the firm were operating as a limited liability partnership.

3. Brad, a paralegal, has been told that if he bills 1,500 hours by January 1 of next year he will receive a bonus. On December 1, Brad realizes he is within 200 hours of reaching this goal. What are some of the risks that Brad and the firm may face regarding this policy?

4. Carol, a new paralegal, is concerned that it took her two hours to draft a letter to a client. Because she doesn't want to appear inefficient, Carol entered one hour for this task on her timesheet. Do you agree with this decision? Discuss.

5. What are some of the advantages and disadvantages of entering time in quarter hours rather than tenths of hours?

WebWork

1. Review NALA's Web site and access its 2004 National Utilization and Compensation Survey Report.

   a. Review Section 2, Table 2.1. How has the percentage of paralegals working in private law firms changed in the past ten years?
   b. Review Section 2, Table 2.10. What percentage of paralegals works in firms with between 76 and 100 attorneys?
   c. Review Section 3, Table 3.2. What percentage of paralegals is expected to bill between 36 and 40 hours per week?

2. Review IPMA's 2005 Utilization Survey.

   a. Review Section 11. What percentage of respondents indicated that their firms had no billable hours requirements for their paralegals?
   b. Review Section 11. What percentage of paralegals is expected to bill between 1,500 and 1,599 hours per year?
   c. Review Section 12. What percentage of firms or employers allows pro bono work to count as billable work?

Chapter 8

Keeping Your Job and Advancing in Your Career

Far and away the best prize that life offers is the chance to work hard at work worth doing.
—Theodore Roosevelt

Chapter Overview

This chapter discusses some basic workplace rules of the road. You not only want to keep the job you worked so hard to get, you want to advance in your career. Keeping your job requires as much if not more effort than getting the job in the first place. Once you are in your new job, you must make sure you are a productive and diligent worker so you will be valued by your employer. If workforce reductions must be made, you want to be sure that you are the last one the employer wants to discharge.

In addition to being a productive worker, you want to present a professional appearance and demeanor at all times. You should also prepare and plan for your periodic performance evaluations so your salary and level of responsibility increase.

Finally, you need to devote time to career advancement, including continuing your education as appropriate and taking the initiative so that your job remains rewarding and challenging. You may want to become a paralegal manager or law firm administrator, jobs for which you will be uniquely prepared and qualified.

A. Keeping Your Job

1. Introduction

Getting a job is only the first chapter of your career story. You must work harder at keeping your job than you did to get it. Each day brings the opportunity for you to demonstrate that your employer made the right decision in hiring you. Moreover, you will be far happier if you know that you are doing your job to the best of your abilities, rather than simply "putting in time" behind your desk. While you may lose a job for circumstances beyond your control — economic reasons, a firm merger, loss of a client, and so forth — there is a great deal you can do to ensure that your employer views you as a critical employee. Many of the tips and strategies discussed in this chapter, such as being punctual and being a team player, seem like "no brainers," yet you would be surprised how many workers don't understand the fundamental rules that can virtually guarantee success on the job.

2.   *Strategies for On-the-Job Success*

Although your employer will understand that your paralegal program has given you a thorough grounding in various legal topics and excellent overall paralegal skills, you will need a training period in your new job to learn your employer's policies and preferences. In addition, it will take a bit of time for you to apply the principles you learned in school to the real-life cases on which you will work. Although employers are prepared to train you in a practice field and allow you some time to learn more about a substantive area of law, there are five characteristics you will be expected to possess on the first day — and every day — of your job.

- **Punctuality.** You will quickly discover that lawyers work very hard. If the workday begins at 9:00 A.M., slipping behind your desk as the clock strikes 9:00 every morning will be quickly noticed (and commented upon). Lawyers expect to hit the ground running each day. If every morning begins with your supervisor waiting for you and wondering where you are, you will quickly be shown the door. Come in a few minutes early (at least until you become more comfortable in your job and you build up some credibility with your employer) to read your email, review your pending projects, and plan your day. Then if the day begins with your supervisor immediately questioning the status of a certain matter, you'll be ready to respond rather than needing to shuffle through your paperwork. Similarly, show up a bit early for any office or team meetings. Making others wait for you is arrogant and unprofessional. Take a file or some professional reading materials with you so that if you need to wait for others, you can use the time productively. Finally, if you know you're running a bit late either in the morning or after a break, or for a meeting due to an errand or unexpected emergency, call or send a quick email to let others know. Occasional tardiness is easily understood if others know about it; no-notice absences are treated far more seriously.
- **Diligence.** Work hard. Clock-watchers are the exception rather than the rule at almost all law offices. If you routinely break for lunch exactly at noon and leave for the day at the stroke of 5:00 p.m., no matter what the status of your projects, your professionalism and

work ethic will be questioned. The client's needs are paramount; leaving in the middle of a critically needed task is unacceptable. If you give your work your best effort and commitment, it will be noticed. Give every project your full attention. Keep working on a project until you are satisfied that it is of the highest quality possible.

- **Competency.** Clients expect the best results from their legal team. You will be expected to know how to perform tasks routinely performed by paralegals, such as cite-checking, preparing certain documents, and communicating effectively. It's equally important to understand what you don't know. If you are presented with an unfamiliar task, ask for advice on how to start the project. Review the file. Conduct some basic research. The standard in law firms is not "good enough"; the standard is excellence.

- **Collegiality.** It is highly unlikely that you will work alone or in a completely isolated environment. You will be expected to be a team player. Your entire team has one goal: to help the client. Thus, you need to get along with your teammates. Share information. It is not enough to simply do your assigned portion of a project. Offer to lend a helping hand. Establish rapport with others. You will undoubtedly need help from others during your career. Work on building up a reservoir of goodwill so that others will want to help you as you have helped them. It is entirely possible (and highly likely) that there will be difficult people in your organization. Try and avoid becoming so focused on their difficult behavior that you cannot work together productively. Try to find some common ground. If you've been slighted by someone, try to forgive, and avoid holding a grudge. Understand that your work environment is not a social setting. You should not expect to be best friends with everyone at work. Keep your focus on the client's needs, and work on establishing professional relationships. If social relationships and friendships develop, that's an added bonus, but the primary reason you are at work is to help your employer assist clients.

- **Respectfulness.** Treat everyone in your work environment with respect. Although your immediate supervisor will be the one to make decisions about your salary and career advancement, every person in the office, from the receptionist to the copy room employees to the kitchen helpers to the most senior partner should be treated with dignity and courtesy. Respect the opinions of your colleagues even if you disagree with their approach. Listen respectfully, and try to help others reach a compromise or consensus if there is disagreement on your team. Respect the client by working diligently and keeping time accurately and honestly. Respect your employer by using the workday for work assignments. Do not use the Internet for personal use or to conduct personal business (although an occasional personal email is probably acceptable). Be honest with regard to other employer-owned resources, such as supplies and equipment. Respect your specific work location by keeping it neat and organized so that others can find a needed file. Remember the adage to give an honest day's work for your wages.

3. *Professional Appearance and Demeanor*

In addition to the characteristics just discussed, there is one more attribute you will need to succeed in your job: You must be professional in every respect. The way you present yourself speaks volumes to those around you. Until you have been instructed otherwise, dress for work the way you did for your interview. Clients expect their legal team to be professional and crisp in both attitude and dress. Appearance *does* count. The legal profession is conservative. When in doubt, err on the side of caution, and dress and act more conservatively rather than less. You can always shed a jacket, blazer, or tie if everyone around you has dressed "down," but if you dress too casually for a meeting, there's nothing you can do to "dress up" in a hurry.

a. Dress to Impress

According to at least one expert, more than half of a person's perception of you is based on your appearance. The following are some suggestions to ensure your appearance underscores and demonstrates your professionalism.

- For men:
  - Wear solid color, conservative suits, in navy, gray, or some similar muted color.
  - Wear white, solid, or muted pattern long-sleeved shirts.
  - Wear a conservative or traditional tie.
  - Wear dark socks and traditional "hard" shoes (no moccasins or "boat" type shoes).
  - Do not wear excessive or showy jewelry.
  - Remove earrings (unless other professionals in the office routinely wear them).
  - Make sure your hair and beard are neatly trimmed and professional appearing.
- For women:
  - Wear solid or muted pattern conservative dresses or suits, or skirts with coordinated blouses. Skirts should be knee-length or longer. Blouses should be tucked in (unless they are designed to be worn out).
  - Wear closed-toed shoes with hosiery.
  - Avoid excessive makeup and jewelry.
- For everyone:
  - Cover any visible tattoos or body piercings.
  - Make sure all clothing is neatly pressed; wrinkled clothes create a horrible impression.
  - Avoid tight-fitting or ill-fitting clothes.
  - Avoid excessive perfume or cologne.
  - Make sure shoes are clean and polished.
  - Avoid unnatural hair colors such as pink or purple.
  - Carry a briefcase or portfolio.

b. The Business Casual Office

Many law firms and offices use a "business casual" dress code, either throughout the entire week, on Fridays only, or during the summer only. What does "business casual" mean? Again, it's better to be over-dressed than underdressed. After you have worked in the office a couple of weeks and have had an opportunity to observe what others are wearing, you'll have a better idea how to fit in, but the following are some basics of business casual dressing. Men usually wear dressy slacks (often khaki-colored) with belts, long-sleeved shirts (rolled up) without a tie, or polo-style shirts with collars (no T-shirts), and casual loafer-type shoes with socks.

Women usually wear casual skirts, dressy pants with nice blouses or sweaters, and closed-toe shoes with or without hosiery. Do not wear jeans, open-toed shoes, athletic shoes, or T-shirts unless and until you have observed several well-respected or senior attorneys wearing them frequently. Clothes should not have any frayed edges, tears, or rips, no matter how fashion-forward you believe them to be.

Some television shows (such as *Ally McBeal*) or movies (such as *Erin Brockovich*) portray female legal professionals in clothing that would be considered inappropriate in nearly every legal office. Take your dress cues from your coworkers and not from Hollywood. Remember that the first word in "business casual" is still "business."

Consider the following true story: One paralegal manager decided to offer full-time employment to a temporary paralegal placed with the firm after it was noticed that the paralegal dressed more formally than required. Even after the temp worker was reminded, "You can dress more casually here," the worker continued to wear dressier clothes. The firm interpreted the worker's dress to reflect a certain level of maturity and professionalism and, as a result, decided to offer the person a permanent position, even though the firm was then required to pay the agency a placement fee. Other paralegals have reported that they are treated more seriously and with more respect when they dress "up" rather than "down." In any event, it's a good idea to keep some extra, dressier clothes at the office so if you are unexpectedly called into a meeting or need to go to court or a client's office, you will be prepared.

Practice Tip: *What Not to Wear*

While many businesses and law firms are becoming more casual, either for the entire week or on Fridays, there are several items of clothing that are not acceptable anywhere. They include: cargo or other baggy-style pants, pants without belts, low-slung pants, ripped or torn clothes, unpressed or wrinkled clothes, low-cut tops for women or scanty tops that show bare midriffs, excessively short skirts on women, tight or suggestively fitting clothes on women, and flip-flops.

c. Professional Demeanor

Looking professional is one part of showing respect at work. The other part is behaving professionally. Your behavior should be no different from that of the senior attorneys. Clients visiting the office should assume you are an attorney until you introduce yourself by name and position. Follow some basic rules: No chewing gum, no slouching in chairs or leaning against doorways, no buttons or other labels that communicate your political views, and no eating in the public areas of the firm. Law offices are relatively quiet workplaces because the legal professionals are engaged in client meetings or confidential calls, researching cases, writing briefs, and the like. As a result, many offices frown upon excessive noise in client areas (although lunch rooms or break rooms are far more casual and social). Before you bring in a radio or your CD collection, check around to see if others listen to music at their desks and, if so, the type of music that's acceptable.

Be alert to the office's culture. Does everyone continue to work while eating lunch at his or her desk? Do most workers come in early and leave late? Do people come into work even on "snow days"? How much personal chat is acceptable? Be a careful observer and adjust your behavior accordingly. If you want people to take you seriously, you should demonstrate that you are serious about your workplace and treat it and your coworkers with respect. A polished appearance and demeanor will signal that you are worthy of trust and responsibility.

B. Performance Evaluations and Salary Negotiations

1. The First One Hundred Days

During the interview process you may have negotiated or requested a performance review after three or six months on the job. If not, after you have been in your job for a few months, you can either request a mini-performance review or conduct your own self-evaluation by taking stock of your performance so far. Just as politicians are often evaluated after their first one hundred days in office, try to get some feedback as to how you are performing. If there's something you could be doing better, this mini-review will be your wake-up call so you can correct any deficiencies, and put yourself in the best possible position to get the raise you deserve at your official evaluation.

This first review does not need to be particularly formal. Simply ask your manager or supervisor to meet for 15 to 20 minutes. Mention that you have been employed for about three months, and ask if your work is satisfactory and whether there are any areas in which you could improve. Keep an open mind. Realize that, even if you have significant experience in other work environments, if this is your first legal work environment, there are bound to be a few bumps in the road. If there are several areas that need improvement, adjust your work habits accordingly, and make a point of frequently communicating with your manager or supervisor. For example, after you finish a task, send a quick email message noting in some way that your work or approach was in accord with the comments made to you at the mini-review. These messages will serve as reminders to your manager that you are trying to meet the goals set for you. It will provide another opportunity for your manager to get you back on track if your work isn't quite meeting expectations.

Avoid saying anything negative about the firm or its personnel at your mini-review. If your supervisor asks whether you are satisfied, find something positive to say about how much you are learning, how you have enjoyed the work, and so on. If you are unhappy, withhold that comment at this point. Work for at least four to six months before you make a determination that the situation isn't satisfactory (unless you have observed unethical conduct or been the victim of some form of harassment, in which case, you should raise the issue with a supervisor, or start making arrangements to find other employment).

2. *Planning for Your Performance Evaluation*

During your employment, you will be evaluated on a continuing basis. Every project or task you work on is an opportunity for your supervisor to review your work. At some time, however, you will receive a more formal evaluation of your performance, usually in conjunction with a salary increase or career development plan. Some employers conduct performance evaluations annually or semiannually while others conduct them on a more sporadic basis. In large law firms, the review process is more formal, while in a small firm, the process could consist of a casual chat over coffee, primarily because these small firms might not have a paralegal manager or supervisor. In some firms, you will be asked to complete a self-appraisal prior to the evaluation. The self-appraisal is the forum in which you make the case for a promotion or salary increase. Whatever the nature of your work environment, you should be ready for your performance review.

Remember that attorneys are often poor managers and are typically so busy that they don't have time to assist paralegals in their professional development. Paralegals need to take their professional development "in their own hands" and develop strategies to obtain the feedback and performance evaluation they need.

During the course of the year, ask for feedback from those with whom you work. When a case or project is completed, ask what could have been done better or more efficiently. Don't wait until the end of the year to find out that your manager is unhappy with something you do or don't do.

The best way to prepare for a formal performance review is to keep accurate records of your accomplishments. The person who makes the final determination as to whether you receive a salary increase or a promotion may not be entirely familiar with your work. The attorney you worked with most closely may move to a new firm just before your review. Thus, you must be your own advocate. Keep notes on the projects you worked on, indicating the type of work you performed and the results achieved for the client. Perhaps a client's transaction was completed in record time. Perhaps an appeal was filed on a tight deadline. Perhaps you worked on a case with continuing crises that required you to work significant overtime. If you receive any emails from clients or others complimenting your efforts and work, print them out and keep them in a file folder marked "Performance Review." These "kudo" letters and notes from others can be invaluable in demonstrating your capabilities and value to the firm.

Keep track of your billable hours. If your hours are lower than the firm's stated minimum, be prepared to explain why. Perhaps a partner asked you to help write a nonbillable article or speech. Such an assignment shows that your writing skills are valued and explains why your hours are lower than the average.

Keep a list of any out-of-the-ordinary tasks. Did any cases require travel or overtime? Did you attend any classes or seminars? If so, keep copies of the syllabus and any certificates of completion. Attending classes or seminars shows you care about your career and are continuing to learn. Tell your supervisor if you have participated in your area's paralegal association, if you have written any articles or newsletters, mentored any other paralegals, or mastered new software or systems. Have you had any ideas that saved the firm or its clients time or money?

You will be well prepared for your review if you maintain a working or personal portfolio, which should contain copies of the documents, briefs, memos, and other matters you worked on during the year. Just as job-hunters should keep a job-hunting notebook so they are prepared to showcase their talents when they are looking for a new job, you should be prepared to showcase your accomplishments by keeping a performance portfolio.

3. *Learning from Your Performance Evaluation*

Although it is possible that your salary increase and performance rating may simply be announced to you, it is far more likely that you will sit down in a face-to-face meeting with your paralegal manager, or supervising attorney, or both. Many firms insist that two reviewers participate so that there will be no confusion later about the topics discussed during the review.

Try to learn as much as possible from your review. Listen carefully and don't be defensive. Remember that it is in your employer's best interest that you be as productive as possible. The employer wants this for you just as much as you do. Graciously accept any criticism. If a particular problem area or weakness is noted, ask for specific suggestions on how to improve. Ask to be directed to a mentor who possesses the desired skill so you can remedy the weakness. For example, if you are informed that your files are disorganized, offer to take a class on organization skills, and ask whose files in the office are a model of organization. You can then speak with that person and learn how to improve. Showing a positive outlook and taking the initiative to improve shows maturity and will impress your employer.

If your performance evaluation discloses several weaknesses, ask to meet more frequently with your supervisor — perhaps every six or eight weeks — so you can mutually determine whether you are achieving the goals established during your review. If a problem is noted during your performance review and there is no indication later that you are attempting to remedy the problem, you could very well lose your job.

If you feel that you are struggling, ask your paralegal manager to assign you to a mentor or more senior paralegal. A mentor can help you learn the ropes, serve as a role model, and provide advice. Pay close attention to advice given by your mentor; it is probably advice from the firm itself that the mentor has been asked to pass along to you. Thus, if your mentor comments, "most of us get in by 8:30," understand that the firm is really telling you, "you need to get in by 8:30."

During the performance review, you will probably have an opportunity to comment on your work environment. If there is a particular issue that needs to be solved, don't merely present the problem — politely suggest a possible solution. If you would like more challenging work or greater responsibility, say so. Volunteer to work on other projects. Offer to assist another practice group to sharpen your skills. Do not use your performance review, however, to critique other workers or make negative remarks about office management.

End the review by thanking the reviewer for his or her time and comments, and indicate that you will immediately set about correcting any weaknesses. Send a follow-up email to confirm. Impress the reviewer with your professionalism in a difficult situation.

Practice Tip

If your performance evaluation has left you disappointed, take the comments from the meeting and let them "percolate" for a few days. Then come up with a plan to remedy any of your weaknesses. For example, if your oral communications skills are weak, join Toastmasters International and learn the art of public speaking and presentations. If your written communications skills were noted as being deficient, take a class or two at your local community college or through adult education classes. Be creative and proactive about improving your skills. Develop a strategy to fix any problem areas. Once your plan is in place, make sure to tell your supervisor exactly what you are doing to remedy the problems noted. Your initiative will be a sign of your professionalism and maturity and will be remembered during your next performance evaluation.

4. Salary Negotiations During Your Performance Evaluation

The issue of a salary increase will likely arise during your review. Just as for a job search, do some advance "homework" to be prepared for the discussion of a salary increase. Review the national surveys released by the National Association of Legal Assistants (NALA), National Federation of Paralegal Associations (NFPA), *Legal Assistant Today*, and International Paralegal Management Association (IPMA). Check with your local paralegal association to determine the average salaries in your market for paralegals with your level of experience and in your practice area.

Check with colleagues as to what the average increase has been in your locality during the preceding year. While sharing specifics of salary information is generally awkward, or even taboo, most colleagues will volunteer the average percent increase—between 3 and 5 percent, for example.

Be judicious when reading salary survey information. Review the survey information indicating how many respondents participated in the survey, the level of experience of the respondents, and other factors that may influence salary outcomes. Some paralegal experts believe that salary surveys may present slightly inflated numbers (possibly because the majority of the respondents are paralegals whose employers, typically large law firms, pay their organization dues).

The firm may have already released information as to an expected range of salary increases. Thus, if the firm announces that raises will be between 3 and 7 percent, based on performance, then you have some guidelines. When such an announcement is made, generally only extraordinary performance will result in a raise at or above the stated maximum.

Review your billable hours and compare them against the average in the firm. Consider the nature of your work. If your team participated in a complex merger or your job required travel, these could be factors that would justify an increase at the upper end of the range. Don't just say that you need a raise; provide facts to show that you deserve one. If your raise is a disappointment to you, take a day or two and consider whether the firm offers other benefits (matching 401(k), telecommuting, flex-time, paid parking, and the like) that offset a lower-than-average raise.

Be realistic about the firm's financial position. If the economy is weak, your firm lost a major client, or downsized during the year, you should be prepared to forgo a raise this year. Read the legal journals and newspapers for your locality to determine whether the market is strong or weak and which firms are enjoying success. Be knowledgeable about the external factors that influence your compensation.

Be realistic about your work performance. If your learning curve was longer than anticipated and your billable hours were low, understand that your raise will be on the lower end of the scale.

Negotiating for a salary increase after you are employed is usually far easier than negotiating a salary when you interview. Once you are employed, you will have some understanding and knowledge about salaries in your area, market conditions, and firm finances. Based on performance feedback you have gotten within the year, you will likely have some idea whether you are on track or whether you need improvement in some areas. Employers understand that employees generally expect annual salary increases. Thus, in all likelihood, you will not truly be "negotiating" for an increase but rather discussing how much of an increase you will be given. Lawyers are primarily evidence-driven people. Thus, you should be prepared to demonstrate why you have *earned* an increase based on your job performance and successes. Be prepared to specifically discuss your performance. Review your files and timesheets to remind yourself of cases you worked on. Keep congratulatory emails or notes from your colleagues and provide copies to the person evaluating you. Such "evidence" could be instrumental in helping you get the raise you deserve.

If you work in a setting in which there are few, if any, formal evaluations, be sensitive about the timing of your request for a salary increase. If you have just completed work on a successful transaction or have been assigned additional duties, this may be an excellent occasion to request an increase. On the other hand, if your firm just lost a practice group and several clients to a competitor, this is not the time to make demands.

If you are disappointed with your raise or weren't given one, ask what you can do to ensure that you will receive one at the next review. Confirm the duties expected of you. Verify the number of hours you are expected to bill. Set a date for another review to make sure you are on the right track. Instead of asking for more money, ask for additional responsibility. Increased salary will usually come along with increased duties. Consider whether there is some form of compensation other than salary (extra vacation or flexible hours) that you would accept in lieu of a monetary increase. Don't threaten to leave unless you are prepared to do so. Employees who threaten to quit are usually invited to do so.

C. Advancing in Your Career

1. Strategies to Ensure Advancement

There is more to your job than your salary. You need stimulating and challenging work. If your firm has an established career track and your work is exemplary, you will advance to a senior paralegal position. If you wish to advance in your career, you need to take an active role. Consider the following strategies.

- **Ask for more responsibility.** A common complaint among paralegals is that they are underutilized by their employers. It is possible that your employer simply does not realize what you are capable of doing and does not know how well your paralegal program trained you. Volunteer to summarize a deposition, cite-check a brief, or draft correspondence. Indicate that you will do this on your "own time" as a learning experience and will not bill the client for this. Ask for a review of or comments on your work. Once your employer sees what you are capable of, you will likely be given more challenging tasks.

- **Continue learning.** Continue your education. Take some classes, whether these are substantive legal classes or classes on time management, organizational skills, or software tools and applications. Let others know about the classes you take and the knowledge you have gained. Attend any firm seminars with enthusiasm. Send a quick email to your team members about a pending change in local court rules. Offer to draft a newsletter or bulletin for clients if there is new legislation that will affect them. Read the same publications and journals that your supervising attorney does so that you will be current in the field. Subscribe to online journals and newsletters to stay informed of new developments. Many Web sites, such as FindLaw (www.findlaw.com), will send you a daily legal news bulletin. If you are in a specialty practice area, subscribe to an online newsletter devoted to your field. For example, those working on intellectual property issues often subscribe to GigaLaw's daily newsletter (www.gigalaw.com), which reports on cutting-edge IP issues.

- **Take the initiative.** Write an article for publication in a paralegal journal (and give a copy to your paralegal manager and supervising attorney). Get involved in your local paralegal association. Serve on one of its committees. Run for an office or set up a seminar. Perhaps you could arrange for your firm to host a "brown bag lunch" at which someone speaks on a topic of interest to your firm. Serve on one of your firm's committees. Organize a charity event at the firm (after clearing it with the human resources department and your paralegal manager). Volunteer to be a mentor to a new worker. Perform pro bono work. Volunteer to help out when you see that a practice group or colleague needs assistance. All of these activities demonstrate initiative and leadership.

2. *Career Paths in a Law Office*

a. Introduction

Larger law firms often have defined paralegal career tracks with several "tiers," each with its own name. For example, the firm may use the terms "project assistants," "paralegal," "senior paralegal," and "paralegal specialist," each of which refers to a certain level of experience. Other firms — usually smaller ones — do not have defined categories that represent different skill or experience levels. In those firms, a paralegal's title may remain the same for 20 years. What will change is the amount of responsibility given to the paralegal, which will steadily increase.

b. Senior Paralegals

Senior paralegals are experienced paralegals who generally have at least five years of experience. Although they usually perform the same types of tasks as more junior paralegals (drafting documents, conducting research, working with clients, and so forth), their senior positions require them to work far more independently than other paralegals. Additionally, their communications skills are such that the documents, pleadings, and agreements they draft often need little review and revision. Finally, most senior paralegals engage in some supervision and management of more junior paralegals.

Senior paralegal: Experienced paralegal who generally has at least five years of experience.

Ethics Alert

As you become more experienced, you will likely work without a significant amount of supervision and will likely have increased client contact. Such situations can often lead to the "unauthorized practice of law." All states have statutes that prohibit nonlawyers from practicing law. To avoid the unauthorized practice of law:

- Always disclose your status as a paralegal.
- Do not give legal advice. Always indicate that information you provide to clients is from the attorney.
- Request and ensure that attorneys supervise and review the materials you draft and that they sign opinion letters and court documents.

---

c. Taking Control of Your Career

If your firm does not have defined career paths for its paralegals, take the initiative and meet with your paralegal manager or supervisor to map out a plan for your professional development. Figure out what it will take to get to the next level. Confirm your career plan in writing. Follow the plan, and periodically meet with your manager to ensure you are progressing on the path to success. At a minimum, take the following steps to excel in your career.

- **Continue your education.** Many experts believe that as the paralegal profession grows, each generation will be better educated than the one before it. Moreover, continuing legal education is a component of certification—NALA's Certified Paralegal or NFPA's Paralegal Advanced Competency Examination (PACE) Registered Paralegal designations, for example. In addition, some state registration schemes—such as California's statutes regulating paralegals—also impose continuing legal education requirements on paralegals. To make sure that you keep up, take classes, attend seminars, and share your knowledge with others. Stay current with technological developments. If new paralegals know software applications that you don't, you may be passed by. Ask your manager to help you get training on new applications.

- **Find a niche.** As the practice of law becomes more specialized for attorneys, paralegals are also expected to specialize. If you become an expert in an area of law, whether it is securities, trusts and estates, or communications law, you will be more valued by your firm (and will definitely find it easier to land your next job, if you need to). Consider what you most enjoy doing. Learn as much as you can about this area of law. Become the "go to" paralegal in this specialty area.

- **Distinguish yourself.** Volunteer to help out on a busy project, make yourself available to others, or be a mentor. Become active in your local or statewide paralegal association. Write articles. Teach a class. Take NALA's or NFPA's exam and become certified. Proudly wear your pin designating you as "PACE Registered Paralegal" or as a NALA "Certified Paralegal." Office colleagues will ask what it means to be "registered" or "certified," and you will have the opportunity to explain that you have demonstrated competency in various substantive legal topics and have obtained a certain level of experience. Notice who is successful in the office, and observe what traits and characteristics make them valued. Adopt those characteristics. Find a mentor who can be an advocate for you at review time.

Practice Tips

There are several ways to be identified as a valuable worker in your firm. Anything you do that saves the firm time or money will be noticed. Consider the following:

☐ If you work in a practice field such as communications law or energy law, each of which has its own citation formats and for which *The Bluebook* provides little information on citation, develop a firm practice manual. Survey the attorneys and other paralegals and develop a citation manual or style guide for your group. Include numerous examples so that the firm's approach to citation form is clear and consistent.

☐ Develop a "best practices" manual for new paralegals. Include samples of forms, lists of valuable Web sites, tips on billing and timekeeping, and any other information that a new paralegal joining the firm needs to know.

☐ Volunteer to review old forms and agreements and organize them into a useful, easily accessible form bank. Prepare an index to all of the forms and agreements and distribute it to all attorneys and paralegals.

☐ Prepare short status reports on various cases and projects and distribute them to everyone in your group.

The next time something in your work environment frustrates you or takes up a significant amount of time, don't seethe about it. Solve it. Look for something that's broken and fix it. Whether it's a matter of organizing files or simplifying an office procedure, your initiative and interest in the firm's efficient operation will set you apart.

d. Paralegal Managers

Many paralegals find that moving into management is a natural step in their career development, and most paralegal managers come from the ranks of paralegals. After several years of front-line experience, working as a paralegal, and after obtaining the trust and confidence of your colleagues, you may have the opportunity to become a paralegal manager. **Paralegal managers** (sometimes called *paralegal coordinators*) usually have nearly sole responsibility for all issues relating to the firm's paralegals, from hiring to firing. Although duties vary from firm to firm, paralegal managers generally have the following responsibilities:

> **Paralegal manager:** Paralegal who manages other paralegals.

- Recruiting, interviewing, hiring, and training new paralegal employees
- Preparing and managing the budget for the paralegal program at the firm
- Coordinating the day-to-day activities of paralegals, including managing workflow, work assignments, and staffing needs for both permanent paralegals and temporary staffers
- Identifying areas of needed training and implementing training programs and seminars for paralegals
- Evaluating paralegals' work performance, monitoring billable hours, conducting reviews, and terminating paralegals, if needed
- Managing vendors, such as litigation support software vendors and audio-visual support for trial preparation and courtroom exhibits
- Administering the firm's paralegal program, including long-range planning and analyzing paralegal staffing needs

Typically, overtime and travel are the norm for paralegal managers. Some large law firms will employ a paralegal manager for each branch office and then a director of paralegals who supervises the branch office managers and the entire paralegal staff. Smaller firms may require the paralegal manager to bill some number of hours each year in addition to carrying out managerial duties. In some firms, the paralegal manager reports to the human resources department; in other firms, the paralegal manager reports to the firm's managing partner.

One of the best ways to become a paralegal manager is to combine on-the-job experience as a paralegal with specific training and education. Many paralegal programs offer specific courses in paralegal management; others offer advanced degrees. For example, Marymount University in northern Virginia offers a post-graduate Master of Arts degree in

Legal Administration for those who want to pursue careers in paralegal management. Contact your local paralegal association to find out what programs and courses are offered in your area, or check with the ABA Standing Committee on Paralegals (www.abanet.org/legalservices/paralegals) to determine if there are any programs in your area.

e. Legal Administrators

Legal administrator: Individual who manages nearly all aspects of a law firm and its personnel.

Legal administrators differ from paralegal managers in that they manage the overall day-to-day operations of the entire firm, rather than manage only the paralegal staff. Legal administrators report directly to the managing partner or management committee. They supervise all hiring (usually with an emphasis on support staff hiring), handle banking relationships, manage payroll and benefits administration, ensure tax reporting and legal compliance, supervise technology systems and supplies, plan for future space needs, and so forth. Because experienced paralegals have an intimate knowledge and understanding of the way a law firm operates, legal administration positions are often a natural career fit for them. Just as there are specialized courses and programs to become a paralegal manager, there are also courses and programs for those who want to become a legal administrator. See the Association of Legal Administrators Web site (www.alanet.org/home.html) for additional information.

3. *Alternative Career Paths for Paralegals*

Traditional paralegal: A paralegal who works under the supervision of an attorney, usually in a law firm, corporate law department, or government agency.

Because of the need for cost-effective legal services, the paralegal profession has steadily grown since its inception. Thus, there are a variety of employment opportunities for paralegals in both the private and public sectors and in both law-related fields and non-law-related fields. Although most paralegals work in law firms, there are also paralegals who work in corporate legal departments and various government agencies (both federal and state). In fact, the term **traditional paralegal** is usually used to refer to a paralegal who works under the supervision of an attorney, usually in a law firm, corporate legal department, or government agency.

Freelance paralegal: A self-employed paralegal who works as an independent contractor for attorneys on an as needed basis.

In contrast, a **freelance paralegal** (sometimes called a *contract paralegal*) is a self-employed paralegal who works as an independent contractor, hiring himself or herself out to attorneys for specific projects or tasks — for example, to coordinate discovery in a large class action case. When the project or case is finished, the freelance paralegal moves on to another contract situation. Freelance paralegals provide assistance to attorneys on an as-needed basis, so the attorney does not need to hire a full-time, permanent employee. In all instances, the paralegal is supervised by an attorney.

Independent paralegal: A paralegal who works directly for consumers without supervision by an attorney, generally preparing documents for consumers.

An **independent paralegal** works directly for consumers without supervision by an attorney. Generally, these paralegals complete forms and agreements (often related to family law) and participate in real estate closings. California's statutory scheme refers to these individuals as "legal document assistants." The terminology used can be quite confusing.

Consider the fact that some freelancing paralegals title themselves "independent paralegals" and that California's statute provides that the terms "independent paralegal" and "freelance paralegal" are synonymous. NFPA, however, recognizes that independent paralegals are those who provide some services directly to the members of the public. Consumers, members of the bar, and paralegal associations such as NFPA are concerned that independent paralegals may engage in the unauthorized practice of law, and so regulation of independent paralegals is a key issue facing the paralegal profession.

California is presently the only state in the nation that statutorily regulates the paralegal profession. Statutes in California define the term paralegal, impose educational requirements for paralegals, and identify the services that paralegals may perform. Similarly, California requires legal document assistants to register with county authorities. These individuals directly assist the public in completing various forms, such as wills and divorce petitions. Thus, in California, paralegals work under the direction of attorneys, and legal document assistants (sometimes called "independent paralegals" in other states) work directly for the public in preparing certain legal documents.

Consider working in the public sector. The 2004 NALA Survey reported that about 14 percent of its respondents were employed by either the federal or various state government departments or agencies. Within the federal government, the Department of Justice is the biggest employer of paralegals, followed by the Social Security Administration and the Department of Treasury. Other federal agencies employ paralegals as well, including the U.S. Patent and Trademark Office, the U.S. Tax Court, the Equal Opportunity Employment Commission, the FBI, and the CIA.

Experienced paralegals have numerous traits that are valuable to employers other than law firms. Paralegals are independent and organized workers who have a keen eye for detail. They are often valuable team players in any number of organizations. Note, however, that the number of paralegals employed by various nontraditional employers is small: The 2004 NALA Survey reported that combined employment of paralegals in banks, insurance companies, court systems, and nonprofit associations was only 5 percent of all paralegals.

As will be discussed in more detail in Chapter 11, there are a variety of employment opportunities for paralegals outside a traditional law firm, including the following:

- Alternative dispute resolution paralegal
- Bank, insurance, or trust department paralegal
- Consumer group advocate
- Court clerk
- Editor or journalist
- Executive assistant to corporation presidents and other officers
- Government or public sector paralegal
- Health care or medical specialist
- Human resources specialist
- Independent paralegal

- In-house paralegal
- Law librarian or research specialist
- Legal aid paralegal
- Legal recruiter or placement agent
- Legislative aide
- Lobbying organization paralegal
- Nonprofit corporation or foundation paralegal
- Paralegal teacher
- Self-employed or freelance paralegal
- Title searcher or other real estate-related paralegal
- Trade association paralegal

NetWorks ▬▬▬▬▬▬▬▬▬▬▬▬▬▬▬▬▬▬▬▬▬▬▬▬▬

www.nala.org; www .paralegals.org	The Web sites of the National Association of Legal Assistants and the National Federation of Paralegal Associations offer excellent information on issues of interest to paralegals, including career advice, resources on current compensation and benefits, information on certification, and job banks where you can post your résumé and review job notices.
www.paralegalmanagement .org	The Web site of the International Paralegal Management Association provides thorough information about the paralegal manager profession as well as notices of seminars and classes, salary surveys, and job listings.
www.alanet.org	The Association of Legal Administrators' Web site offers a variety of information about the legal administrator profession.
www.opm.gov	The Office of Personnel Management's Web site posts paralegal job vacancies for federal government positions.

Case Illustration

Termination for Poor Performance

Case: *Camp v. Jeffer, Mangels, Butler & Marmaro,* 41 Cal. Rptr. 2d 329 (Ct. App. 1995)

Facts: The plaintiffs, law firm employees and their spouses, brought an action against their former employer for wrongful termination. The law firm contended that the plaintiffs were "at will" employees who could be fired for any reason or no reason, that they had failed to disclose their felony convictions when they were hired, and that they were fired for poor performance (excessive errors in typing documents and using company time and resources to work on personal matters).

Holding: The defendant employer was entitled to summary judgment. There was no wrongful termination. The employer had the right to terminate the employees because they were at will employees, had engaged in résumé falsification, and were poor performers.

Chapter Summary

- In order to achieve job success and career advancement, paralegals must be punctual, diligent, highly competent, collegial, and respectful.
- Paralegals should always maintain a professional appearance and demeanor. When in doubt, dress more formally than others. You will be respected and admired.
- During the course of your job, your performance will be evaluated. Prepare for formal evaluations by maintaining a list of your projects and work products. Conduct research about salaries in your locality so you are prepared to engage in salary negotiations. Don't be defensive about performance improvement suggestions made to you, and take prompt action to remedy any identified weaknesses.
- To advance in your career, ask for more responsibility, continue learning, and take the initiative to work on new projects.
- Among the career paths for more experienced paralegals is a position as senior paralegal. Take control of your career by continuing your education, finding a specialty or niche practice area, and distinguishing yourself at your job.
- Many paralegals move into management positions as paralegal managers (who manage the paralegal staff) or legal administrators (who manage the entire office).
- There are numerous employment opportunities for paralegals outside traditional law firms. Paralegals may engage in freelance work, may be employed in the public sector, may be employed by in-house legal departments, and may be employed by banks, insurance companies, title companies, or other employers.

Key Terms

Senior paralegal: Experienced paralegal who generally has at least five years of experience.

Paralegal manager: A paralegal who manages other paralegals; also called a *paralegal coordinator.*

Legal administrator: An individual who manages nearly all aspects of a law firm and its personnel.

Traditional paralegal: A paralegal who works under the supervision of an attorney, usually in a law firm, corporate law department, or government agency.

Freelance paralegal: A self-employed paralegal who works as an independent contractor for attorneys on an as-needed basis; also called a *contract paralegal.*

Independent paralegal: A paralegal who works directly for consumers without supervision by an attorney, generally preparing documents for consumers.

Bits and Bytes

- The 2004 NALA Survey reported that of paralegals who were employed more than five years, 80 percent reported an increase in their duties and responsibilities.

- The 2004 NALA Survey reported that 8 percent of its respondents worked as paralegals in the public sector.

- A 2002 survey by Altman Weil reported that there are approximately three paralegals for every ten attorneys in government agencies.

Discussion Questions

1. At your last performance review, you were given a lower raise than expected and informed that you need to be "more professional." What should you do to ensure you receive an increase at your next review?

2. Your paralegal manager has commented that your billable hours are "a bit low." What should you do to ensure you meet the firm's requirements?

3. You have been considering becoming a paralegal manager. What are some things you can do to determine if this is the right career path for you?

4. You are concerned that you are being given more and more responsibility. What actions can you take to make sure that you are not engaged in the unauthorized practice of law?

WebWork

1. Review the 2004 NALA Survey cited throughout this chapter.
   a. Review Section 4, Table 4.3. What is the average salary for paralegals who have received the Certified Legal Assistant designation? What is the average salary for those who have not been so certified?
   b. Review Section 4, Table 4.4. What percentage of paralegals receives a salary increase once a year?

oftentimes the only way to significantly boost your compensation is to leave your current job for a new one.

Before you put yourself through the usually emotionally wrenching act of quitting, spend as much time analyzing why you would like to leave as you did getting your job in the first place. Perform another self-assessment. Write down the pros and cons of your current situation. Be honest. Although you may be at a low point in your job—overwhelmed by excessive work demands or travel—the job likely has some benefits and advantages. Don't ignore these merely because you're currently suffering from job burn-out.

Similarly, do not, under any circumstances, quit on a no-notice basis over a single incident. No matter how upset you are over an issue or event, no matter how sure you are that you deserved a raise or acted appropriately in a situation, you must invest in your future and handle difficult situations with maturity and professionalism. Tell yourself that you will begin looking for another job in three days if you still feel the same way. Give yourself a cooling-off period to determine whether you have a legitimate reason to leave or whether you were letting your emotions get the best of you during a stressful time.

Review your original self-assessment. What were your goals and desires before you obtained your first paralegal job? Did you meet these goals in your current job? Have your goals changed? If so, how? Why? What have you learned in your first job that has caused your goals to change?

Take another sheet of paper, and list your accomplishments at your current job. What skills have you learned? What software programs and applications have you mastered? Did you work on any significant or well-known cases? What classes have you taken? Identifying these achievements will help you determine whether your skills are transferable to a new place of employment and will also help you when it is time to revise your résumé.

2. *When You May Quit*

The conventional wisdom is that employees should stay in a job for at least one year before making a change. Otherwise, you could appear to be someone who lacks stability or cannot be satisfied by a job. There are, however, some exceptions to this general rule.

- If you are miserably unhappy and cannot find a solution to a work problem, go ahead and start looking for another job.
- If you are the victim of unwanted sexual advances or some other form of workplace discrimination, you may well need to resign. You must, of course, inform your paralegal manager or the human resources group about the situation so the employer has the opportunity to remedy the situation. It is an unfortunate fact of life, however, that the victim of discrimination often is made to feel so uncomfortable that he or she feels the only solution is to find another job.
- If the reason you want to quit your job is for some "external" purpose that is not related to your current job, such as moving closer to relatives, continuing your education, or relocating so

your spouse or partner can begin another job or educational program, you can leave at any time (upon giving reasonable notice, of course). These reasons for leaving a job are readily explainable and easily understood by future employers.

Before you quit, take out your résumé and mark the dates of your employment with a highlighter. If you had several jobs that lasted less than one year (unless these were summer or temporary jobs you held while you were a student), you should reconsider quitting. Try to make your current position work for a while longer. Constant job-hopping sends a message to employers that you are undependable. Conversely, if your résumé shows several jobs of moderate or long duration, a one-time job change after a few months won't necessarily be devastating. Nevertheless, you must always be prepared to explain why you left a job after such a short time, and you must be prepared to do this without making negative comments about your employer.

3. *Can This Job Be Saved?*

In many instances, there is only one negative factor about a job, but it colors the worker's feelings about the entire work environment. Carefully review your list of pros and cons. Can you fix the cons? Don't make the crucial mistake of forgetting that there will be difficult colleagues, unreasonable deadlines, bureaucratic red tape, and boring tasks at *any* job. If your immediate boss is the only problem, consider whether you can save your job by changing to a different practice field within your firm. Perhaps you can take a class in intellectual property or trusts and estates and then ask to transfer to that working group. Perhaps your firm has another branch or office location where you can work. Remember that your goal is not merely to find a different job — it is to find a better job. Fill in the blank in this sentence: "The primary reason I want to quit is _____." If the problem can be fixed, then do it.

Review your self-assessment. Focus on the parts of your job that make you the happiest and make you feel most productive. See if there is a way to integrate more of these tasks into your daily routine.

You must be honest with yourself. Review your résumé and ask yourself one question for each job you have left: Why did I leave that job? If every time you left a job it was because your coworkers were difficult to get along with or your boss was overly demanding, it may be possible that your expectations are unreasonable or that you are part of the problem. Understand that while the attitudes and personality traits of others certainly play a part in your day-to-day job happiness, no one has as much control over your career and outlook as you do.

Consider some of the following possible fixes for common work problems:

- **Too much stress.** Take a stress reduction class. Your employer may have an employment counseling program you can use. Meet with one of the counselors (don't worry — it's confidential) and discuss ways you can reduce stress.

- **Work is too demanding.** It is possible that you are working on a case that is complex and demanding. Deadlines are tight and there is always a crisis. Don't forget that all cases eventually come to an end. If this one case is the problem, consider whether your supervisor will give you a "vacation" from the case for one or two weeks while you work on another project. A short break from the case may refresh you. Be careful not to quit a job because of one case; this is making a permanent change to fix a temporary problem.
- **Too much travel.** Meet with your supervisor and discuss the situation. Be specific. Don't just say, "I travel more than anyone else." Have the facts and figures — for instance, "In the last 4 months, I was on the road 10 weeks. I've got several commitments at home and with my [family] [theatre group] [education], and I'd like to reduce my travel for the next few months. Would that be possible?" Ask if someone else can be assigned to the team so that you can switch off traveling.
- **Supervisor is too difficult.** Once again, see if you can transfer into a different practice group. Be honest with yourself, and consider whether you are letting a few odd or quirky mannerisms get "under your skin." Try a one-week attitude adjustment: Be as enthusiastic and noncritical as you can for one workweek, and see if your own changed attitude produces some positive changes. Sometimes our own negativity makes a merely difficult situation seem intolerable. Brainstorm with some friends, and ask them for their suggestions for dealing with difficult co-workers. They may have been in a similar situation and be able to offer invaluable advice.

Consider whether you simply need some rest and relaxation. Take a few days (or more) vacation and treat yourself to a change of pace. Force yourself not to think about your job for a few days. Force yourself to disconnect; don't constantly review your email, voice mail, or text messages to find out what's going on at your office. It's not a vacation if you're still working. After some much-needed rest, you may find that you're ready to return to your job with newfound enthusiasm.

4.   *Career Counseling*

Just as many couples go to marriage counseling before they separate or divorce, consider whether career counseling could save your job. There are several individuals who can serve as career counselors: your friends, colleagues (those who are not employed by the firm), former teachers, a former program manager, or peers you have met through your local paralegal association. Of course, there are professional career counselors as well, but your friends and paralegal peers probably know you well enough to offer on-target advice.

If none of these individuals can help with career advice, consider working with your mentor at the firm. Understand, however, that once you disclose your job unhappiness in any way, your mentor will in all likelihood discuss this further up the chain of command. You could also consider meeting with your paralegal manager or supervising attorney. Express your concerns about your job, but be sure to raise some possible solutions as well. Be specific. A general complaint that "there's too much work," is not as effective as demonstrating that your team is tasked with working overtime far more than any other team in the office. Explain that you want to make the situation work because you like your job and the firm. Otherwise, your discussion may convey the impression that you are threatening to leave. Additionally, make sure that you have evaluated the job market before you burn any bridges. If the market is weak, you may have to be patient and continue trying to resolve the problem from within.

Many experts note that the most critical issues for most workers—advancement and compensation—are also the most difficult to discuss. Thus, many employers have no idea that employees are unhappy until the employee presents a resignation letter. Consider whether you will stay with your employer if your employer tries to keep you by giving you a raise. In some instances, an employee who resigns and then retracts the resignation goes on to have a healthy working relationship at the firm. In many instances, though, the employee is viewed as disloyal and as having bullied his or her way into an out-of-sequence raise. Of course, staying with your employer is not an option if you have already accepted a job offer at another firm or place of employment.

B. The Resignation Process and Your Resignation Letter

1. Six Ways to Leave Your Lawyer

Quitting a job is almost always difficult and emotional. If, however, you can do this with professionalism and dignity, you will reduce the stress of the situation and be able to leave with grace, whether you are leaving a small firm, a mid-sized firm, or a megafirm. Follow these six tips to leave with your reputation intact and without burning any bridges.

- **Be professional.** Meet with your paralegal manager or supervising attorney and indicate that you are leaving. Do not give advice on how the firm could be better managed. Resist the temptation to settle scores. The fact that you are leaving speaks for itself. Moreover, the legal community is small, and you never know when you may encounter your colleagues in the future. Walk out on your last day with the same professionalism you walked in with on your first day.

- **Give appropriate notice.** Give at least two weeks' advance notice, which is the generally accepted standard. Plan on giving more notice if you are at a critical juncture in a task, you work in a niche or specialty area, or if you know that your employer will have a difficult time replacing you. Never walk off a job with no notice to the employer (unless, again, you are the victim of a legitimate case of workplace harassment or discrimination, in which case you must still meet with a supervisor to explain why you cannot stay in the work environment).

- **Be prepared to leave.** It is unusual, but possible, that you will be asked to leave immediately on giving notice, and you will not be allowed to work the usual final two weeks. Unless you have an employment agreement, your employer is free to terminate you at any time, for any reason or no reason. Plan for this contingency, and make sure you have sufficient accrued vacation time or savings to meet your financial obligations until you receive your next paycheck.

- **Ease the transition.** Work out a reasonable transition plan, promise to complete critical projects, and mutually agree on your final date. Organize your files so that your colleagues won't be inconvenienced by your departure. Prepare a short memorandum on the status of each matter on which you have been working. Indicate what tasks need action and when. Place a separate copy of the memo in each file and give another copy to your supervisor. Forward emails to the appropriate employees who will be taking over for you. Everyone will remember how you left. Use this opportunity to create a good last impression.

- **Respect your current employer.** After submitting your resignation letter, tell your colleagues that you have resigned rather than letting them find out through the office grapevine. Your final two weeks should be devoted to your current employer, not your future one. Remember that the documents you created for clients belong to the firm. Do not take or copy any confidential documents. Pleadings and other documents that have been filed with courts or other government agencies are public documents, however, and you should be able to keep copies of these.

- **Stay in touch.** Leave on a positive note, and stay in touch with your colleagues, managers, and supervisors. Send email messages, links to legal stories of interest, and holiday cards. This is not only the right and courteous thing to do, but it also creates a good impression. One legal professional left her position with a law firm for an in-house legal job. On her last day, she made a point of leaving nicely wrapped gifts and thank you notes for all of her mentors and managers. For years, the firm continued to invite her to its holiday parties and seminars. The relationship was mutually beneficial for both the professional and the firm. You never know when you might need future advice, mentoring, a recommendation, or another job.

2. *Your Resignation Letter*

a. Introduction

You can prepare your letter of resignation before you meet with your manager or supervisor and hand it to him or her during your resignation meeting, or you can wait to prepare your letter until after the meeting, when you have mutually agreed on a departure date. Remember that your letter of resignation will be the top item in your personnel file, so you want it to provide continuing evidence of your professionalism. Moreover, your written letter confirms that you voluntarily resigned rather than being terminated. There is no need to explain in the letter why you are leaving, although if you are leaving to continue your education or because of a relocation, you might want to include that information.

b. Contents of Your Resignation Letter

A resignation letter generally includes five elements (in addition to the standard components of a letter, such as letterhead, date, salutation, and so forth): statement of resignation, confirmation of last day of employment (if already set), your commitment to ensure a smooth transition, a parting expression of good wishes to your employer, and your contact information so that you can be contacted, if needed. If you want to add that resigning was a difficult decision for you to make, you may do so. Similarly, you may want to offer to train other paralegals to ensure that clients' needs are met. If you feel strongly that you should indicate your reason for leaving, keep it vague; merely state that you are leaving to pursue other opportunities. There is an element of risk in indicating that you are leaving for more challenging work: It clearly implies that your current job is boring. Thus, the best approach is to keep it simple, brief, and nonspecific.

Your resignation letter should always be typed, not handwritten. Make sure to hand deliver your letter to your immediate supervisor (and hand deliver copies to other individuals in your chain of command). Keep a copy for yourself, and organize a file for this employment position that includes your offer letter, all details about your job (starting date, salary, vacation time, and so forth), and a list of contacts at the firm, so you can easily provide this information to future employers, if needed. See Figure 9-1 for a sample resignation letter.

3. *Final Steps in the Resignation Process*

Clean out your office. Return extra supplies to the supply room. Box up and remove your books and personal files. Delete any personal emails and any "bookmarks" or "favorites" you had set on your computer. Meet with the information management team and ask what, if anything else, you need to do to the information on your computer. Return any other office-owned equipment (laptop, PDA, and the like) to the appropriate individuals.

Arrange a final meeting with your paralegal manager and supervisor. Ask if there is anything else needed from you. Hand deliver copies of

Figure 9-1
Sample Letter of Resignation

Denise J. Kimball
123 Elm Street
Edison, New Jersey 08512
Telephone number
Email address

September 13, 2007

Ms. Jacqueline Alvarado
Jacobson & Sanders, L.L.P.
1885 Avenue of the Americas
Suite 2600
New York, NY 10012

Dear Ms. Alvarado:

This letter is my formal letter of resignation from my position as a paralegal with Jacobson & Sanders, L.L.P. As we discussed, my last day will be September 30, 2007.

I will do everything possible to ensure a smooth transition during my remaining time here. I have enjoyed working for the firm and appreciate the opportunities I have had to learn about trusts and estates.

I wish both you and the firm continued success, and I thank you for allowing me to part of the Jacobson & Sanders team. Please let me know if there is anything I can do to assist you in making sure that my remaining time here is productive. If you should need to reach me, my contact information is provided above.

Sincerely,

Denise J. Kimball

Cc: Henry Sanders, Esq.

your status reports for the files on which you are working. Hand deliver a sheet that includes your contact information (name, address, telephone number, and email address). In some law firms, this final meeting is a true **exit interview**, meaning you will be asked specific and direct questions about your work experience at the firm and why you are leaving. An exit interview is typically done for the employer's benefit, not the employee's. It gives employers a chance to find out why individuals commonly resign so they can remedy any common work complaints. Again, resist the temptation to badmouth your employer, supervisor, or co-workers. If you are asked directly if you are leaving because of any difficult people or situations, try to finesse your answer. You might say, "Yes, sometimes there was conflict on Jack's team, but that often arose from the stressful nature of the case involved. I'm really leaving to do more corporate work."

Exit interview: Final interview of employee who is voluntarily resigning; designed to inform employer of workplace problems.

After this final meeting, send one last email to your manager, supervisors, and colleagues. Thank them for their help, assistance, and mentoring. Promise to stay in touch. Repeat your contact information. Then set your sights on your new job.

Practice Tip

When should you resign? Many employees prefer to resign first thing in the morning so they do not have to spend the day dreading the resignation meeting. Similarly, you should resign as soon as you accept another position so you can reduce the stress inherent in knowing that a difficult situation is pending. Role-play the resignation meeting with a friend or colleague so you are prepared for any questions or comments that may arise. Expect your manager to be surprised or even a bit upset. Keep repeating your "script": Say that you are resigning to work in another field or for some other neutral reason. Don't get personal.

C.   Handling a Job Loss

1.   Introduction

Even the most diligent workers get fired. In many instances, the situation is out of the employee's control. Perhaps the attorney you worked with relocates or goes to another firm, and your firm doesn't have enough work to keep you. Perhaps the economy suffers a downturn. Perhaps your practice field (such as intellectual property, bankruptcy, or mergers and acquisitions) is highly subject to swings in the economy. Perhaps your firm loses a significant client or case and must downsize, and you are the most junior person.

In other instances, the firing may be more personal. Perhaps you had an irreconcilable personality conflict with a more senior staffperson at your office. Perhaps a client complained about your work, and to keep the client happy, the firm terminated you. It is important to understand that you are not alone. Many brilliant, hard-working, diligent individuals get fired. For example, in early 2005, President and Mrs. Bush fired the White House Executive Chef, who had been in the job for approximately 12 years. New York City Mayor Michael Bloomberg has been fired. So has Lance Armstrong. So was Carly Fiorina, former chief executive officer of Hewlett-Packard. Actors and actresses are routinely fired from television shows. Every election brings politicians the possibility of being unceremoniously put out of a job. Famous and highly competent corporate executives are fired every day — and many of those firings are very much in the public eye.

2. *Your First Steps Forward*

If your employment is terminated, you might be immediately escorted from the building. Your office and personal effects will be packed up and sent to you. Do not interpret this as a signal that you are untrustworthy. Many offices routinely employ this policy, and it is not a personal reflection on you or your honesty.

If you are not required to leave immediately, gather together your personal papers, delete personal email and files from your computer, and then request a follow-up meeting with your supervisor or human resources director. Find out the benefits to which you may be entitled. Does the employer owe you for accrued vacation time or sick days? Is there a severance policy? Don't allow your pride to get in the way of what you need. File for unemployment. Terminated employees are generally entitled to unemployment benefits upon termination; don't forget that you have been contributing to your state's unemployment fund. Secure health insurance coverage. Ask if your firm provides outplacement services.

If you are fired because of a poor economy or firm downsizing, the firm may well allow you to use your office, firm email account, and other firm support services from which to conduct your job hunt. Using these firm resources "camouflages" the fact that you have been fired because the appearance from all of your documents and correspondence is that you are still with the firm. Ask for a letter verifying and explaining that you were terminated due to an economic downturn, or the like, rather than poor performance. Don't be afraid to ask for these critical tools. Be sure to ask for them right away, when the firm and its employees still feel bad or guilty that they had to let you go. They will be more inclined to help you as much as possible.

3. *Rebounding from a Setback*

Most individuals who are either fired or laid off suffer some period of depression. Don't be surprised if it takes you a bit of time to adjust and to overcome doubts about your self-worth. Try to remind yourself of all of the successes you have had. You have been a successful student, employee, colleague, and friend. Review your résumé and focus on your achievements. The most important thing is to take control — immediately. Don't let your feelings of anger, guilt, and doubt get in the way of the most important work you now have: getting another job. If depression persists, get some help. It is possible you are entitled to use your former employer's employee assistance program for counseling.

4. Rebuilding Your Network

One of the first things you need to do if you are fired or laid off is to contact your network. Call your colleagues, former supervisors, student peers, and anyone else who may be able to help you. Do not be ashamed. Tell them simply and clearly what has happened and ask for their help. Indicate that because this situation has arisen so unexpectedly, you need to find a good job immediately. Ask them if there are jobs available at their office, if they have heard of any openings, and if they will spread the word to their friends and supervisors that you are in the job market. Once again, don't let your pride or guilt get in the way of what you need. Ask for and accept help. You will be surprised how many people want to help others who are temporarily in a tough spot. Even if some of the individuals in your network cannot help you with job leads, they will probably be a good source of comfort and support as you go through the difficult process of rebounding after a career setback.

Don't restrict yourself to a legal network. Tell everyone you know that you're looking for a job. Paralegals have reported getting job leads through their personal trainers, hairdressers and barbers, tennis partners, and church acquaintances. Let the world know you're looking!

Understand that job hunting after graduation is somewhat isolating. You no longer have your fellow students to talk to and brainstorm with. If you have been laid off, you may feel awkward about contacting those at your former place of employment. Understand that the process of finding a second job is likely "lonelier" than that of finding your first job.

If you haven't yet joined your paralegal association, do so now. It will provide you with access to a job bank, new contacts, and possibly some comfort as you learn that you are not the only paralegal to ever have been terminated.

5. Moving On After a Job Loss

Just as the best cure for a broken heart is a new relationship, the best cure for a job loss is another job. Your first steps at moving forward will reenergize you. Review the information in Chapter 5 about how to locate a job. Follow the same strategy for finding a job after a termination as you did for your first job. Update your résumé, grab the "want ads" of both your local legal newspaper and general newspaper, go online, and begin your search.

Contact your local placement agency and accept a temporary paralegal job. It will provide a source of income, additional contacts, and may turn into a permanent job.

There will undoubtedly be a few "blank" days between when you send out some résumés and when you are scheduled for interviews. Use this time productively. Write an article for one of the paralegal journals or magazines. Attend a seminar or lecture. Learn a new software application. Volunteer at your local legal aid society. These activities serve three purposes: They keep you busy, expand your network of contacts, and enhance your résumé.

Once you have had an interview or two, your spirits will rise and you will gain self-confidence. You will begin to see a solution to your setback and may even begin to feel excited about embarking on a new job. On interviews, avoid bitterness and don't blame others. Explain what you have learned from the situation.

Once you have a job, don't forget the professional courtesies of letting your network know where you landed and thanking everyone for their help and support. Then plunge into your new job with a great attitude, and demonstrate that the new firm made the right decision in hiring you. Remember not to criticize the employer who fired you (even if criticism is justified). If asked, simply say, "That was a really difficult time for me. I don't even like to think about it. I'm just happy to be here. Now, what's next?"

Practice Tips

While you are looking for a new job, plan and prepare for how you will respond to the question why you were fired or laid off. The issue will arise during your interviews. Role-play with your friends. Surf the Internet and get some ideas how to respond to the difficult questions you will face. If you were laid off, the explanation is far easier. If you were laid off for economic reasons or because of a firm merger, other firms will undoubtedly have heard the news and will accept your simple explanation. (For example, you could say, "My firm merged with Smith & Brown, and because I was the most junior paralegal, I was laid off.")

If you were fired for a more personal reason, you must be honest and forthcoming and state that you were fired. Don't become defensive and don't over explain. Keep your explanation as simple as possible. Consider whether either of the following statements will work for you:

❑ "When I was hired, I probably had less experience than the firm needed. As the case became more complex, it became clear that a much more senior paralegal was needed, and so my position was eliminated."

❑ "Unfortunately, a personality conflict existed between me and one of the attorneys. This was a shock because it had never happened to me before, and I have always been a team player who can get along with anyone. Possibly, the high stress level of the case we worked on was a contributing factor as well."

If possible, try to counter the reason you were fired with a solution for it. For example, explain that you have recently completed a stress-reduction class, that you have learned a new software application, or that you have taken a class to address time management or organization skills. These efforts on your part demonstrate initiative, professionalism, and problem-solving skills.

D. Getting the Next Job

1. Introduction

Getting a second or later job is usually substantially easier than getting your first job because you will have the one asset required by many employers: real-world experience. In some instances, a job may fall into your lap through your network of personal contacts. Alternatively, legal recruiters or headhunters are known for calling currently employed paralegals and inquiring if they know anyone who might be interested in a great job opportunity. (This is the universal signal that *you* are being recruited.) Additionally, you will have a wider network of contacts because of your time spent in the legal scene in your area.

You may be ready for a change or a different field of practice. You may have reached the top of the salary range or career path at your present job. These are all valid reasons for changing jobs.

Your résumé should always be ready to go. Each time you receive an award or recognition, update your résumé. Each time you receive a verbal or email compliment, put a note in your personal file to jog your memory when it comes time to revise your résumé or go on an interview. Each time you work on a new or complicated project, include a description of your work in your résumé. Each time you take a class or attend a seminar, include it in your résumé. If you are then called by a friend who tells you that his or her firm has an immediate opening, you will be ready to respond right away.

2. Looking for the Next Job

The process of obtaining your next job duplicates that of getting your first job. Establish your objectives. In most cases, this will be easier for you than when you did this before your first job. With the experience you have gained from your current employment, you may have some definite ideas on the size of the firm you want to work for, the type of work you would like to do, and the benefits and perks that are important to you. In addition, as a working member of the legal community, you now have a better grasp of how strong the market is in your area, which fields of practice are up-and-coming, and which firms are known for certain specialties (or for their onerous billable hours requirement).

After you set your objectives, review your original job-hunting notebook and consider the strategies that worked well for you last time. Review Chapter 5 about where to look for a job. Step one of any job search is to let your friends, family, and colleagues know that you are looking for a new job. If you do not want your present employer to know you are looking for another position, you need to make it clear to your contacts that your search is confidential. Networking alone may land you a job. In fact, it is common for individuals to be recruited for jobs by their former colleagues.

Review advertisements placed in legal newspapers and general newspapers, look at the job bank postings of your local paralegal association, and see if your school placement office offers job support services for second jobs. Because you now have experience, you will be able to use the services of a legal placement agency. A general employment agency may also be able to place you. Look at online job postings. Review the legal directories (such as *Martindale-Hubbell Law Directory*).

Review the Web sites of area law firms. In an era of increasing emphasis on the bottom line, some firms are reluctant to use legal recruiters or placement agencies. Many firms now post their open positions on their own Web sites.

Consider whether you want to explore something entirely different, such as working in-house, teaching, working for a nonprofit association, being a paralegal manager, working as a law librarian, and so forth.

3. *Your Cover Letter and Résumé*

Your cover letter and résumé will look substantially similar to your original cover letter and résumé, with a few minor exceptions:

- Because you now have experience, find a way to highlight it in your cover letter. Tailor the description of your experience as closely as you can to any job advertisement you respond to.
- If your present employer does not know you are looking for a new job, you must mark both your cover letter and résumé with a notice of its confidentiality (discussed in more detail below).
- Because your experience makes you highly desirable, consider whether you should reorganize your résumé sections and place your experience front and center, moving the education section to the end of your résumé. The more time that has passed since you completed your education, the less important it usually becomes. Your experience should be prominently showcased and discussed in detail.

4. Some Special Concerns When Looking for Another Job

There are five key items that are relevant only to second and subsequent jobs.

- **Blind ads.** Many ads placed by law firms and employers are **blind ads**, which means that they do not identify the employer by name. For example, the ad may simply say, "large, nationally known firm is seeking experienced litigation paralegal," and you will be directed to respond to a newspaper post office box. Imagine your embarrassment if you find out you are responding to your own law firm's ad. Imagine what your paralegal manager will say when she or he finds out that you are looking for another job. This has happened. Most job sections of newspapers tell you how to handle this, generally by marking your envelope with a notation like, "Do not give to the law firm of Jacobson & Sanders." Rather than risking this situation, though, it may be better to respond only to ads that identify the employer.

  Blind ad: Advertisement that does not identify the person or firm that placed it.

- **Confidentiality.** When you send your résumé to a potential employer, write "Confidential" on both the cover letter and your résumé. In the cover letter include the statement, "Please do not contact present employer without prior notice." This will help to ensure that the hiring manager who receives your résumé doesn't immediately contact your present employer and ask why you are leaving. Interestingly, a confidentiality notice is a signal to others that you are employed, that your present employer values you, and that you are leaving your present employment situation voluntarily.

- **Writing samples.** You will likely have a number of real-world (rather than purely academic) writing samples to provide to prospective employers. You may have, for example, drafted a partnership agreement, minutes of a corporation board of directors' meeting, complaints and other litigation documents, and settlement agreements. Although these documents make excellent writing samples and showcase your experience, in many cases they are confidential client documents. Thus, after you receive permission to use any documents, you will need to **redact**, or black or white out, any information that identifies the client. Include the notation "Redacted for Confidentiality" at the top of any such document. Documents filed with courts (for example, complaints and briefs) and those filed with public agencies (for example, articles of incorporation) are public records and can usually be freely provided to others.

  Redact: Striking out of material on a document, usually for confidentiality reasons.

- **Client conflict list.** You must always maintain a current conflicts list so that a potential employer can determine whether hiring you would pose an ethical problem or disqualify the firm from representing a client. Always keep your conflict list up to date.

Be realistic: Although a firm may want to hire you, it will probably not do so if it would cause a conflict, even if the conflict is one that a client might waive.

- **Use of current employer's email.** Do not use your present employer's email or other systems to send your résumé, confirm an interview, or engage in negotiations or any other activities related to your search for a new job. Such practices are disloyal and unprofessional. Use your cell phone, personal laptop, and personal email account to conduct your job search. Use only authorized breaks and lunch breaks for job-hunting activities. If you must send your résumé or other documents by facsimile, use the services of a local, consumer copy store. It is acceptable to maintain your updated résumé and conflicts list on your office computer because these might be needed in your present employment.

5. *Finessing "No Reference" Rules*

If your job search is necessitated by a geographic location or some "external" factor (rather than your own desire to change jobs), your employer might agree to give you a reference. Few employers will ever provide a blanket letter of reference — a letter addressed "to whom it may concern" rather than addressed to a specific individual — because they do not want to lose control over a reference letter that you could then use for several years.

When a prospective employer calls your current or former employer to ask for a reference, the current trend nationwide (probably due to fear of litigation) is for the provider to merely confirm three basic items of information: the dates of your employment, your title, and your most recent salary. This is usually referred to as the **no reference rule**. Employers are extremely reluctant to provide information regarding an employee's work habits, performance, or competence. Note, however, that potential employers are savvy about reading between the lines: If you list someone at your current firm as a reference, this is a signal that you are leaving your firm voluntarily (rather than being fired); conversely, if you list only employers from previous jobs as references, potential employers might assume you have been terminated from your present job. Similarly, many prospective employers will ask your previous or current employer if he or she would rehire you. The answer to this question is a reference in and of itself.

There are a few approaches that might help you get around a no reference rule:

No reference rule: Policy of employers to provide only basic information about terms of employment rather than discussing employee's performance.

- Try to locate a supervisor or manager who is no longer with your employer. These departed employees are often comfortable giving references.
- Stay in touch with your teachers and previous employers (in your nonlegal jobs) because these people will usually speak more freely about your competence and work habits.

- If you have developed a good working relationship with several individuals at your firm, meet with them privately and ask whether they will serve as personal references. Your paralegal manager or human resources director will likely never budge from a no reference rule; however, the attorneys and senior paralegals you worked with (and helped out in a crunch) may be willing to comment on your performance, even it is merely a confirmation that they would be willing to hire you again.

- Your paralegal colleagues and peers in your firm, other firms, and paralegal associations may vouch for you. Although they may not be able to give a great deal of information about your work product (because you didn't work directly for them), they may well be able to speak of your general work habits, such as punctuality, organization skills, willingness to work hard, and so forth. Similarly, if you do any volunteer work, those with whom you work may provide a reference for you.

- Consider whether a client could serve as a reference as to your competence and diligence.

- Provide a copy of your latest performance evaluation to show your progress at your previous place of employment. If you do not have a written performance evaluation, create your own detailed summary of your job history at your previous job, indicating promotions and advancements, to demonstrate your success on the job.

6. *The Interview, Offer, and Negotiation Process*

In all likelihood you will be far more comfortable in the interview process for your second job than than you were for your first. You have experience to refer to, you are accustomed to being questioned by attorneys, and you know what questions to ask. Be prepared to explain why you are leaving your present job, but never badmouth your current employer. Not only is such a practice unprofessional, it will also make prospective employers wonder if you will treat them with the same lack of respect the next time around. It is acceptable to say that you are looking for new opportunities, that you want to change to a new practice field, that you are seeking additional responsibility, and so forth. As you did for your first job, send a thank you note after any interview and keep your job-hunting notebook updated. (See Chapter 6, Figure 6-3, for sample entries from a job-hunting notebook.)

Unless you are desperate to leave your current job, remember that you are interviewing prospective employers just as much as they are interviewing you. You want to be certain that making a job switch is the right thing to do; making a mistake at this point and having to change jobs within a few months could derail your career. Contact your friends and colleagues and ask if they have any "inside" information about the prospective employer. In many instances, a firm or employer will have a reputation for insisting on overtime, for having unreasonable standards for billable hours, or, conversely, for being a great place to work with high retention of employees.

You probably will feel more adept in salary negotiations at this point because you have a baseline (your current salary) from which to judge an offer. It is highly unlikely that you will be offered a mere match of your current salary. Most employers understand that a job change always brings with it a salary increase. Once again, give careful consideration to the nonsalary aspects of a job. Are you willing to trade a slightly lower salary for lower stress? Is the location or reputation of a firm important to you? Again, once you accept an offer, you may not renege on it.

After you start your new job, send email announcements to everyone in your network, and thank everyone who helped you or put in a good word for you. If you left your previous job on good terms, send an email announcement to your former paralegal manager, supervising attorneys, and colleagues. Tell them where you are, stating that you are excited about the new opportunity and thanking them for all they did for you in your previous job. You will impress them with your thorough professionalism.

NetWorks

www.paralegals.org	The National Federation of Paralegal Associations (NFPA) offers an excellent "Career Center" that provides both job-seeker services (allowing you to post your résumé and search available jobs) and a legal resource center with tips and articles on job hunting.
www.aapipara.org	The American Alliance of Paralegals offers job-search services, including a job bank and job posting service.
www.paralegalmanagement .org	The International Paralegal Management Association (IPMA) Web site lists job openings for paralegals and allows posting of résumés by paralegal job seekers.
http://careerplanning .about.com/od/ jobseparation	The site "About" offers excellent articles on a variety of career topics, including losing a job and resigning from a job.

Case Illustration

Discharged Employees Must Inevitably Disclose Reason for Discharge

Case:	*White v. Blue Cross & Blue Shield of Massachusetts, Inc.*, 809 N.E.2d 1034 (Mass. 2004)
Facts:	White, a former employee of Blue Cross, sued Blue Cross for defaming him while he was with Blue Cross. White himself later communicated the allegedly defamatory statements to prospective employers, believing he was "compelled" to tell prospective employers why he had been fired.
Holding:	There was no defamation because the allegedly defamatory material was not communicated by the alleged defamer to any third party. The court also refused to recognize the doctrine of "self-defamation." The court remarked that performance evaluations are a standard feature in workplaces and are widely endorsed as valuable to both employers and employees. If employers could be sued for defamation for what they said to employees in performance evaluations, they would be unlikely to tell employees why they were being fired. The court noted specifically, "there is surely nothing more harmful to a discharged employee who must tell a prospective employer, 'I don't know why I was fired. I was never given a reason.'" Moreover, it is "all but inevitable" that a discharged employee

will be called upon to explain the circumstances of his or her discharge to prospective employers. If this disclosure were actionable as slander, the calculation of damages for such slander would be highly unpredictable and totally within the terminated employee's control.

Chapter Summary

- Try to remain in a job for at least one year before quitting. Quitting a job requires a great deal of planning. Consider whether your job can be saved.

- If you must resign, do so professionally and with dignity. Give appropriate notice, and work to ensure a smooth transition of your responsibilities to other employees. Don't burn any bridges at your current place of employment.

- Always prepare a written letter of resignation because it will be the top item in your personnel file. It also provides verification that you resigned rather than being terminated.

- If your employment is terminated, rebuild your network and get busy with your job search as soon as possible. Be prepared to honestly explain why you were terminated, but do not be defensive or bitter.

- When you are ready to look for another job, reevaluate your goals and interests. The experience you gained in your first job should make it easier to get a second or later job. You will have a wider source of contacts, and placement companies will be willing to work with you.

- When you look for a later job, be careful not to disclose confidential information or documents from your first job. You must prepare a current list of clients to allow prospective employers to check for conflicts of interest.

- Interviews, offers, and salary negotiations are usually easier during the search for a second job because you have gone through the process once before and are now familiar with the questions that will be asked.

Key Terms

Exit interview: Final interview of employee who is voluntarily resigning; designed to inform employer of workplace problems.

Blind ad: Advertisement that does not identify the person or firm that placed it.

Redact: Striking out of material on a document, usually for confidentiality reasons.

No reference rule: Policy of employers to provide only basic information about terms of employment rather than discussing employee's performance.

Bits and Bytes

- The average annual employment turnover rate in the United States has been estimated at about 12 percent.

- Thirty-four percent of job searchers under the age of 34 use the Internet to locate a job.

- The cost to an employer of replacing an employee is usually estimated at approximately $10,000.

- Donald Trump, Larry King, and Muhammad Ali are among the famous people who have been fired from jobs.

Discussion Questions

1. Your firm has just lost its biggest client, and you are the most junior paralegal in your practice group. You are concerned that you might be laid off. What should you do?

2. You have decided to resign from your current job because your salary is too low. When your colleagues ask you why you are leaving the firm, what should you tell them?

3. You have accepted a job offer for a job that requires you to begin in five days. What should you do with respect to your current employer?

4. You were fired from your last job for failing to meet deadlines. How will you respond to an interviewer who asks, "Why did you leave your last job?"

WebWork

1. Review the Web site for the Bureau of Labor Statistics and review the information for employment for paralegals. How much growth is projected for the paralegal profession through 2016?

2. How does the Bureau of Labor Statistics define a "displaced worker"?

3. Review the 2004 NALA Survey (Section 1, Table 1.9). What percentage of respondents had been with their current employer one to five years? Six to ten years? Eleven to fifteen years?

Trading in Your Backpack for a Briefcase: Strategies for Success in the Workplace

Real success is finding your lifework in the work that you love.
—David McCullough

Chapter Overview

Because learning does not stop when you leave the classroom, this chapter discusses skills and attributes you need to be successful on the job. Successful practicing paralegals share several characteristics: reliability, competency, and flexibility. They have mastered communications skills and learned how to navigate the often-difficult task of working in groups. This chapter provides some approaches to consider when you receive an assignment at work and concludes with strategies for time management.

A. Success in the Workplace

1. Introduction

Not surprisingly, most of the skills and techniques that students use to achieve success in the classroom work equally well in workplace settings. Moreover, because paralegals these days perform a great deal of the work that was formerly performed by attorneys, paralegals need to possess the professionalism and attributes of their attorney colleagues. This section of the chapter discusses some of the common skills and attributes of successful practicing paralegals.

2.   *The Team Approach*

In most instances, students are responsible solely for their own work product. Although group projects may be assigned, generally, students work on their own to learn and master the subjects in a paralegal program. The legal work environment is quite different: You will generally be working very closely with other paralegals and with attorneys and support staff. Moreover, you will interact on a daily basis with clients, witnesses, vendors, court personnel, and other members of your legal team. Your ability to do your job well will be critically compromised if your interpersonal skills are lacking.

The people you work with may be under a great deal of stress. Clients could be going through a difficult divorce or could be engaged in a sensitive business transaction. They may be anxious and, as a result, abrupt. Other clients rightly believe that they are paying a great deal of money for legal services and may be highly demanding. Lawyers are notorious perfectionists. The clerical staff is usually overwhelmed with work and is underappreciated. All of these people will be making demands on you.

Be sensitive to others' working styles. Other workers may have cluttered desks or odd working hours. Just because their method of approaching tasks is not one that you would use does not mean it is not effective.

You will be a productive team player with strong working relationships if you do three things:

- **Treat others with courtesy.** Treat every individual with whom you interact with respect and courtesy. Be polite when asking for something. Be appreciative when you get it.
- **Pull your weight and more.** It's not enough to do only what you have been assigned to do. Do more if you can, and do it in a timely manner. Don't make your team members wait to complete their tasks because you haven't yet completed yours. Work collaboratively, and make sure you at least do your fair share. Be the person everyone wants on a team.
- **Volunteer.** Volunteer to help when you see a need. You will quickly make yourself invaluable. Take the initiative, and work on a task that needs completion. Don't ever say, "It's not my job."

3.   *Attributes of Successful Paralegals*

Successful paralegals share the following characteristics:

a.   **Reliability**

Successful workers can be relied on to get the job done. They do not need to be micromanaged and reminded to do their work. They arrive early to work and to meetings and can be counted on to stay until the work is completed. They understand the need to keep client confidences. They are self-starters who continually demonstrate their commitment to their profession, colleagues, and clients. When a task is assigned to them, they can be depended upon to keep working until it is completed — accurately and on time.

b. Competency

Paralegals who are respected in the workplace have earned that respect by showing they are knowledgeable about the core competencies required of all paralegals: research and writing skills, communication skills, analytical skills, interviewing skills, and general understanding of the basic legal principles and fields they studied in their paralegal programs. If they are assigned a new or unfamiliar task, they diligently learn how to do it and remember the next time around. They pay attention to the details, knowing that an error in a decimal point could be fatal and that misspelling the client's name will attract more attention than anything else in a document.

c. Flexibility

Successful paralegals know to expect the unexpected. You can be certain that a crisis in a case will arise, a client will forget to respond to interrogatories, a needed file will be missing from its place. Flexible paralegals understand that there are numerous ways a task can be handled. They aren't afraid to abandon a method that isn't working in favor of a creative solution. They are resourceful in tackling problems and finding needed information. They know how to move seamlessly to a new task when their work is interrupted by a phone call or crisis that requires their attention to a new matter. They understand that their workday will be filled with interruptions and distractions and they plan some "wiggle room" into their daily schedules to accommodate the unexpected.

B. Three Critical Workplace Skills

Although there are many skills that effective paralegals possess, there are three that deserve special attention: organization skills, communications skills, and computer skills.

1. Organization Skills

Being organized requires more than merely being neat. It means that you complete all your assigned tasks in the most efficient manner and in the least amount of time. Law firms and law offices are busy places. You will work on several different tasks and files during the course of each day. You will likely have several bosses. Thus, staying organized is critical. If you are organized, you can achieve more during your workday, minimizing the need to work overtime and freeing up time for leisure. Finally, if you are organized, you will be able to manage stress more effectively because you won't spend time worrying that you won't be able to find an important document or that you'll miss a deadline. That "worrying energy" can be put into your work product.

There are two components to being organized: having the right tools and having the right systems.

a. Organization Tools

You will need some basic tools to be well organized. You will need a calendar — either a traditional paper or desktop calendar or a personal digital assistant (a "PDA," such as a BlackBerry®, which includes a calendar function). Consider investing in a large, wall-mounted dry erase calendar so you can see upcoming deadlines at a glance. Your desktop computer will likely have a calendar (such as Microsoft's Outlook®), which includes the option of electronic messages and prompts to remind you of meetings and due dates. Your calendar will help you track assignments and ensure critical commitments are met.

Use different colored file folders to serve as instant visual cues. For example, use a red folder for "hot" projects, a yellow folder for projects on hold or projects for which you are awaiting a response from others, a blue folder for critical phone numbers, and so forth. Make sure that when you need something quickly, the answer is at your fingertips. Use colored sticky flags to serve as visual cues. Use any tools or supplies that help you work efficiently and productively.

b. Organization Systems

Develop a few methods or systems to keep yourself and your work organized. The best approach is to maintain a "to do" list that identifies tasks that need completion. Prioritize the tasks as high, medium, or low, depending on the immediacy of the due date or the overall importance of the task. Work on the high-priority tasks with critical deadlines before you work on a low-priority task. Your "to do" list will also serve as an excellent reminder of the projects you have worked on so that when it is time for your performance review, you'll be ready to discuss the cases and projects you worked on during the year. Think about the things you need to know on a daily basis. For example, if you find that you routinely need to look up a client's Federal Express account number, keep it on your desktop in a folder marked "Contacts." Use the "favorites" or "bookmarks" tool in your Internet browser for Web sites that you frequently visit. Keep your list of client and matter numbers handy so you can efficiently enter your time. Don't procrastinate.

Keep your files in order. Eliminate time-consuming searches for documents by using desktop folder organizers. Realize that eventually you will have to file papers away, so file them as soon as you can. There's no point wasting time thinking about the filing you need to do. Moreover, if anyone else in the office needs the file, it will be complete. Even a desktop tray marked "to file" is an improvement over disorganized stacks of paper on your desk. Try to handle mail or other papers just once. Remember an easy acronym to help keep your paperwork organized: OHIO — <u>O</u>nly <u>H</u>andle <u>I</u>t <u>O</u>nce. Otherwise, you'll waste time by picking up the same piece of paper over and over.

As soon as any deadline or due date is set, mark it in your calendar or docketing system. If you let it slide, even for a day or two, it may fall through the cracks. Know how your office operates, so you can tap all available resources.

Keep your own form files of the documents you have drafted so the next time you are asked to prepare an agreement or document that is similar to others you have drafted, you can do so more efficiently and without having to reinvent the wheel. At the end of a project or transaction, prepare checklists of the tasks you completed, the critical phone numbers and contacts you relied on, and a "lessons learned" memo. You can use your checklist or lessons on a future similar project so it proceeds even more efficiently and smoothly. Be the person recognized in your office as the "go to" worker — the one with the best form files, the best sample documents, and the best practices in place. There is no one perfect method of organization, but find a style that works for you and stick with it.

Practice Tip: Your Three Desktop "Must Haves"

There are three resources you should have on your desk at all times. Having these tools at your fingertips will save you time and make your job much easier. Although it is simple to maintain this information on your computer or PDA, many paralegals like to keep color-coded folders within easy reach.

❏ **Client contacts directory.** Make your own phone book. Keep an alphabetized list of the individuals you contact most frequently. Include the correct spelling of names, phone numbers, addresses, email addresses, and billing numbers. Include an extra column for your notes and impressions. Remembering the names of clients' children or special accomplishments will help cement your relationship with the client.

❏ **FAQ folder.** You may find that you need to refer to some items of information on a routine basis. For example, trademark paralegals need to know the various fees imposed by the U.S. Patent and Trademark Office. Litigation paralegals need to know court filing fees, clerk names, and contact information. Almost everyone needs to know the name and number of the firm's LEXIS or Westlaw representative (and the passwords to access the systems). If you routinely go to court, you need to know where to find the best parking spot. Keep a folder with fee schedules, maps, vendor names, and other information so it is ready at a moment's notice.

❏ **Need-to-know folder.** If you work with several attorneys, keep a running list of their preferences. Know which attorneys want their case names underscored and which want their case names italicized in their briefs. Note which ones leave early on Fridays, which ones eat while working at their desk, and which ones like revisions made with green rather than red pens. Gather and share this "intelligence" with your paralegal colleagues.

2. *Communications Skills*

a. Introduction

The foundation of the legal profession is communication — communication with a colleague, client, adverse party, or judge. Some of the communications skills discussed in this section have undoubtedly been mentioned in other classes you have taken, particularly your writing classes. Remember that there are at least two parties in every communication, and so there is the possibility for misunderstanding on both sides. It is probably true that in a law office setting, there is no such thing as too much communication. Each of the following four methods of communication requires attention to detail and care, but each method also has its own special characteristics.

b. Written Communication Skills

Written communications must be accurate in every aspect. Not only must the provided information and conclusions be accurate but also the "details" must be accurate: names, dollar amounts, numbers, and so forth. Use a style manual and a dictionary to ensure that the mechanics (grammar, punctuation, and spelling) are correct, and follow your office's desired format for letters, memos, and the like. Remember that a written document will remain in a file and continue to reflect on you and your abilities long after your work on a project is completed. Even handwritten notes placed in a file should be accurate, complete, and legible. Every piece of writing conveys not only information but also information about you. Be sure that even informal methods of communication, such as emails, are accurate and professional. If an email is going to a very senior team member, consider printing it out and reviewing a hard copy to make sure all your *i*'s are dotted and *t*'s are crossed.

Providing status reports is an excellent way of communicating not only the nature of the projects you are working on but these reports also serve to keep your name in front of your supervisor and reminds him or her that you are diligently working on a variety of matters. Once you prepare a standard format or template for status reports, you can continually add matters or modify the form as needed. Most attorneys greatly appreciate receiving status reports because they serve as reminders of tasks they need to complete as well and serve as an easy reference if a client calls asking for information about his or her case.

c. Speaking Skills

Speaking well requires not only that you use proper grammar and that you accurately convey information but also that you are attentive to the listener. Watch for body language and nonverbal cues suggesting that the listener does not understand your message. Be attentive to the subtle signs that listeners are bored, need a break, or lack comprehension. If you have any concerns that a listener has not fully understood your message, follow up with a written memo or email.

Tailor your remarks to your audience. If you are explaining a concept to a client, you must use plain English and avoid legalese. On the other hand, if you are speaking with your supervising attorney, expressions such as "The TRO was served yesterday" will be easily understood. Exercise tact and diplomacy. If conflict arises, avoid negativity. Explain your point of view calmly and suggest alternative approaches. Try to find a solution that works for everyone.

d. Listening Skills

Communication is a two-way street. Be attentive not only to the words of a speaker but also to subtle messages given by a speaker's body language and other nonverbal cues. Take notes. Ask for clarification when needed. Focus on the message being conveyed to you and not on the messenger or his or her particular mannerisms. Active listening is a style of communication that lets the speaker know that you have heard what has been said. It includes strategies such as making eye contact with a speaker and nodding to let the speaker know you are paying attention, using verbal cues such as "yes" or "go on," and repeating or restating what the speaker has said. This type of active listening is effective in engaging the listener in a discussion.

e. Reading Skills

There is usually a great deal of reading in a law firm or office. Documents seem to reproduce by themselves. Attention to detail is critical when you review and proofread documents prepared by your office. You may spend much of your time proofing documents, checking figures, and locating differences between documents. Learn to sharpen your focus by giving your full attention to tasks. Reduce or eliminate distractions.

3. *Computer Skills*

Paralegals must be computer savvy to be successful in today's law firms and legal offices. You will be expected to have some of the following computer skills.

a. Word Processing and Related Skills

At a minimum, you will be expected to be familiar with preparing and revising documents using a word processor. Some law firms prefer the WordPerfect® word processing program but most use Microsoft Word.

In fact, according to a recent survey commissioned by IPMA, about 99 percent of the legal professionals who responded indicated that they frequently use Microsoft Word. You will be more efficient if you know not only the basic features of each program, but also some of the tricks, shortcuts, and other features of each program to improve your ability to produce documents quickly and effortlessly. You must understand how to access the firm's wide array of files, forms, and documents so you can easily prepare similar documents. You will undoubtedly be expected to understand the firm's "redlining" software, the tool that allows users of documents to show changes they make to documents and allows others working collaboratively to accept or reject those changes. If you need to improve your word processing skills, take classes through adult education. You can also check with computer stores near you because they almost always offer low-cost introductory word processing classes. In addition, many free tutorials are offered online. Try doing an Internet search for terms such as "Microsoft Word tutorial" and the like.

Remember that while word processing makes producing a new document easy (because you can often use one of the firm's earlier documents as a model), there is also a high likelihood of error. You may inadvertently import another client's name or information. You must use your proofreading skills and computer aids (such as the "Find and Replace" feature of your word processing system) to ensure correctness. Be cautious when using your word processor's built-in spell check function, which will not always catch correctly spelled but misused words (e.g., "form" instead of "from").

b. Skills in Other Software Applications

The more software applications you can use, the more valuable you will be to your employer. Law firms use Microsoft PowerPoint® to make presentations both to clients and in courtrooms, Microsoft Excel® to create spreadsheets and graphs, and a host of other applications to streamline law office practice. You will be expected to be able to use your firm's time and billing software so you can track time. Some of the time and billing software and litigation software support tools were discussed in Chapter 7. Law firms share documents and allow real-time collaboration, use conferencing systems for virtual meetings, and perform conflicts checks using software tools. Legal professionals make extensive use of automated calendaring, docketing, and reminder systems, and use various technology tools to set up meetings and conferences, confirm attendance, and send reminders before the meeting begins. Many discovery requests require production of electronically stored evidence. Complex litigation cases rely upon paralegals' familiarity with automated case management tools. For example, many attorneys use sophisticated litigation software packages to manage documents. Four of the most commonly used litigation support software packages are Concordance®, Summation®, CaseMap®, and LiveNote® (product descriptions and demos are available at http://law.lexisnexis.com/concordance, www.summation.com, www.casesoft.com, and www.livenote.com, respectively). These software packages streamline electronic and paper discovery, generate deposition summaries, and allow annotation or marking of electronically stored documents. The provider of LiveNote® was awarded contracts to automate documents for the plaintiffs in the Enron civil litigation and was expected to organize, store, and disseminate more than 20 million documents.

c. Email Skills

You will be expected to use the firm's email system to communicate with your colleagues and with the firm's clients. Moreover, you will need to know how to attach documents to your email communications. Email is an excellent method of communicating information in the office and giving your supervising attorney a quick overview of your pending cases. Make sure that your email communications are error-free and professional. The informality of email often leads to careless errors.

d. Internet Skills

The American Bar Association (ABA) has reported that nearly all legal professionals in the United States have access to the Internet at their offices. Paralegals use the Internet to obtain phone numbers, addresses and directions, conduct investigations, perform legal research, and provide information to clients. Legal professionals routinely take continuing legal education classes through the Internet, and keep current on legal news through legal Web sites, e-journals, and newsletters. Additionally, more and more courts and agencies are accepting documents submitted electronically. For example, more than 95 percent of all trademark applications filed with the U.S. Patent and Trademark Office (USPTO) are now submitted electronically. Trademark paralegals are expected to be familiar with the USPTO Web site, understand how to retrieve the form template for a trademark application, complete it, attach an electronic signature to it, arrange for electronic payment of the trademark filing fee, submit the application to the USPTO, and monitor the application electronically throughout the entire trademark registration process.

Although employers will be willing to provide some training, the more familiarity you have with technology, the more likely you are to get the interview, the job, and the promotion you want. Most law firms have an **intranet**, a secure internal network within the firm that allows everyone in the firm access to certain shared documents and information but does not allow access to anyone from outside the firm. Many law firms also use an **extranet**, a secure private network in which firm information and files are shared with those outside the firm (such as clients and co-counsel) on a select, confidential basis. Clients must have a password to gain access to documents relating to their cases.

Although you may not need to know all of these technology applications, the more you do know, the more valuable you will be to an employer. Make a point of learning as much about the firm's technology systems as you can. Ask the firm's technology personnel how to obtain training on some of the applications and software packages. Alternatively, as mentioned earlier, take classes through adult education or at your community college. Hire a tutor. Go online to see if free tutorials are available. Your résumé will be enhanced when you can say you have mastered several

Intranet: Internal computer network within an office that allows workers to share documents.

Extranet: Computer network within an office that allows file sharing and some limited access to those outside the office.

commonly used technology tools. Moreover, your ability to communicate with your firm from remote locations may enable you to telecommute if your office permits it.

C.   What to Do When You Get a Work Assignment

During the course of your paralegal career, you will routinely be asked to perform certain tasks and assignments. In some cases, the assignment will be clear or very familiar to you. In other instances, the assignment will require you to perform a new task. In the latter case, follow these seven tips to ensure you satisfy the requirements of the assignment.

- **Take notes.** If the assignment is given to you in person or at a meeting, take notes. Use two columns, placing your substantive comments in one column and any questions you have in the other. Include the date of the assignment and the name of the assigning individual.
- **Find out the due date.** In some cases, your supervisor will tell you when an assignment is due. If not, ask for a due date. Otherwise, the project will languish in your inbox until it is specifically requested. If your supervisor persists in giving you vague comments, such as "within the next several days," take the initiative and go public: Announce that you will have the task completed by next Monday, for example. Once you have announced a public due date, you will find a way to honor your commitment.
- **Ask for clarification.** If there is any part of the assignment that is unclear to you, ask for additional clarification. If you get bogged down during the course of the task, either ask for a meeting with your supervisor or send a quick email with your questions. Don't be afraid to ask questions. No one expects you to know everything. Consider the following approaches:
  - "Is there any particular part of this task you'd like me to work on first?"
  - "Do you have any preliminary thoughts as to the best place to begin [my research or drafting the complaint]?"
  - "Is there any file that I should check first that might serve as a model for the agreement I will be drafting?"
    Similarly, consider sending an email or short memo to your supervisor confirming your understanding of the task and outlining how you plan to approach it, especially for an extensive project. Your supervisor will then have the chance to redirect you if your plan of approach makes it clear that there's some confusion about the task. Attorneys often assume everyone is as familiar with a case as they are. A confirming memo will ensure you don't waste your time and the client's money.

- **Provide status reports.** Give a quick status report when you are about a quarter of the way through your work. This accomplishes two things: It lets your supervisor know that you are working on the project, and it allows the supervisor to correct you if you have drifted off track. Similarly, if you have reached a stumbling block, say, "I'd like to give you a brief overview of what I've done so far and ask for a few suggestions." Your supervisor would prefer to know as soon as possible that you are having some difficulties with the task — not after you have billed 40 hours to the client without making any progress.
- **Anticipate what is needed.** If, during the course of the assignment, you come across other avenues of interest, take the initiative and prepare a list of related tasks. Ask your supervisor if you should follow up on these items as well.
- **Communicate your results.** Prepare a memo or other document with the results of your research or investigation. Handing your supervisor a sheaf of photocopied cases with a sticky note saying, "Here's what you wanted" is neither helpful nor professional. Prepare a formal memo or summary explaining what you have done, providing your results, and attaching any relevant documents. Make sure that the client and matter number appear on all documents, and identify any particular file name or path so your supervisor can retrieve the pertinent documents from the computer himself or herself.
- **Keep a "chron" file.** Most legal professionals maintain a separate file with a copy of every document they prepare. This file is called the **chron file** because it provides a chronological record of their work. The most recent document is placed on top. Keeping a chron file allows ready access to all documents you have worked on in the event a question arises about a client matter. If you have a secretary, ask the secretary to maintain this file for you.

Chron file: A file of all documents prepared by an employee in a law office, kept in chronological order.

D. Time Management Strategies

1. Introduction

We each have 24 hours in a day, yet some of us accomplish far more than others. Why? Some workers are simply more efficient and productive with their time. Managing time in the work world is often more difficult than managing time in the academic world. In school, your class time is scheduled, your syllabus tells you what to expect when, your exams occur on a specific day, and then you graduate. In the work environment, however, projects and assignments are far more fluid. No one can predict the course of a case, whether it will go to trial or whether it will settle, or what obstacles will occur during a transaction. You will not meet with your supervisor on a regular basis the way you did with your instructors, and, in some instances, you may have little or no supervision. Missing a deadline in class might have resulted in a point deduction; missing a deadline in a law firm can result in a malpractice suit. Thus, learning to be productive on the job requires a different approach to managing your time than the one you use in school.

2. *Setting Priorities*

One of the common complaints of paralegals is that all of the tasks given to them are denoted as critical. Every attorney who gives you a project will likely think that his or her assignment is the most important task you have. There are a few techniques you can adopt to establish priorities among competing projects:

- **Ask the assigning attorney or individual.** Always ask the individual who gives you the assignment what its priority is or whether there are any deadline dates associated with the project.
- **Review the files.** Review the various files to determine if any correspondence or pleadings indicate a due date. Any statutory deadline or court due date will take priority over other matters. Review the correspondence files to see if commitments have been made to clients or opposing counsel as to when they will receive a document. A careful review of the files may disclose the proper ordering of the tasks you must perform.
- **Ask your paralegal manager.** If you find that your projects still have conflicting priorities, ask your paralegal manager to help you establish the priorities for the work. Paralegal managers are expert in this area and will work with the attorneys involved to separate tasks and sort out conflicting priorities.
- **Prepare a status report.** If your office does not have a paralegal manager, prepare a status report of the tasks you have been assigned and circulate it to each attorney who has given you work. Indicate the case name, assigning attorney, brief description of task, and due date. It is highly likely that attorneys in the firm are unaware that you are being overwhelmed with conflicting tasks. Your status report will serve as a wake-up call and will give them a cue to redistribute your workload or reestablish the priorities of the tasks you are to perform. Add a quick cover memo to the report asking for input on setting the priorities of the various conflicting matters.

3. *Time Management Techniques*

The following are some of the most common suggestions for using your time more efficiently.

- **Use a "to do" list.** Almost all productivity experts recommend that workers prepare a list of the tasks that must be completed. Once all of the tasks are listed, identify each task as a high, medium, or low priority. If three categories are not sufficient, use a grading scale of A to F. If too many tasks are marked "high," you will need to review the list and demote some tasks to a lower priority.

- **Formalize your to do list.** Once each task has been assigned a priority, prepare a log or calendar, with tasks assigned to different days and times. Be realistic. Don't think you can cite-check an appellate brief in one hour. Identify the amount of time you think it will take to complete each task, and schedule this time on your calendar. Use whatever method or calendar that works best for you, whether it is a conventional desktop calendar or diary, an electronic calendar (e.g., part of Microsoft Outlook®), or a PDA. Allow some time for unexpected interruptions or delays. Revise your calendar or schedule as needed. Some workers maintain two separate lists, one for weekly goals and another for long-term goals.

- **Break down your projects into smaller parts.** If certain projects seem overwhelming, break them down or "chunk" them into more manageable tasks. View each small task as important and reward yourself for completion. Avoid negative thoughts such as, "I'll never get this done." Challenge yourself to complete one of the small tasks in one hour. Remind yourself of how much you have done, and do not focus on how much there is left to do.

- **Use your to do list.** Your to do list will only work if you use it. Preparing the list is not your goal. Once the list is prepared, keep it handy, revise it as needed, and check off completed tasks. Keep the list nearby so that if your supervisor asks how the project is coming along, you will be ready to provide an overview of the tasks that have been completed.

- **Adopt strategies for success.** Consider the following techniques to improve your efficiency as a worker.
  - **Find the right time to do your work.** Try to figure out when you are most productive. If you have more energy in the morning, do your most difficult tasks then. You will not only get the hard work out of the way, but you will have a sense of accomplishment. Do routine tasks such as filing in the afternoon when your energy levels are lower.
  - **Set realistic goals.** You may want to complete ten tasks each day, but this may be unrealistic. Don't set yourself up for failure and stress by scheduling too many tasks during the day. Decide what can reasonably be accomplished during the day, bearing in mind that unexpected tasks will arise and that you need some time for work breaks and lunch.
  - **Don't procrastinate.** The most effective workers are the "do it now and do it once" types. These workers read an email message and immediately decide whether to respond to it or delete it. They don't continually revisit old emails while they decide when might be a good time to respond. They handle their mail once rather than continually reshuffling it. They respond to their phone messages promptly rather than accumulating a stack of messages.

Much procrastination occurs because workers view a task as overwhelming. They know the task will take a full day to complete and they cannot then allocate that time to work on one project. Again, break the project into smaller units. Work 30 minutes if that's all the time you have. Don't allow yourself to become paralyzed by the thought of a big project. Do some part of the project—any part of the project—even if it is merely photocopying the exhibits or preparing the Federal Express envelopes. At least you will have made some forward movement toward completing the overall task. Recall that if you go public and announce to your supervisor that you will have the project completed by a given date this will force you to honor your spoken commitment. If you find that procrastination is a continuing problem for you, see if you can figure out what you are trying to avoid.

○ **Move on if you're blocked.** If you find that you encounter an obstacle or are completely blocked, move on to another task. Perhaps a quick break will refresh you so you can return to the task energized. Brainstorm with colleagues for ideas on how to approach the task. Move to another project that is completely different. You may suddenly get a great idea about how to approach the first task.

○ **Reduce interruptions.** Efficient workers know they cannot eliminate all interruptions, but they also know they can structure their environment in such a way as to reduce them. Although you need to be accessible to your colleagues, there is nothing wrong with closing your door on occasion or asking for your calls to be held while you work on a critical part of your project. You may need to be aggressive in carving out time for yourself and your work. One attorney who is much admired by his colleagues for being efficient refuses to take any phone calls (other than for emergencies) during the first hour or so of his workday. He closes his office door, plans his day, and begins work on his most important tasks. Clients and colleagues know that the attorney is simply not available until 10:00 A.M. each morning. Try to finish one task or segment of a project before moving on to the next. There will be plenty of interruptions you cannot control so try not to interrupt yourself. Otherwise, you will need to reorient yourself to start again by retrieving the first file, figuring out where you left off, and so forth. If you are interrupted, jot down a few notes (either on a pad of paper or on a sticky note you can put on your computer screen) as to what you planned to do or write next. These notes will jog your memory when you return to the first task.

○ **Make your environment work for you.** Reduce any distractions that might impair your ability to work efficiently. Move your desk or computer so that you cannot see the flow of traffic in the hallway near your office. Move to a quieter place if your office is near the break room. Make sure you have the necessary supplies to do your work. Know what makes you most productive, whether it is frequent breaks, small rewards, background music, or adequate lighting.

○ **Multitask.** There are many occasions when you can save some time by doing two tasks at once. While you are on hold on the phone, review your email. Bring a file with you to every meeting, so if the meeting starts late or there is a break, you can do some work. Keep professional journals with you so that if you are waiting for an appointment, you can catch up on your reading.

○ **Manage stress.** Stress is part of every work environment. Stress in law firms is thought to be higher than in many other workplaces. This is due in part to the combination of extremely high standards and critical deadlines in the legal profession. Also, there are at least two groups (attorneys and clients) making demands of paralegals. Some workers are stress addicts and will create tension even if none exists. Law firms probably encourage stress due to the emphasis on billable hours and productivity. To keep stress manageable, eat right, get sufficient sleep, exercise, and remember to take breaks and reward yourself. Don't obsess over mistakes. Learn from your mistakes, resolve not to repeat them, and move on. Studies show that 75 percent of all worry is over possible events that never occur, but the stress generated speculating about these events wastes a significant amount of time. Don't forget to enlist the support of your colleagues. Ask for help. Work with a mentor who can coach you through difficult moments. Realize that you will probably never omit tension entirely from your job, but if you learn how to manage stress, you will find that you can be a more efficient and productive team member.

E.   Some Closing Thoughts

Although this section of the chapter has focused on skills and techniques to ensure success in the workplace, there are four final items you should learn if you want to be admired and respected by your colleagues.

- **Understand that all work has value.** Understand that there are boring and mindless tasks in any job. There may well be times when you feel you are being underutilized. Remember that all of the client's work has value. If documents need to be copied or envelopes need to be prepared, do it. The most senior partner in any law firm is willing to do the most mundane task to make sure the client is satisfied. You should be too.

- **Acknowledge mistakes.** You will undoubtedly make a mistake at some time. Own up to it as soon as possible, take responsibility for it, and do not deflect blame onto someone else. Avoid making excuses. Simply acknowledge that you made a mistake, state that it will not happen again, learn from it, and don't agonize over it. Similarly, learn to accept constructive criticism. Try to be objective, and commit to making improvements suggested to you.

- **Commit to excellence.** Decide that your professional standard will always be excellence. Make sure every project you submit is one in which you have pride. Pay attention to detail. Take charge of your own career. Take classes. Subscribe to online newsletters to keep current in your field. Write articles. Be a mentor. Prepare to be an excellent paralegal by being an excellent student.
- **Give back.** Give back to your community by volunteering or engaging in pro bono work. Participate in your employer's pro bono program, if it has one; if it doesn't have one, suggest it to your supervisor. Call your local paralegal association or bar association to find out about volunteer opportunities in your area. You will achieve great personal satisfaction, expand your horizons, and help others in need. Check the ABA's Web site for its Standing Committee for Pro Bono & Public Service (http://www.abanet.org/legalservices/probono/home.html) to find out what opportunities are available for you to help those in need of legal services.

The paralegal field is filled with both challenges and opportunities. Be excited by your profession and your role in it. Remember that you play a vital and indispensable part in helping clients. You will be rewarded not only monetarily, but also, more importantly, by having a career that brings you emotional satisfaction.

NetWorks ▬▬▬▬▬▬▬

www.aafpe.org/core.html	The American Association for Paralegal Education identifies the core competencies required of successful paralegals.
www.abanet.org/ careercounsel/home.html	The ABA offers tips on finding jobs and maximizing a legal career. Articles related to career planning and success in the workplace are also provided.
www.couns.uinc.edu/ Brochures/time.htm	The University of Illinois offers excellent advice about time and stress management.
www.mindtools.com	The Mind Tools site provides information on important life and career skills, including time management, stress reduction, and communications skills.

Case Illustration

Standards for Legal Professionalism

Case: *Florida Bar v. Weinberger*, 397 So. 2d 661 (Fla. 1981)

Facts: After suffering adverse rulings in two cases, a new attorney made several public statements denigrating the courts and the administration of justice.

Holding: The attorney's professional misconduct warranted a public reprimand. Although the attorney later apologized and exhibited remorse, his conduct cannot be condoned. The court noted that the behavior was professional misconduct.

Chapter Summary

• Successful paralegals are those who are reliable, competent, and flexible. They work well in teams by respecting other team members, pulling their own weight, and volunteering to help when needed. They possess excellent organization skills, communications skills, and computer skills, so they can be efficient and productive workers.

• When receiving a work assignment, take notes, determine the due date, ask for clarification when needed, provide status reports to the assigning supervisor, anticipate what is needed, and communicate your results in a professional manner.

- To manage time effectively, set priorities, prepare a "to do" list, break up projects into manageable tasks, set realistic goals, avoid procrastination, establish a good working environment, multitask when possible, and manage stress.
- Successful paralegals understand that all work has value, acknowledge their mistakes quickly, commit to maintaining the highest possible standards of excellence for themselves and their work product, and give back to their community.

Key Terms

Intranet: Internal computer network within an office that allows workers to share documents.

Extranet: Computer network within an office that allows file sharing and some limited access to those outside the office.

Chron file: A file of all documents prepared by an employee in a law office, kept in chronological order.

Bits and Bytes

- IPMA's 2005 Utilization Survey reported the following percentage of paralegals frequently used these technology applications:

Microsoft Word	95%
Corel WordPerfect®	7%
Spreadsheets	57%
Databases	57%
Presentation software	33%

- Many experts estimate that most individuals lose one hour of productive time each day due to disorganization.

- Many time management advisors state that the biggest "time bandit" is not decision making but the procrastination that comes from decision avoidance.

Discussion Questions

1. You have been given four "top priority" projects by four different attorneys in your law firm. What should you do?

2. At your last performance review, your paralegal manager commented that your only weakness was disorganization. What can you do to improve your organization skills?

3. You have noticed that when you work with your bankruptcy team members, you are seldom given any of the challenging work. What should you do?

WebWork

1. Locate IPMA's 2005 Utilization Survey. Review Sections 18, 21, and 24.

   a. What percentage of respondents frequently used the Internet to conduct legal research?
   b. What percentage of respondents frequently used LEXIS? Westlaw?
   c. What percentage of respondents offered their paralegals laptops?

2. Locate Tufts University's Organizational Development and Training Web site. Locate the "tip sheet" on time management. What are the first three items identified in the action plan to manage time more effectively?

3. Access the Web site "FabJob.com" (www.fabjob.com). Select "Advice" and review the information relating to dealing with difficult people at work. What four pieces of advice are given?

4. Access IPMA's Web site. Access the "Job Bank." What qualities do prospective employers say they deem most important in a legal assistant or paralegal candidate?

Alternative Career Paths

*They always say that time changes things, but you
actually have to change them yourself.*
—Andy Warhol

Chapter Overview

A wide variety of career options exist outside of a traditional law firm
setting. Paralegals work in the public sector, in in-house legal departments, in banks, for real estate title companies, and in legal clinics.
This chapter explores many of the alternative careers that are open to
paralegals. Many of these career paths are in law-related fields (such as
working as a law librarian or working in a courthouse). Other careers,
such as human resources specialist, build on and take advantage of a
paralegal's legal education and training. Still others are nonlaw related,
such as management positions and counseling. Some paralegals opt to
work as freelance or contract paralegals, working for attorneys or firms
on a case-by-case basis. When a case or project is complete, the paralegal
moves on to another firm. Still other paralegals work independently
for consumers rather than for attorneys. Independent paralegals must
exercise caution to ensure they do not engage in the unauthorized practice
of law. No matter which career path you pursue, your paralegal education,
skills, and training are highly transferable to other professional settings.

A.   Thinking Outside the Box

Although most paralegals work in law firms, there are a number of other
career opportunities for paralegals. Some are in law-related fields, and others
are in nonlegal fields but are jobs for which a paralegal education provides
useful training. If you have no interest in working in a law firm or decide to
make a change after working in a law firm, there are several career choices
open to you. As you plan your next career move, consider four specific items:

1. **Give some thought to the specific tasks you enjoy most.** Out
    of all of the work you perform, what gives you the greatest

satisfaction? Is it working with clients? If so, perhaps you have excellent people skills that would allow you to adapt easily to a job in the human resources sector or working for a legal placement firm. Do you most enjoy researching and working in the library? Consider working as a freelance researcher or law librarian. Have you been working in the firm's energy group? You may be well qualified to work for a nonprofit environmental group. Focus on the tasks you most enjoy, and then consider what career fields would give you the opportunity to do more of these tasks.

2. **Keep an open mind as you read job listings.** Although your first review of some job postings may lead you to think that you don't have the background or requirements specified, remember that your paralegal education and training at a law firm are excellent springboards from which to launch a new career. Potential employers will know you have received a well-rounded education from your paralegal program and that at your firm you have developed critical workplace skills, including attention to detail, crisis management, and learning how to work hard in an ever-changing environment. These skill sets are highly portable and valuable in any number of other fields.

3. **Remember your background and any special skills you have.** If you know sign language or are fluent in another language, you could serve as an interpreter for court proceedings. If you have a scientific background, you could easily transition into one of the numerous jobs related to the environment, from land conservation, to preserving wetlands, to working in any of the Environmental Protection Agency (EPA) research labs around the country. If you have some medical training, you could work as a nurse or medical consultant. If you have a background in economics, working in your city or county budget planning office may be a good fit.

4. **Don't be afraid to make a complete change.** If what you're doing isn't making you happy, find what will. Be creative. Don't assume that because you have four years of litigation experience, you can only do litigation work. Think outside the box. Understand that the skills you used in the litigation field (persistence, organization, proofreading, flexibility, and so forth) are marketable commodities in other fields as well. For example, the ability to keep track of masses of documents, which is common in litigation, is a skill that applies to paralegal jobs in other legal fields (such as securities and insurance) and is also valuable in most large companies, no matter what the type of business.

B.   Switching Career Tracks

Generally, this chapter addresses the desires of paralegals who have worked in a law office environment for some period of time and then wish to change career tracks. For example, although a new paralegal may start working in a human resources (HR) department, it is far more likely that an experienced paralegal eventually transitions into HR work. Once paralegals have some on-the-job experience in a certain field, a transition to another field is far easier.

Many paralegals eventually go to law school. In some instances, they have been given a great deal of responsibility by their firms and they realize that if they are often doing "attorney" work, they might as well get paid an attorney's salary. For others, working closely with attorneys helps them realize that they really want to be the one arguing a case in court or negotiating an important contract.

Many experts believe that a law-related background affords great flexibility in employment opportunities. Legal professionals are generally trained to be organized, detail-oriented, and thorough, making them ideal candidates for a number of different types of jobs. Moreover, legal issues permeate many employment fields. For example, HR professionals need to know various workplace laws, such as laws relating to workplace discrimination. Title searchers need to know certain real estate concepts. Paralegals who work in banks need to understand corporate and securities concepts.

Before you leave your law firm, think carefully about why you are leaving. If you are suffering from burnout, maybe a transfer within the firm to another practice group will solve the problem. If you're bored and need a change of pace, maybe a transfer to one of the firm's other offices will restore your enthusiasm. If you absolutely hate tracking time and worrying about meeting the firm's billable hours requirements, working in-house may be the answer.

C. Alternatives to Working in Private Practice

Although approximately three-fourths of the nation's paralegals work in law firms, there are several alternatives to working in private practice, many of which use and build on the legal skills you already possess.

1. In-House Legal Work

A number of companies have legal departments, usually called **in-house legal departments**. These can range in size from one attorney to a staff of more than 300 legal professionals in some of the nation's "blue chip" corporations. In some instances, the attorney, called the **in-house counsel** (or **general counsel**, if he or she is the most senior attorney in the corporation), performs most of the company's legal work. In other instances, the in-house counsel performs only some of the work, delegating

In-house legal department: Group within a company that performs legal work for the company.

In-house counsel: Attorney employed directly by a company to perform its legal work.

General counsel: The most senior in-house attorney in a company.

significant work to either one law firm or several who represent the company in a variety of matters.

Paralegals are employed at some of the nation's corporate giants, such as E.I. DuPont de Nemours and Company, FedEx Corporation, and Exxon-Mobil Corporation. They are also employed by media companies, such as AOL-Time Warner, and by smaller companies. In fact, the 2004 National Association of Legal Assistants (NALA) Survey reported that 14 percent of its responding paralegals were employed by corporations. Moreover, while the conventional wisdom is that pay is usually higher for paralegals employed in private law firms, a 2007 salary survey by *Legal Assistant Today* shows otherwise, reporting that the average salary for paralegals in law firms was $50,666 compared with $59,453 for paralegals in corporate environments.

Although the work performed by paralegals in in-house law departments may be similar to that performed by paralegals in law firms, there are some notable differences. Perhaps the most significant difference is that paralegals working for private companies do not generally track their time. There are no minimum billable hours, and legal professionals usually devote as much time as they believe is warranted on a task, with no artificial budget constraints. Most paralegals find that being "freed from the clock" is liberating. Perhaps the downside to not billing time is that paralegals who work in corporate law departments seldom receive overtime compensation. Altman Weil's 2007 survey on paralegal compensation reported that more than 80 percent of paralegals in law firms received overtime compensation while only approximately 30 percent of paralegals in law departments received compensation for overtime work.

A hidden benefit of working as part of an in-house team is that although there may be many different tasks, there is only one client, the company. An in-house paralegal has the opportunity to get to know everything about a company, including its finances, its vision for the future, and its culture. Paralegals who work in-house frequently attend various corporate meetings and are encouraged to offer ideas and suggestions for the overall benefit of the business. The ability to witness a company in action firsthand and learn about finance, business, and marketing is attractive and can lead to interesting employment opportunities in other fields. Finally, many companies offer educational benefits such as tuition reimbursement. Thus, paralegals who plan to take additional courses might be able do so at the company's expense.

In addition to working in the company's legal department, paralegals may work in the company's HR group or its government relations or lobbying group, or may serve as administrative or executive assistants to company officers, jobs that all call for the organizational skills and flexibility paralegals possess.

Paralegals who work in-house assist the in-house counsel with a variety of tasks, including the following:

- Drafting and reviewing employee and vendor contracts
- Reviewing leases

- Preparing shareholder agreements, stock option plans, and employee benefit plans
- Administering employee benefit plans
- Calendaring deadline dates for corporate matters, such as the filing of various state-required reports, payment of annual taxes, filing of periodic reports with the Securities and Exchange Commission (SEC), and so forth
- Maintaining corporate records, including the corporate minute book, and recording resolutions and taking minutes at corporate meetings
- Filing required corporate forms, such as annual corporate reports, with the secretary of state
- Developing various in-house compliance policies, such as policies relating to Internet use, display of company trademarks, and workplace harassment
- Working closely with the company's HR department and assisting in hiring, firing, and ongoing employee-related issues and disputes
- Assisting in employee training to ensure compliance with various government regulations and laws, such as training to avoid sexual harassment, compliance with the Family Medical Leave Act, and so forth
- Serving as a liaison, monitoring matters being handled by outside counsel, including litigation involving the company

2. *Public Sector Employment*

The NALA Survey reported that about 8 percent of all of its respondents were employed in the public sector or for a government branch or agency. Within the federal government, the Department of Justice is the largest employer of paralegals, followed by the Social Security Administration and the Department of Treasury. Other federal agencies employ paralegals as well, including the U.S. Patent and Trademark Office, Equal Employment Opportunity Commission, and the Central Intelligence Agency. A 2002 Altman Weil survey reported that there are approximately three paralegals for every ten attorneys in government agencies. Paralegals also work for state governments and state agencies.

According to the Bureau of Labor Statistics (BLS), although the duties of paralegals who work in the public sector vary within each agency, in general, they "analyze legal material for internal use, maintain reference files, conduct research for attorneys, and collect and analyze evidence for agency hearings. They may then prepare informative or explanatory material on laws, agency regulations, and agency policy for general use by the agency and the public."

Because the "client" is the governmental entity, paralegals generally do not track their time. Paralegals working in the public sector usually work closely with attorneys. In many instances, their work is a mirror image of the work performed by paralegals in private law firms.

For example, in a lawsuit brought by the SEC against a corporation for insider trading or some other violation of securities laws, paralegals on both sides will perform much of the same type of work, including conducting legal research, indexing documents, coordinating pretrial discovery, reviewing documents produced, and assisting at trial. In one case, the paralegal will be employed by the plaintiff agency, the SEC, while in the other, the paralegal will be employed by the defendant's private law firm.

Because paralegals may appear before administrative agencies and because most government agencies are always looking for ways to save money, paralegals in the public sector often perform a wide array of interesting and challenging tasks. BLS has reported median annual earnings of just over $56,000 for paralegals working for the federal government. BLS has also noted that paralegals in the public sector usually work a standard 40-hour week, which is often far less than the hours required of paralegals in the private sector. Additionally, BLS has estimated that job opportunities for paralegals will expand in the public sector to provide assistance to the poor, aged, minorities, and middle-income families. Keep in mind that pay structures for government jobs are fairly rigid; for example, federal jobs pay according to the standard General Schedule, or "GS," rates.

Visit the Web sites of various government agencies. Look for information relating to jobs and careers. In many instances, you can review agency job openings and submit your résumé in one easy step. You need not live in Washington, D.C., to work for the federal government. Most agencies have regional, branch, and local offices. For example, the SEC has regional and district offices in 11 cities, and the EPA has 10 regional offices and 16 research labs scattered throughout the United States. One of the best places to look for job openings in the federal government is through USAJOBS (www.usajobs.opm.gov), a one-stop source for information on job openings with the federal government. It allows you to post your résumé online to allow federal employers to contact you.

Don't forget that your state and locality are also possible sources of employment. Most states, counties, and cities now post job openings on their Web sites. Access your state's homepage (start at USA.Gov, www.usa.gov) or your county or city homepage.

3. *Banks, Insurance Companies, and Trust Companies*

Banks, insurance companies, and trust companies all employ paralegals. Because these fields are so carefully regulated by both state and federal statutes, much of the work relates to ensuring compliance with these regulations. Because many banks and insurance companies have stock that is publicly traded, paralegals perform many duties that are similar to those performed by paralegals engaged in business and corporate work. For example, paralegals in these fields research SEC regulations and coordinate the various required SEC filings; they prepare trust documents; they help administer trust accounts; and they serve as liaisons to clients and others.

4. *Real Estate and Title Searching*

Nearly everyone buys or sells real estate during a lifetime. The transactions are document-intensive and require great attention to detail. For those reasons, the work is a perfect fit for organized and diligent paralegals. Paralegals may work for real estate companies (helping with the actual purchase or sale of property) or for title companies (helping ensure that title to the property is free of any liens or encumbrances, such as tax liens, and making sure that title insurance is obtained to protect the lender or owner against a loss in the event of a dispute relating to ownership or title to the property). Some paralegals work for property management companies, helping to ensure that apartment buildings or condominiums are appropriately managed, that rents are collected and fees are paid, and that the property is kept in good order.

Paralegals can perform nearly all functions related to various real estate transactions. They help draft the agreements by which real estate is sold or leased. They prepare loan documents and the deeds by which property is transferred. They conduct title searches. They review the description of the property and check this against the various maps and documents on file with county officials to ensure that the description of the property in the agreements and deeds is correct. They appraise property being purchased. They coordinate and assist in the "closing" or settlement of transactions relating to the purchase and sale of real estate. They ensure that the appropriate documents are recorded with the office of the county recorder so that the official records reflect current ownership of the property. They arrange for title insurance so that if there is a later claim against the property, sufficient insurance exists to clear the title. They prepare the closing binders that contain copies of all pertinent documents.

5. *Human Resources*

Paralegals who have managed or supervised other paralegals often develop an interest in a career in human resources management. Because so many HR issues are intertwined with legal issues, many paralegals transition into HR positions. HR professionals deal with nearly all workplace issues, from recruiting and staffing, to performance reviews, to employee training, to employee compensation and benefits, to workplace diversity, to employee terminations. HR professionals manage nearly every issue related to personnel. They usually work closely with senior managers in a company and help plan for the company's future. Because paralegals are skilled in research and writing, they understand which questions are illegal to ask during a job interview, how to draft an offer letter to a potential employee, and how to respond to a claim of discrimination in the workplace. They readily understand the importance of compliance with federal and state labor regulations and the workplace implications of the Americans with Disabilities Act or the Family and Medical Leave Act. The work is interesting and is a good fit for paralegals who have excellent interpersonal skills.

6. Legal Research

Some paralegals complain that they do not get a chance to perform as much legal research as they would like. These paralegals often seek employment at a company specializing in legal support services. Numerous companies provide legal research services both to corporations and to law firms (usually smaller law firms or sole practitioners). They help companies and lawyers research case law, draft court briefs, conduct cite-checking, and review documents.

7. Law Librarian Jobs

Some paralegals choose to work in their firm law library and, of those, many decide to continue their education and become a professional law librarian. Law librarians are employed by law schools, private law firms, and government agencies. While about 85 percent of law librarians have graduate degrees in library science, many paralegals work in law libraries as assistants. They maintain the books and other resources, work closely with vendors (including publishers both of traditional print resources and of electronic resources, such as LEXIS and Westlaw), they train new paralegals and attorneys on the use of technology, and perform legal and other research. Today's law librarians are expected to be familiar not only with traditional print books but also electronic resources and the Internet. They often conduct factual research as well as legal research. For example, they may help locate statistical information, articles, government information, and so forth to help attorneys who are drafting court documents. They are expected to be able to get their hands on needed information quickly and efficiently. For paralegals who enjoy legal research and the "treasure hunt" aspect of investigatory work, law librarian positions are fulfilling and rewarding.

8. Legal Recruiting Work

Many paralegals move into the field of recruiting and headhunting. With an extended network, a list of valuable contacts, and firsthand knowledge of the way law firms work, they can readily transition to helping law firms "staff up" for projects or find legal professionals. Legal recruiters need good people skills because they interact both with law firms who need professionals and with the professionals who are looking to be placed in a firm. Placements may be either temporary (as is the case when a law firm has a complex document production and needs several paralegals to help out for several days or weeks) or permanent. In some instances temporary jobs become permanent ones. Paralegal recruiters may be paid a straight salary by their legal search firm employers or may receive a combination of salary and commission for each placement made. Because paralegals have an insider's view of what is expected of parale-gals on the job, they are uniquely qualified to work as recruiters or for placement companies. Some recruiting companies focus solely on parale-gals, others work exclusively with attorneys, and still others help to place all legal professionals. Paralegals who work in the field of recruiting talk with employers to determine their needs, interview prospective candi-dates for placement, conduct background checks on the candidates, and monitor the placement after it is made to ensure that the worker is performing and meeting the firm's needs. Large cities that are home to some of the nation's megafirms usually have several thriving and compet-ing legal placement companies.

9. *Writing and Teaching*

After working in a law firm, you may discover that you love writing briefs, corresponding with clients, and drafting memos setting forth the results of your research and investigation efforts. Similarly, you may realize that you enjoy mentoring new paralegals and assisting in various training programs in your law firm.

It can be somewhat daunting to enter the writing field. Start small. Track legislation that affects some of the firm's clients, and then write a brief memo about it that can be sent to the clients. Write an article about a change in the law or an emerging trend and see if your law firm will post it on its Web site. Write a column for your local paralegal association. Submit an article to *Legal Assistant Today*, *Facts & Findings* (NALA's quarterly journal), or *National Paralegal Reporter* (NFPA's bimonthly magazine). All of these publications accept articles on ethics, technology, and breaking news and provide practical tips that help paralegals in the workplace. Once you have some publication experience, you can contact some legal publishers and inquire about writing a textbook or practical manual for paralegals on the job. Note, however, that writing a book may be more a labor of love than anything else; authors are typically paid based solely on sales of the book, and it can take quite a while for a book to gain a following.

Other writing opportunities do exist, however. Consider working for the company that publishes the legal newspaper in your area. Perhaps you can obtain a job as a legal editor. Your proofreading skills and attention to detail would make you a good hire for legal publishers.

Test the teaching waters. Volunteer to present a seminar on a topic of interest at your law firm or for your paralegal association. Help set up your paralegal association's annual conference, and teach one of the mini-classes that will be offered. Volunteer to help your paralegal coordinator work on the firm's paralegal training program. Contact your paralegal school, and offer to speak at orientation, graduation, or in class to tell the students about "real life" in a law firm. These teaching opportunities may land you an offer to teach at your paralegal program. If an opening doesn't yet exist, offer to team-teach an existing class with another instructor. Attorney-paralegal teaching teams are good combinations. The attorneys often instruct about substantive areas of law, and the paralegals speak about the practical aspects of the work and instruct students on real-life assignments they are likely to see in the workplace.

10. *Legislative Assistants and Lobbying Work*

Working as a legislative assistant or for a lobbying group is exciting and challenging. Unfortunately, the jobs are generally restricted to certain locations. Most of the jobs are either in Washington, D.C., or near state capitals. One of the best ways to get your foot in the door is to volunteer to work on a political campaign. Many legislative offices have active internship programs, and you may be able to secure an internship. Your legislative representatives may be able to help. To locate your federal or state representative, access the USA.Gov Web site (www.usa.gov). This site lists all nationally elected representatives and provides access to each state's homepage.

Lobbyists are individuals or companies who act as advocates. Most major corporations and political interest groups engage professional lobbyists to promote their interests. Lobbyists may meet with lawmakers and legislative staff, provide analysis to legislative offices, engage in media activity, and promote letter-writing campaigns. Lobbyists are required to file registration statements for each client they represent. These registration statements are on file with the U.S. Senate (www.senate.gov), allowing you to find out who the major lobbyists are so that you can apply for jobs with them. Keep in mind that law firms often act as lobbyists as well, so you may want to begin your lobbying career by working for a law firm that does significant lobbying work. Alternatively, many large corporations have government or public relations departments, whose function it is to act with paid "outside" lobbyists. Working in-house for one of these corporations may provide you with the lobbying experience you desire.

11. *Trade Association Work*

Nearly every industry has a professional trade association to promote the interests of its members. From the American Banking Association to the American Medical Association to the Snack Food Association, these groups often have large staffs, including in-house attorneys and paralegals. In some respects, these groups are similar to lobbying groups because they often advocate for and against legislation that affects them. They also, however, respond to their members' needs for support and continuing education. They hold educational conferences and publish newsletters and journals to keep their members informed of developments that might affect them. You could work directly for a trade association or for a law firm that represents the trade association. For example, the law firm Covington & Burling represents more than 100 trade and professional associations, including the American Automobile Association. Law firms provide advice to the associations on compliance with federal and state laws, help develop their codes of ethics, and provide advice on changes in the law that might affect them. A good Web site that provides links to numerous trade associations is the Internet Public Library's "Associations on the Net" (http://www.ipl.org/div/aon).

12. *Nonprofit Associations*

Nonprofit associations are generally tax-exempt organizations that serve the public interest (rather than their members' interests, as is the case with trade and professional associations, although these are usually tax-exempt as well). They usually promote charitable, religious, educational, or scientific purposes. The Web site "Idealist.Org—Action Without Borders" (http://www.nonprofits.org/) maintains a list of nearly 50,000 nonprofit organizations throughout the world. The site offers job searching, and the organization will email you with job listings that respond to your interests. Before you interview with a nonprofit entity, review its Web site so you understand its goals and internal structure.

13. *Courthouse Employment Opportunities*

Paralegals are also employed by federal and state courts. They serve not only as paralegals to judges but also as court clerks, assistant law librarians, court officers, court administrators, case specialists, and records technicians. To find these jobs, access the Web site for the federal court closest to you (by using www.uscourts.gov) or the courthouse in your county, township, or parish. Most courts now post job openings on their Web sites.

14. *Alternative Dispute Resolution Work*

Alternative dispute resolution (ADR) is the term given to an umbrella of activities that are designed to resolve disputes without trial. Because going to trial is expensive, time-consuming, and stressful, a number of disputing parties elect ADR. ADR may take the form of **mediation**, in which a neutral third party acts as a facilitator to help parties resolve their differences, or **arbitration**, in which a neutral third party renders an actual decision, much like a judge at trial. A number of commercial companies provide ADR services. Two of the largest are JAMS (formerly Judicial Arbitration and Mediation Services, Inc.) and the American Arbitration Association, which hires paralegals to work as case managers. Ask

Alternative dispute resolution: Method of resolving disputes without trial.

Mediation: Process by which a neutral third party attempts to help parties resolve their differences.

Arbitration: Process by which a neutral third party renders a decision affecting disputing parties.

litigation attorneys which ADR firms they recommend in your area and apply for jobs with those firms.

15. Criminal Law Opportunities

Both your local prosecutor or district attorney's office and your public defender's office likely employ paralegals. Paralegals also work as probation officers, social welfare caseworkers, and child advocates in abuse and juvenile justice cases. Because most of the "employers" are in the public sector, review your state, county, or city Web site and review its job postings. Alternatively, seek an internship at the prosecutor's or public defender's office. You will probably develop some contacts, or the internship itself could lead to an offer of permanent employment.

16. Legal Support and Vendor Services

After working in a law firm, you will likely have experience with LEXIS, Westlaw, software applications such as TimeSlips, Concordance, Summation, and other products and services that make the practice of law more efficient and less expensive. You may have developed unique skills in setting up the firm's live video conferences with its other offices. You may discover that you have sales skills and would like to sell and demonstrate these services and products to those in the legal profession. In all likelihood, you probably already know whether or not you are a good salesperson. If so, consider whether your intimate knowledge of these systems and products would make you an effective spokesperson for them. Salespeople often work on commission, and the work can be lucrative. Moreover, the work is typically more routine in nature and seldom requires the overtime that law firms typically do. If you are interested in transitioning to this field, make a list of the services and products with which you are familiar, and apply to the companies that offer them. Meet privately with the vendor representatives with whom your firm is working. Tell them of your interest, and get some inside information about their profession. Because you will have firsthand knowledge of how the products and services can streamline work in a law firm, you would be an ideal candidate to market them to other firms and offices.

17. Legal Clinics

Many paralegals find meaningful employment by working at legal clinics. Some legal clinics are private firms that offer affordable legal services. Many advertise and depend on a high volume of cases, often personal injury and family law cases. Other legal clinics are operated by governmental agencies or communities and offer legal services to the poor, elderly, or disabled. Although paralegals often work at these legal aid clinics on a pro bono basis, to engage in meaningful work and to obtain experience, many clinics offer full-time permanent positions. Your local bar association will likely have a list of legal clinics that employ paralegals. Read your local newspaper to determine which groups in your area help the underserved. Perhaps a church or synagogue would have a list of such organizations. Many impoverished people need legal services. They may be homeless, they may need an advocate to help them obtain health care, they may have a dispute with their landlord, they may be struggling to regain custody of their children. All of these issues might seem insurmountable to them, but you will have the training, contacts, and resources to help.

D. Freelance and Independent Paralegals

1. Traditional, Freelance, and Independent Paralegals

According to NFPA, there are three general categories of paralegal practice:

- **Traditional paralegal.** A traditional paralegal is one who works under the supervision of an attorney, usually in a law firm, corporate law department, or governmental agency. Most paralegals are traditional paralegals.
- **Freelance or contract paralegal.** As discussed earlier, a freelance paralegal (sometimes called a contract paralegal) is a self-employed paralegal working as an independent contractor who hires himself or herself out to attorneys for specific projects or tasks — for example, organizing exhibits in preparation for trial. When the project or case is finished, the freelance paralegal moves on to another contract situation. Freelance paralegals provide assistance to attorneys on an as-needed basis, so the attorney does not need to hire a full-time employee. In all instances, the paralegal is supervised by an attorney. One of the advantages of freelancing is that it provides significant variety and allows you to "try on a job" before committing to an employer. The disadvantages, of course, are that you will seldom receive health or other benefits, and your case (and employment and your salary) could end at a moment's notice.
- **Independent paralegal.** An independent paralegal works directly for consumers, without supervision by an attorney. Generally, these paralegals complete forms and agreements (often related to family law matters) and participate in real estate closings. Consumers, paralegal associations, and members of the bar are concerned that independent paralegals might engage in the unauthorized practice of law and, thus, regulation of independent

paralegals is a critical issue facing the paralegal profession. All states have statutes that prohibit nonlawyers from practicing law so that members of the public are protected from incompetence. As discussed in Chapter 8, California regulates those individuals who provide independent services as Legal Document Assistants (and unlawful detainer assistants). Independent paralegals enjoy a significant amount of autonomy. They truly run their own businesses. The disadvantages of operating as an independent paralegal are usually a lack of paid insurance and other benefits and a lack of employment stability. Nevertheless, acting as an independent paralegal can be gratifying and challenging work.

2. *Legal Placement Agencies*

Headhunter:
A recruiter who places candidates for employment.

Most communities have placement agencies, also called recruiting firms or **headhunters**, devoted exclusively to placement of lawyers, paralegals, and legal secretaries. Paralegals are usually placed with law firms or other employers on a temporary or contract basis; once a project is completed, the placement ends, and the paralegal is free to accept another freelance position. Check your telephone directory to locate these placement services. Alternatively, your paralegal program office will know of several legal placement services in your area. Law firms and companies looking for legal professionals contact the agency and identify their needs. The agency attempts to fill the vacancy by sending several candidates to the prospective employer for interviews. If a candidate is accepted, the employer pays the agency a placement fee. Some placements are for temporary independent contractors while others are for full-time permanent employment. In large cities, there may be agencies devoted solely to the placement of paralegals. These agencies are extremely knowledgeable about required skills, salary levels, and career opportunities for paralegals. Agency fees are typically paid by the employer and not the employee; be especially wary of any agency that asks you for a fee to place you with an employer. There is one significant barrier to obtaining employment through a legal placement agency: Most will place only those with some experience. Thus, many of them will not work with paralegals looking for their first job. Most placement agencies will carefully screen candidates before sending them on interviews. Thus, be prepared to take quizzes on proofreading, cite-checking, and computer skills. Additionally, these agencies will check your references before sending you to any interview. Working with an agency can be helpful because the agency knows the firm needs a paralegal and will be able to help you prepare for the interview, polish your résumé to target the firm's specific needs, and assist in salary negotiations. It is acceptable to work with more than one agency, although you should disclose this fact.

Some agencies place paralegals on a temporary basis with firms that need help only for a specific period of time (perhaps to handle one production of documents or prepare for a trial) and also on a permanent basis. Temporary placements might turn into full-time jobs; however, there is no guarantee of this. Typically, a law firm that wants to extend an offer of full-time employment to a temp worker must pay a fee to the agency.

E. Paralegal Specialization

Just as in many fields, paralegals are becoming highly specialized. For example, several institutions now offer certificates in **Legal Nurse Consulting** (also called Nurse Paralegal programs). These programs are offered to registered nurses who then apply their nursing knowledge to legal services. Required courses include medical and legal malpractice, health care administration, and worker's compensation. Nurse paralegals are often employed by large law firms with sophisticated injury or illness practices; these highly specialized paralegals provide expert in-house assistance and review doctors' charts, nurses' notes, and medical testimony. Paralegals without nursing degrees who have an interest in health care may work for health care organizations, hospitals, and insurers, such as Blue Cross Blue Shield.

Legal nurse consultant: A registered nurse who is trained as a paralegal (also called a nurse paralegal).

A few institutions offer master's degrees in paralegal studies, legal studies, and legal administration. As discussed in Chapter 8, graduates usually manage law offices or paralegal departments within large law offices. They recruit, hire, supervise, and terminate paralegals, coordinate workflow, prepare annual budgets for their departments, establish paralegal salaries and billing rates, monitor billable hours, and coordinate training and education for the group.

One of the newest trends in the provision of services by paralegals is offered by "We the People," a franchise offering computerized legal document preparation services. We the People has approximately 150 franchised offices in more than 30 states, often staffed by paralegals, and compares its services to those offered by H&R Block (the preparer of tax forms for consumers), in that it offers affordable services to people who need help with their legal documents (especially in the areas of divorce, business incorporations, and wills). In 2003, We the People processed 20,000 bankruptcy petitions throughout the United States. Although We the People has been challenged in a number of lawsuits and has been accused of engaging in the unauthorized practice of law, it is advocating for state or federal legislation, or both, that would permit it to operate without continual legal challenges. In fact, in mid-2005, We the People agreed with the U.S. Bankruptcy Court for the Southern District of New York not to engage in the unauthorized practice of law, and agreed not to advise customers on when to file bankruptcy or distribute how-to books or guides on filing for bankruptcy. A Department of Justice attorney characterized We the People as "a typing service." Its Web site is www.wethepeopleusa.com.

F.   Nonlegal Jobs

There are a number of nonlegal jobs you might want to consider, including the following:

1.   Becoming an Entrepreneur

Many people dream of owning their own business. You may have a passion for catering, decorating, computer technology, or some other field and may want to launch your own business rather than working in someone else's. You may want to start a business related to law, perhaps your own legal placement company or a company providing litigation support services to law firms in your area.

Your paralegal education and training provide you with some basic information, including a working knowledge of the different types of business structures, so that you can intelligently decide whether to operate as a sole proprietorship, partnership, or corporation. You will have gained excellent communications skills, which are needed by any entrepreneur. Your training will have allowed you to witness firsthand how a business operates and will have given you familiarity with software and technology applications, billing, personnel decisions, and many other issues common to any kind of business. If you are thinking about launching your own business, use the numerous resources available to help you conduct some research. Start with your local chamber of commerce or with your state's secretary of state to obtain some basic business knowledge and information on starting a business. Talk to others who have started their own businesses, and find out what strategies they have adopted. Join a local business group to gain inside information into the possible pitfalls of operating your own business.

2.   Management Positions

The excellent organization skills possessed by most paralegals often provide a sound foundation for management positions. You may have been in charge of organizing and maintaining thousands of documents, leading a litigation team, or some other activity that requires resourcefulness, leadership, and competence. These skills easily transfer to any business setting. Review the job notices in your local newspaper. Read the business section to find out what businesses are "up and coming" in your area. Sell yourself. You may find that you need to first start as an assistant. For example, you might work as the executive assistant to the president of a company. This position allows you to observe at firsthand critical business decisions and executive leadership. You may eventually need a degree or advanced degree in a business-related field, but your on-the-job training within a company will serve as an excellent foundation for any later formal education.

3. *Counseling*

As you have proceeded through your paralegal program and worked in a law office, you may have discovered that others often seek you out when they have a problem or crisis. You may have a unique combination of empathy and pragmatism that makes you good at helping others solve their problems. Thus, working in a setting in which these skills are critical (such as an HR department) or working as a life coach, career coach, or career counselor could be the next chapter in your career story. You will probably need to obtain specialized training in counseling, but the satisfaction and enjoyment you gain from helping others will make the additional investment of time and money the best investment you ever make.

4. *Writing and Teaching*

Although legal writing and teaching in legal settings were described earlier, don't forget that your communications skills may easily translate into nonlegal writing, editing, and teaching. Perhaps you have been doing a great deal of "ghost writing" for the attorneys in your office or have been in charge of your firm's training program. If these activities give you great enjoyment and fulfillment, consider whether your heart leads you to writing or teaching in a nonlegal setting. Review the section above and follow the suggestions listed there. For example, submit an article to your local newspaper, volunteer to teach a class at your church or for a local nonprofit organization, such as a shelter. These first steps will help you determine if a career in writing and teaching are for you.

NetWorks

www.bls.gov/oco/ ocos114.htm	The Department of Labor's Bureau of Statistics provides information about the paralegal profession and the nature of the tasks performed by paralegals.
www.paralegals.org	The NFPA Web site provides an excellent review of the roles and responsibilities of paralegals in more than 20 separate fields. Select "CLE" and then "Paralegal Responsibilities."
http://careerplanning.about .com/od/careerchoicechan/	The Web site "About" offers valuable articles and resources relating to career choices and career changes.
http://www.quintcareers .com/career_change.html	The QuintCareers.com Web site offers an excellent article entitled "The 10-Step Plan to Career Change," with valuable advice about assessing your transferable skills.

Case Illustration

Recovery of Outsourced Paralegal's Fees

Case: *Sandoval v. Apfel*, 86 F. Supp. 2d 601 (N.D. Tex. 2000)

Facts: A social security claimant sought to recover attorneys' fees he had incurred after his successful appeal of a denial of his disability benefits. His original attorney had outsourced some of the work to an attorney and a paralegal who worked for a Florida-based legal aid society as independent contractors.

Holding: The claimant can recover fees for services that his attorney outsourced to the lawyer and paralegal who worked as independent contractors. They should be reimbursed at reasonable hourly rates according to the prevailing market for their services. The paralegal performed valuable services that might otherwise have been performed by the attorney at a higher hourly rate. An attorney is not necessarily more efficient in performing certain tasks than an experienced paralegal. The fact that the attorney and paralegal were functioning as independent contractors should have no bearing on compensation for their valuable services.

Chapter Summary

- Although most paralegals work in law firms, there are numerous other job opportunities available for paralegals. Paralegals usually have excellent organization skills and communications skills, making them valuable in a variety of work settings.
- Switching careers requires you to assess your likes and dislikes and then consider which of your skills are transferable into other work environments.
- There are numerous law-related jobs for paralegals who choose to work outside of a traditional law firm setting. Paralegals are employed in in-house corporate legal departments, in the government and public sector, banks, trust companies, insurance companies, real estate and title companies, trade associations, alternative dispute resolution groups, legal aid clinics, and court systems, among other places.
- Paralegals who work in-house or for government agencies generally do not track their time because they have only one client: the company or the agency, respectively.
- Some paralegals work as freelance or contract paralegals. These paralegals are self-employed and work as independent contractors, hiring themselves out to attorneys for specific projects or tasks. When the task is complete, the freelance paralegal moves on to another contract situation. In all instances, the freelance paralegal is supervised by an attorney.
- Some paralegals work as independent paralegals, meaning they work directly for consumers without supervision by an attorney. In many instances, these paralegals function as document preparers. Many consumers, paralegal associations, and members of the bar are concerned that independent paralegals may engage in the unauthorized practice of law, and so regulation of independent paralegals is a key issue facing the paralegal profession.
- Paralegals who choose to perform nonlegal work might start their own businesses, engage in counseling, serve in management positions, or write or teach.

Key Terms

In-house legal department: Group within a company that performs legal work for the company.

In-house counsel: Attorney employed directly by a company to perform its legal work.

General counsel: The most senior in-house attorney in a company.

Alternative dispute resolution: Method of resolving disputes without trial.

Mediation: Process by which a neutral third party attempts to help parties resolve their differences.

Arbitration: Process by which a neutral third party renders a decision affecting disputing parties.

Headhunter: A recruiter who places candidates for employment.

Legal nurse consultant: A registered nurse who is trained as a paralegal; also called a *nurse paralegal.*

Bits and Bytes

- One expert estimates that the average worker changes careers (not just jobs) at least five times over a lifetime. Many individuals change careers even more frequently.

- The 2004 NALA Survey disclosed that in order to develop and grow professionally, 10 percent of respondents developed opportunities for freelance work, and 8 percent authored educational articles for law-related publications.

- The Department of Justice is the largest federal employer of paralegals.

Discussion Questions

1. Discuss some advantages and disadvantages of working in an in-house legal department rather than a law firm.

2. Discuss some advantages and disadvantages of working in the public sector (for example, working for the Department of Justice) rather than a law firm.

3. Sarah, an independent paralegal, is preparing a petition for divorce for a consumer. The consumer asks Sarah whether it would be wise to seek joint custody of the couple's children. What should Sarah respond?

WebWork

1. Access the Web site of the EPA. Use the search box to locate résumé tips. Review the résumé tips provided. What four items must your résumé include or address?

2. Access the Web site for USAJOBS. Select "Apply for Jobs," then "Search Jobs," and then "Series Search." What is the occupational series number that has been assigned to "paralegal specialist" jobs?

3. Access NFPA's Web site. Select "CLE" and then "Paralegal Responsibilities." What is the first task listed for paralegals engaged in Alternative Dispute Resolution work?

Job-Hunting Resources

Government — Federal

U.S. Federal Government Official Job Site
http://usajobs.opm.gov

Central Intelligence Agency (CIA)
http://cia.gov

Federal Communications Commission (FCC)
www.fcc.gov/jobs

Fedworld
www.fedworld.gov

U.S. Department of Justice (nationwide)
www.usdoj.gov

Legal Job Sites

LawyerShop
www.lawyershop.com

Law Crossing
www.lawcrossing.com

Paralegal-Jobs.com
http://paralegal-jobs.com

National Federation of Paralegal Associations (NFPA) Career Center
www.paralegals.legalstaff.com

Findlaw
http://careers.findlaw.com

LawJobs
www.lawjobs.com

General Jobs Sites

America's Job Bank
www.jobbankinfo.org

Career Builder
http://careerbuilder.com

Craigslist
www.craigslist.com

Monster.com
www.monster.com

Yahoo! Hot jobs
http://hotjobs.yahoo.com

Directories

Martindale-Hubbell Law Dictionary
www.martindale.com

Yellow Pages
www.bigyellow.com

**American Bar Association/AMB Young Lawyers Division
(career information and job listings)**
www.abanet.org

Hieros Gamos (law-related links)
www.hg.org

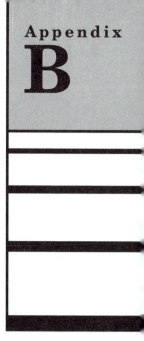

Sample Résumés

Beginning Paralegals

Taylor D. Wade
123 First Street*
* Columbus, OH 12345 * 555-555-1234*
<u>hireme@emailaddress.com</u>

Education

2005	**Ohio State University,** Columbus, OH <u>Paralegal Certificate Program</u>, ABA Approved Business and Environmental Law Specialty Coursework: Introduction to Law, Legal Research, Corporate Law, Civil Litigation, Real Estate Law, Environmental Law, and Computers in the Law Office.
1999-2003	**Ohio State University,** Columbus, OH B.A., Sociology

Experience

Feb 2005-May 2005	**Paralegal Intern** <u>Law Office of Jim Ward</u>, Columbus, OH Organized medical records for personal injury cases. Prepared answers to form interrogatories. Prepared demand letters. Filed correspondence and pleadings
Sept 1999-May 2002	**Loan Office Assistant** <u>Ohio State University — Controller's Loan Office</u> Columbus, OH Updated loan payment spreadsheets in Excel. Checked accounts for delinquency. Updated account information in database. Deposited loan payments with the University Cashier. Filed confidential documents.
June 1997-June 1999	**Courtesy Clerk** <u>Piggy Wiggly</u>, Columbus, OH Greeted customers and assisted them in locating specific products. Packaged groceries and loaded them into customers' cars. Addressed public's questions and concerns.

Achievements

1999 & 2000	United Food and Commercial Workers Union Scholarship

Volunteer

2000	De Colores Program — Traveled to Tijuana, Mexico to help construct elementary school. Worked with children at La Gloria Orphanage.
2000-2002	Special Games — Athlete Coach

Patricia L. Pollack
Cell: 123-456-8910
Ineedajob@emailaddress.com

1234 Second Street
Los Angeles, CA 92222
Phone: 123-456-8910

556 Elm Street
San Diego, CA 92111
Phone: 123-456-7891

Education   Dec. 2003   **Los Angeles Community College**   Los Angeles CA

Paralegal General Litigation
- Studies included Family Law, Criminal Law, Civil Litigation and Legal Research
- Learned how to draft appropriate documents
- Learned how to use research tools
- ABA approved program

Work   Fall 2003   **Smith, Smith & Trowbridge, LLP**   Los Angeles, CA

Intern, Personal Injury
- Prepared demand letters
- Helped to prepare complaints
- Corresponded with clients

June 2000-Aug. 2000   **Office of State Senator**   San Diego, CA

Intern
- Scheduled appointments for Senator and updated daily calendar for entire staff
- Performed legislative research for Senator and staff
- Conducted constituent tours on U.S. Capitol Building
- Performed other duties including writing letters, faxing, answering phones and greeting constituents
- Became proficient with Microsoft Outlook

Volunteer
Experience   Feb. 2002   **Los Angeles Community College** Los Angeles, CA

Student Ambassador
- Liaison between University and Special Olympics organizing committee

5567 Baker Blvd   (123)-456-7890
Seattle, WA 12345   paralegal@emailaddress.com

JENNIFER SERENE

Education

2007	**Seattle Community College**, Seattle, WA Paralegal Certificate Program General Litigation Specialty Coursework: Introduction to Law, Legal Research, Civil Litigation, Real Estate Law, Criminal Law, Family Law and Computers in the Law Office

Experience

Mar. 2007- Apr. 2007	**Paralegal Intern** Geier Law Group, Seattle, WA • Researched and contacted experts for construction defect case • Organized pleadings, discovery, correspondence, and medical records for personal injury case • Drafted press releases • Created Excel spreadsheets for payroll, annual business expenses and client expenses • Prepared service of process and contacted Attorney Service to serve parties
Mar. 2006- Feb. 2007	**Tour Conductor** Historic Tours of America, Seattle, WA • Narrated a two-hour city tour • Drove trolley bus • Earned "Safe Driver's" award
Skills	Windows 2000/XP, MS Word, Power Point, Excel, Outlook, LEXIS, CaseMap
References	Available upon request

Experienced Workers

AIDAN TEDROW
1599 Hiram Lane #183, Cedar Falls, IA 55867♦ (123) 345-678♦ paralegal@email.com

Education:

01/07-5/07   **University of Cedar Falls**, Cedar Falls, IA
                    Paralegal Certificate Program ABA Approved
                    Specialty: Business Litigation
                    Relevant Coursework: Civil Litigation, Contracts, Corporations,
                    Intellectual Property, and Legal Research

Employment:

03/07-5/07   **Legal Aid Society**, Cedar Falls, IA
                    Paralegal Intern
                    • Met with clients. Conducted legal research regarding bankruptcy
                      and tax issues. Drafted a memorandum to staff concerning
                      unlawful detainers and bankruptcy. Prepared letters to clients
                      for attorney signature. Reviewed and updated various databases.

10/05-01/07   **Mason City Financial Advisors**, Mason City, IA
                    Wealth Management Assistant
                    • Acted as primary liaison with financial institutions, such as
                      brokers/dealers, mutual fund companies, money managers, and
                      insurance companies
                    • Initiated, tracked and expedited new account process, fund
                      transfers and trades
                    • Reviewed all new account applications and all other correspon-
                      dence and paperwork submitted to financial institutions to
                      ensure completeness and accuracy
                    • Prepared monthly and quarterly reports for advisors
                    • Maintained compliance-related files
                    • Assisted in coordination and scheduling of practice marketing
                      efforts

03/03-03/05   **Ottumwa Trust Company**, Mason City, IA
                    Trust Assistant
                    • Processed client cash requests and reconciled client accounts in
                      accounting system
                    • Researched and resolved various account and accounting prob-
                      lems
                    • Handled recurring client information requests and responded to
                      client inquiries
                    • Prepared Excel spreadsheets for distributing stocks, mutual
                      funds, and cash to trust account beneficiaries

- Was liaison between the Trust Department, the Legal Department, Accountants and Personal Investment Counselors, as well as their assistants

09/94-03-03   **Perault & Trowbridge, Inc.**, Mason City, IA
Director, Performance Measurement (1997-2003) ♦ Portfolio Admin
(1994-1997)
- Implemented procedures for compliance reporting to the NASD, SEC in various states
- Responsible and accountable for client reporting service
- Calculated client performance and ran monthly performance intervals and well as created and validated data for use by principals

Michael Perez

1243 39th St.
Hiram, OH 44234

(555) 123-4567
paralegal@email.com

Education

May 2007   Lakeland Community College   Mentor, OH

ABA approved Graduate Level Paralegal Certificate
- Business Litigation Emphasis: Corporations, Contracts, Intellectual Property

June 2004   Hiram College   Hiram, OH

History B.A.
- Minor in Political Science

Work Experience

Feb. 2007-Apr. 2007   Jennifer Conyers, Attorney at Law Hiram, OH

Paralegal Intern
- Drafted complaints, demand letters, and client correspondence
- Researched legal issues, conducted discovery, investigated defendants

Nov. 2004-Nov. 2006   Hiram College   Hiram, OH

Mail Processor
- Processed first-class, presort mail, UPS and Fed Ex shipments using various machines
- Sorted, bundled, and delivered U.S. and interdepartmental mail
- Trained new full-time employees and student helpers

Feb. 2000-Feb. 2003   Apple Co.   Solon, OH

Sr. Internet Analyst
- Analyzed and categorized Web site content for Internet filtering database
- Supervised, trained, and assisted new Internet analysts
- Addressed customer concerns and questions regarding Web site categorizations
- Created and updated category definitions.

Sept. 1998-Jan. 2000   Miller, Otto & Lantz   Middlefield, OH

Mail Clerk
- Processed first-class mail
- Opened, sorted and delivered U.S. mail, faxes and client files
- Photocopied legal documents
- Assisted attorneys and other staff members with administrative tasks
- Ordered and maintained inventory of office supplies

Sept. 1994-July 1998   Yoder, Studer & Schertz   Middlefield, OH

Distribution Center Back-Up Dispatcher
- Responsible for dispatching same-day courier packages, including court filings and process servings
- Audited and processed invoices using Excel spreadsheets
- Supervised and trained new employees
- Editor of the department newsletter, *The Distribution Dispatch*
- Processed FedEx, DHL and UPS shipments

**Technical
Skills**   Microsoft Office 2003 Software, LEXIS, Abacus Law

Tyler Yakatoma

12357 34th ST # 12A, San Francisco, CA

(555) 123-1234

Paralegal@emailaddress.com

OBJECTIVE

Excel as a Paralegal professional by leveraging my strong research, interpersonal, communication training and experience within a long-term growth environment.

EDUCATION

2005   **University of San Francisco**
Paralegal Certificate Program (General Litigation)
1996   **San Francisco State University**
Master of Arts Degree — English / Creative Writing
1994   **San Francisco State University**
Bachelor of Arts Degree — English, Cum Laude

PROFESSIONAL EXPERIENCE

06/2005-08/2005   **Sarnoff Law Group, San Francisco, CA**

Paralegal Intern
- Provided litigation support, drafted legal documents, performed courthouse and background research for current cases

08/2002-09/2003   **San Francisco State University, San Francisco, CA**

Instructor of English
- Taught four courses per semester of basic and advanced writing, including drafting and administering assignments, projects, and tests, as well as active participation in faculty committees.

07/2001-07/2002   **San Francisco City School District, San Francisco, CA**

Instructor of English for Students of Other Languages
- Planned, administered, and taught non-native-English-speaking students, including active participation in faculty committees and planning groups

12/1999-07/2001   **Golden State University, San Francisco, CA**

Instructor of Graduate Business Communications
- Taught oral and written communication skills to MBA candidates, including teaching students to strengthen communication skills (such as oral presentation, visual presentation, and accent reduction)

01/1988-08/1991   **KXML FM/WRSD AM, San Francisco, CA**

Associate Program Director
- Worked for television station to create program scheduling. Liaison for affiliate relations, and syndicated program relations, with strict deadlines in day-to-day operations

SKILLS

Experienced in managing pressure and time constraints, with excellent research skills and computer literacy (Word, Excel, PowerPoint, etc.)
References available upon request

Experienced Paralegals

June Trowbridge

1000 Mount Elbrus Ave #102, New York, NY (555) 123-4567 <u>paralegal@emailaddress.com</u>

Professional Experience:

<u>Legal Secretary</u> **McCann, Trevino and Wade, LLP,**   **05/2004-8/2004**
New York, NY

- Provided litigation support for the Chemistry/Bio-Pharmaceutical Patent Department
  - Prepared complex scientific and technical engagement and opinion documents
  - Researched technical references, patents and citations
  - Assisted with document production and trial preparation
- Provided prosecution support for the Electrical Engineering Patent Department
  - Prepared formal patent application documents including Information Disclosure Statements, Assignments and Powers of Attorney
  - Prepared reporting letters and business development letters
  - Audited case files to ensure proper transfer of matters from foreign associates or other firms
  - Transcribed audio files containing utility patent applications

<u>Legal Secretary</u> **Reedholm Co. Inc., New York, NY**   **2001-2002**

- Active in the initial development of the Patent Department
- Prepared formal patent application filings for the United States Patent and Trademark Office
- Provided litigation support to the Patent Department
- Created and maintained the patent database
- Prepared reports based on the patent portfolio
- Managed communications with outside counsel and inventors
- Maintained the department accounts payable

<u>Paralegal Intern</u> **Laurvick Pharmaceuticals, New York, NY**   **2001**

- Completed a paralegal internship in the Corporate Intellectual Property Legal Department
- Prepared a continuation patent application and an information disclosure statement for filing with the U.S. Patent and Trademark Office
- Conducted legal research using the Manual of Patent Examination Procedure

<u>Executive Secretary</u> **Barclay Technology Co. Inc., New York, NY**   **1997-2001**

- Developed and implemented Resource Management database for all engineering projects
- Coordinated engineering project staffing plans with management team and human resources
- Generated weekly project scheduling reports for project activities and milestones

- Budgeted and coordinated the Engineering Department off-site meetings, special events and travel for 700 plus employees
- Provided diverse and complex support to the Vice President of Engineering and his staff
- Promoted twice within a two-year period

Education

New York Community College, New York, NY

- Paralegal Certificate
  Specialty: Civil Litigation
  Coursework: Civil Procedure, Contract Law, Legal Research, Family Law, and Computer Applications

Lola Geier

paralegal@emailaddress.com
555-123-1234

5679 Mount Alvarez Ave.
Rapid City, SD 56447

EDUCATION

Rapid City Community College   **Rapid City, SD**
Paralegal Certificate, ABA approved
General Litigation Specialty, Completed August 2005
Coursework included: Introduction to Law, Legal Research, Family Law,
   Contract Law, Civil Litigation, Criminal Law, and Computers in the Legal Office
Prepared memorandum of law, deposition summaries and complaints

EXPERIENCE

Sheldon & Harrison
Family Law Firm   **Rapid City, SD**
Paralegal/Intern, June 2005- August 2005
Wrote declarations. Prepared answers to form and special interrogatories. Drafted a
postnuptial agreement. Completed income and expense declarations and schedules
of assets and debts.

Viehl & Sullivan, LLP   **Rapid City, SD**
Criminal Law Firm
Legal Assistant/Intern, Summer 2004
Wrote and filed pleading documents. Interviewed clients. Researched and obtained
expert witnesses

District Attorney's Office   **Rapid City, SD**
Victim/Witness Division
Intern, 2003-2004
Attended court to hear outcome of cases. Reported status of cases to victims,
including pleas, future dates and any added charges. Communicated victims' wishes
to district attorneys. Organized and crated outreach projects.

Conyers, Holt, Garcia & Jefferson   **Rapid City, SD**
Worker's Compensation Defense Firm
Legal Assistant /Intern, Summer 2002
Reviewed and summarized medical files. Subpoenaed records. Attended depositions.
Negotiated outstanding liens

COMPUTER SKILLS

Microsoft Word, Outlook, WordPerfect, Excel, TimeSlips, LEXIS & Legal
Solutions

DeAnne F. Robinson
1245 Main Street Apt #4
Charleston, SC 23467
Email: paralegal@email.com
(555) 123-4567

OBJECTIVE: Seeking Paralegal career with a team-oriented Civil and Business Litigation firm or organization

EDUCATION: **CHARLESTON COMMUNITY COLLEGE, Charleston, SC**
ABA-approved Paralegal Certificate

CHARLESTON COMMUNITY COLLEGE, Charleston, SC
80 Units of General Education courses with emphasis in English
(1990-1995) GPA 3.4

EXPERIENCE: **RAMIREZ & ASSOCIATES, Charleston, CA**
2005 *Paralegal*
- Provided administrative and paralegal support for civil litigation firm
- Served as liaison and managed the flow of information between clients and attorney
- Prepared and maintained motions, pleadings, and legal briefs for pending and ongoing actions
- Prepared and served discovery requests and responses to discovery from opposing parties
- Calendared appointments and schedules while maintaining the firm's records and case files
- Processed correspondence to clients regarding litigation claims, new developments and findings
- Timely filed legal documents to federal and appellate courts to maintain statute of limitations

2004- Present **PLANTATION LAW GROUP, Charleston, SC**
Paralegal (Seasonal Employment Position)
- Provided legal assistance for billing analysis, research and reimbursement auditing law firm
- Achieved recognition for superior performance and received a promotion to Lead Paralegal
- Supervised, trained, scheduled, coordinated and evaluated a team of five seasonal Paralegals
- Analyzed the legal billings for mandated school district funding from the state
- Determined the amount of school district time spent negotiating collective bargaining agreements
- Developed a comprehensive spreadsheet outlining the school district's negotiating reimbursements
- Processed, updated, organized and filed automated and alpha-numeric confidential documents

2003-2004   **RAINBOW ROW INC., Charleston, SC**
                       Office Manager
                       • Managed the administrative operations for a manufacturer or
                         specialized farming equipment
                       • Hired, managed, trained, coordinated and evaluated the admin-
                         istrative support team members
                       • Developed operating budgets, job cost accounting, cash flow
                         forecasts and analytical reports

Chronological Résumés

Arthur Hentemann
15667 Main Street #130
Dallas, TX 54456
(123) 555-1235
Email: paralegal@emailaddress.com

WORK EXPERIENCE

Sept.-Dec. 2004   *Paralegal* (temporary assignment)   Sheldon and Assoc.
- Conducted document review of collective bargaining activities for school districts (K-12 and community college statewide)
- Prepared mandate reimbursement claims requiring focus and attention to detail for submission to the State of California.

2002-2004   *Scheduling/Staffing Coordinator*   Texas State University

Reporting to Dean, School of Education:
- Produced statewide academic long-range class schedules with specific course requirements
- Made recommendations to administration based upon analysis of historical data, current admissions, and enrollment trends
- Implemented transition of new courses/promotion activities

2001-2002   *Assistant to Vice President*   Texas State University

Reporting to VP, Marketing & Regional Operations:
- Managed $3 million advertising budget requiring detail for marketing analyses
- Coordinated statewide media schedules for print, television and radio
- Served as conduit for University-wide sponsorship/promotion activities

1999-2001   *Executive Secretary*   Non-Profit Organization

Reporting to President/CEO:
- Worked closely with Development Director to coordinate/execute major fund raising activities, grant proposals, and contract review
- Prepared agendas with related materials for committee and Board of Trustees meetings

1991-1998   *Senior Program Assistant Legal Department*   Intel Inc.

Reporting to General Counsel:
- Developed/implemented processes for $2 million outside counsel fees budget management
- Established nondisclosure agreement administration, and file management processes/procedures, and implemented document standards

EDUCATION

2004	University of Dallas	ABA-approved Paralegal Program
2002	National University	Bachelor of Arts, English
1989	Texas State University	ABA-approved Legal Assistant Program

COMPUTER SKILLS

Microsoft Office 2003, Word, PowerPoint, Excel, WordPerfect

Bethany Holt

(555) 555-5555

12345 Dirt Road
Bakersfiled, CA 99782
mary@address.com

EDUCATION

May 2005   **University of Bakersfiled**   Bakersfiled, CA
                    Certificate, Paralegal
                    ABA-approved graduate level program

September 1991   **California School of Advertising**   Watsonville, CA
                    Certificate, Graphic Art

May 1989   **California State University**   Sacramento, CA
                    B.A., Humanities and Social Sciences

RELATED EXPERIENCE

March 2005 - May 2005   **Arthur J. Geier, Esq.**   Bakersfield, CA
                          Internship: Education law
                          • *Drafted Pleadings*
                          • *Prepared multiple deposition summaries*
                          • *Coordinated, prepared and organized documents for
                            litigation*
                          • *Researched and drafted legal memoranda*

Sept. 1999 - Oct. 2003 **Bakersfield Hospital**   Bakersfield, CA
                          Office Manager
                          • Co-founder of corporation
                          • Increased corporate visibility in the industry by creating
                            image, strengthening public relations and advertising
                            efforts
                          • Prepared and organized case documents for various legal
                            proceedings

Nov. 1991- Nov. 1996   **California Magazine**   Sacramento, CA
                          Art Director
                          • Art Director of magazine of personal adornment
                          • Assisted with implementation and transition to computer-
                            ized system for magazine production

ACCOMPLISHMENTS
                          • Board of Directors
                          • Chair Person

Functional Résumés

Katie Carter
1234 Front Drive, Manassas, VA 20112
Phone: 703-555-1234 Mobile: 703-555-4321
Email: paralegal@email.com

OBJECTIVE: Paralegal/Litigation Support position utilizing strong technology and database management skills

SUMMARY OF QUALIFICATIONS

— Extensive experience in database management and computer software
— Proven analytical and problem-solving skills with exceptional attention to detail
— Demonstrated ability to work well under demanding conditions and to meet deadlines
— Successful in quickly mastering new skills through hands-on experience

PROFESSIONAL EXPERIENCE

Writing

— Drafted and proofread notices of civil penalties for electronic scanner overcharge violations
— Determined correct penalty amounts by applying California Code of Regulations penalty guidelines
— Developed standards and procedures for administering databases

Management and Project Coordination

— Supervised and provided technical leadership for a staff of Database Administrators
— Managed allocation of personnel resources to support multiple concurrent projects
— Acted as the point of contact for database implementation plans for database conversion and migration projects

Training and Mentoring

— Taught courses in Database Administration for customers and employees
— Trained application developers in database programming and SQL tuning
— Mentored customers' staff during database consulting assignments to ensure adequate knowledge transfer
— Assisted end users in developing queries and reports in MS Access

Computer Skills

— Designed databases and assisted application developers in writing database procedures and SQL queries

—Programmed scripts to automate database creation tasks and installed software updates

—Implemented text indexing to enable keyword searching of text documents

—Skilled in relational databases (Oracle, SQL Server, MS Access), Windows, UNIX, Bourne shell scripting, SQL, XML, HTML, Microsoft Office (Word, Excel, PowerPoint, Outlook, Project), Visio, LEXIS

EMPLOYMENT HISTORY

Summer 2005   **Paralegal Intern**
County Department of Agriculture

2001-2005   **Senior Database Administrator**
Virginia Technology Inc.

1997-2000   **Database Instructor and Senior Database Consultant**
Tech Solutions Corporation

1990-1997   **Lead Database Administrator and Database Manager**
Technology International

EDUCATION

Paralegal Certificate: University of Centreville, Centreville, VA
Computer Programming Certificate: Virginia Tech Institute, Arlington, VA
B.A. Sociology: University of New Hampshire, Durham, NH

Dominic Balsamo
555 Wyckoff Street
Paramus, NJ 07652
(732) 555-4567

Education

University of Paramus — Paralegal Certificate Program	2006
Business	
Rutgers University — B.A., Economics	1990

Legal Internship

Bogardus & Associates a PLC, Chatham, NH   2006

- Drafted request for admissions for personal injury cases
- Reviewed and summarized personal injury case files for paralegals and associates
- Organized and assembled prospective client documents

Securities Industry Experience

- Reviewed client requests for control/restricted stock transactions
- Applied SEC rules and regulation to facilitate restricted stock transactions
- Summarized the transactional options for clients within corporate selling agreements
- Researched and verified corporate executive stock transactions via SEC filings
- Prepared and filed legal documents with the SEC on behalf of clients
- Presented written and oral arguments to facilitate loans collateralized by control/restricted stock
- Participated in conference calls with in-house corporate counsel to ascertain which SEC rules apply to our clients needs
- Consulted retail brokers regarding SEC rules and regulations that applied to their corporate executive clientele
- Assisted employees with their corporate stock option transactions
- Assembled marketing materials for corporate meetings
- Organized and maintained client documents for compliance purposes
- Reconciled client cash accounts from changes due to daily market fluctuations

Macy's, Cherry Hill, NJ	2004-2006
American Investment Company, Monmouth, NJ	2003-2004
New Jersey Investment Banking Inc., Neptune, NJ	1995-1998, 2003
Banking Capital LLC, South Orange, NJ	2000-2001
Ranger Investment Corporation, Madison, NJ	1992-1994

Computer Skills
Proficient in Microsoft Office 2003 (Word, Outlook, Excel, Access, PowerPoint), LEXIS, WestLaw, PC Law, Summation, CaseSoft, NASDAQ Workstation II, Autex, Crossing Network

Sample Cover Letters

Response to Advertisement (Beginning Paralegal—No Relevant Experience)

[Your Name]
[Street Address]
[City, ST ZIP Code]
November 19, 2007

[Recipient Name]
[Title]
[Company Name]
[Street Address]
[City, ST ZIP Code]

Dear [Recipient Name]:

I am responding to the advertisement for the Paralegal position with your firm. The course work in the Paralegal Program I have attended has given me the skills needed to start my career as a Paralegal.

As you'll see on the enclosed resume, the coursework has given me experience with _____ I am proficient in many areas of _____, and look forward to learning more about _____.

My instructors from the program have provided me with superior recommendations to aid me in my search. I would appreciate the opportunity to present these to you and to introduce myself as a candidate for the position at your firm.

[Recipient Name], if you will contact me at _____ during the day or evening, we can schedule an appointment.

Sincerely,

[Your Name]

Enclosure

Response to Advertisement (Relevant Experience)

[Your Name]
[Street Address]
[City, ST ZIP Code]
November 19, 2007

[Recipient Name]
[Title]
[Company Name]
[Street Address]
[City, ST ZIP Code]

Dear [Recipient Name]:

I am responding to the advertisement for a Paralegal position with your firm. My work with first-rate attorneys enables me to offer you an exceptional mix of training, knowledge, experience, and professionalism.

As you'll see from the enclosed resume, I have worked for several law firms in the _____ area. I am proficient in many areas of _____ with an additional concentration in _____. As a result, I can offer you an unusual level of expertise in _____.

The attorneys with whom I work have provided me with superior recommendations to aid me in my search. I would appreciate the opportunity to present these to you and to introduce myself as a candidate for the position at your firm.

[Recipient Name], if you will contact me at _____ during the day or evening, we can schedule an appointment.

Sincerely,

[Your Name]

Enclosure

Response to Advertisement
(Different Experience)

[Your Name]
[Street Address]
[City, ST ZIP Code]
November 19, 2007

[Recipient Name]
[Title]
[Company Name]
[Street Address]
[City, ST ZIP Code]

Dear [Recipient Name]:

I am responding to the advertisement for a Paralegal position with your firm. My work experience in other fields allows me to offer you an exceptional mix of training, knowledge, experience, and professionalism.

As you'll see from the enclosed resume, I have worked for several companies in the _____ area. I am proficient in many areas of _____ with an additional concentration in _____. As a result, I can offer you an unusual level of expertise in _____.

The supervisors for whom I have worked have provided me with superior recommendations to aid me in my search. I would appreciate the opportunity to present these to you and to introduce myself as a candidate for the position at your firm.

[Recipient Name], if you will contact me at _____ during the day or evening, we can schedule an appointment.

Sincerely,

[Your Name]

Enclosure

Blind Cover Letter

[Your Name]
[Street Address]
[City, ST ZIP Code]
November 19, 2007

[Recipient Name]
[Title]
[Company Name]
[Street Address]
[City, ST ZIP Code]

Dear **[Recipient Name]**:

I am writing to express my interest in serving as a Paralegal at _____.
I will be graduating (or have graduated) in _____ with a Paralegal
Certificate from _____.

As indicated on my enclosed resume, I was employed at _____
as _____. This experience increased my knowledge of the legal
field, particularly in the area of _____.

In addition to my _____ knowledge, I will bring to my next
employer strong leadership and organizational skills gained through
the coursework and internship from my Paralegal Program.

I would be delighted to begin my career with _____. I will contact
you the week of _____ to see if we can arrange a mutually convenient time to meet for an interview. If you would like to contact me, my
contact information is _____.

I look forward to speaking with you.

Sincerely,

[Your Name]

Enclosure

Blind Letter in Response
to Network Contact

[Your Name]
[Street Address]
[City, ST ZIP Code]
November 19, 2007

[Recipient Name]
[Title]
[Company Name]
[Street Address]
[City, ST ZIP Code]

Dear [Recipient Name]:

I am writing to express my interest in serving as a Paralegal at _____. I heard about the open position from _____, and (s)he suggested I contact you. I will be graduating (or graduated) in _____ with a Paralegal Certificate from _____.

As indicated on my enclosed resume, I was employed at _____ as _____. This experience increased my knowledge of the legal field, particularly in the area of _____.

In addition to my _____ knowledge, I will bring to my next employer strong leadership and organizational skills gained through the coursework at my Paralegal Program and my internship at _____.

I would be delighted to begin my career with _____. I will contact you the week of _____ to see if we can arrange a mutually convenient time to meet for an interview. If you would like to contact me, my contact information is _____.

I look forward to speaking with you.

Sincerely,

[Your Name]
Enclosure

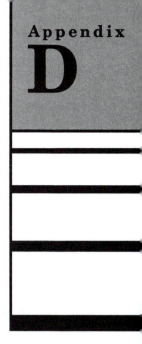

Appendix D

Sample Acceptance and Resignation Letters

Sample Job Acceptance Letter

Your Name
Your Street Address
Your City and State
Your Zip Code
Your Telephone Number

Date

Interviewer Name
Interviewer Title
Firm Name
Firm Street Address
Firm City and State

Dear Mr. [or Ms.] _____:

    I am very happy to accept the offer of family law paralegal with _____, with a starting date of July 1, _____. The position sounds interesting and challenging, and I look forward to being a part of the _____ legal team.

    As you requested, I am enclosing a copy of my signed and dated offer letter, which confirms the terms of my employment. Please feel free to contact me if you need additional information prior to my starting date. I look forward to a long and successful career with _____.

                                       Sincerely,

Encl.   Your Name

Resignation Letter Format

Your Contact Information
First Last Name
Address
City, State, Zip Code
Phone Number
Email Address

Date

Employer Contact Information
Name
Title
Organization
Address
City, State, Zip Code

Salutation
Dear Mr./Ms. Last Name,

First Paragraph
Your letter should say that you are resigning and state when your resignation is effective.

Middle Paragraph
The next (optional) section of your resignation letter should thank your employer for the opportunities you have had during your employment with the company.

Final Paragraph
Conclude your resignation letter (also optional) by offering to assist with the transition.

Close

Respectfully yours,

Signature

Handwritten Signature

Typed Signature

Letter of Resignation Sample

Your Name
Your Address
Your City, State, Zip Code
Your Phone Number
Your Email

Date

Name
Title
Organization
Address
City, State, Zip Code

Dear Mr./Ms. Last Name:

Please accept this letter as formal notification that I am leaving my position as _____ (title) on _____(date).

Thank you for the opportunities you have provided me during my time with the company.

If I can be of any assistance during this transition, please let me know.

Sincerely,

Your Signature

Your Typed Name

Sample Thank You Letters

Interview Thank You Letter: Basic

Your Name
Your Street Address
Your City and State
Your Zip Code
Your Telephone Number

Date

Interviewer Name
Interviewer Title
Firm Name
Firm Street Address
Firm City and State

Dear Mr. [or Ms.] _____:

    Thank you for meeting with me last Friday to discuss the position for a securities paralegal at _____. I enjoyed seeing the firm and meeting you. After meeting with you, I am confident that my education and experience fit the firm's needs. In addition to my qualifications, I will bring excellent work habits and communications skills to the position.

    Thank you again for the opportunity to meet with you. I look forward to hearing from you. Please contact me if you have any questions or comments.

Sincerely,

Job Hunter

Interview Thank You Letter:
Clarification

Your Name
Your Street Address
Your City and State
Your Zip Code
Your Telephone Number

Date

Interviewer Name
Interviewer Title
Firm Name
Firm Street Address
Firm City and State

Dear Mr. [or Ms.] _____:

    I appreciated the opportunity to meet with you last Wednesday to discuss the trusts and estates paralegal position at _____. I especially enjoyed touring your offices and meeting with _____.

    In addition to the information I shared with you during our meeting, I thought of an additional project I worked on during my internship [or previous job] that demonstrates the type of trusts and estates work I have performed. I am enclosing a copy of my work on that project.

    Please feel free to call me if you have any follow-up questions, and, again, thank you for taking the time to meet with me. I look forward to hearing from you.

Sincerely,

Job Hunter

Encl.

Interview Thank You Letter: Additional Information

Your Name
Your Street Address
Your City and State
Your Zip Code
Your Telephone Number

Date

Interviewer Name
Interviewer Title
Firm Name
Firm Street Address
Firm City and State

Dear Mr. [or Ms.] _____:

Thank you for the time you spent meeting with me on Monday regarding the entry-level paralegal position at _____. I am very excited about the position and am confident that my experience and education have prepared me for the job.

I neglected to mention during the interview that I have experience with a variety of software packages used in law firms, including Power-Point, Microsoft Excel, and TimeSlips. I am enclosing an additional copy of my resume, which reflects my experience with these software packages.

Please feel free to contact me if you have any questions or comments. I look forward to hearing from you. Thank you again for meeting with me.

Sincerely,

Job Hunter

Encl.

Interview Thank You Letter:
No Prior Experience

Your Name
Your Street Address
Your City and State
Your Zip Code
Your Telephone Number

Date

Interviewer Name
Interviewer Title
Firm Name
Firm Street Address
Firm City and State

Dear Mr. [or Ms.] _____:

     I enjoyed meeting with you last Tuesday when I interviewed for the corporate paralegal position with _____. I know that you expressed some concern that I have never performed corporate work before, and I wanted to stress that although I am new to the paralegal field, I have excellent organization and communications skills and have a solid academic record in corporate and business law. I am confident that I could hit the ground running at _____ and quickly become a valued member of the corporate legal team.

     I am enclosing some additional writing samples to demonstrate my written communications skills.

     Thank you again for providing me with an opportunity to meet with you and learn about _____. Please feel free to contact me if you have any questions or comments or if I can provide you with any additional information.

Sincerely,

Job Hunter

Encl.

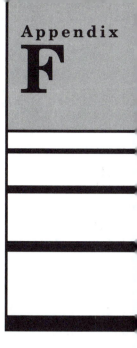

Paralegal Associations

There are many paralegal associations throughout the country. Some are national in scope (for example, the National Association of Legal Assistants (NALA) and the National Federation of Paralegal Associations (NFPA)), while others are regional (for example, the Rocky Mountain Paralegal Association covers Colorado, Nebraska, South Dakota, Utah, and Wyoming), others are statewide (such as the Delaware Paralegal Association), and still others are local (for example, the San Diego Paralegal Association). Many of the smaller associations have no physical address and maintain only a post office box or a Web site to communicate with their members. The contact person identified is often an active member of the association, whose telephone number or address may be subject to change. The following is a list of many paralegal associations, together with an identification of their affiliation with NALA or NFPA (remember that not all paralegal associations elect to affiliate with NALA or NFPA). If the address or telephone number for an association is invalid, try linking directly to its Web site using the Web address given below.

Web Links

A number of Web sites provide direct links to national, state, and local paralegal associations, including the following

www.nala.org/links.htm#afflinks	NALA provides direct links to its affiliated associations
www.paralegals.org/displaycommon. cfm?an=1&subarticlenbr=488	NFPA provides direct links to its member associations

http://www.legalassistanttoday.com/
assoc_links.htm

Legal Assistant Today offers links to national, state, and local paralegal associations

http://www.paralegalgateway.com/
associations.html

ParalegalGateway.com, a general Web site for paralegals, provides direct links to paralegal associations

National Organizations

American Alliance of Paralegals, Inc.
16815 East Shea Boulevard, Suite 110
PBM #101
Fountain Hills, AZ 85268
http://www.aapipara.org/

American Association for Paralegal Education
19 Mantua Road
Mt. Royal, NJ 08061
(856) 423-2829
www.aafpe.org

American Association of Legal Nurse Consultants
401 N. Michigan Avenue
Chicago, IL 60611
(877) 402-2562
www.aalnc.org

**American Corporate Legal Assistants Association,
Houston Chapter**
P.O. Box 941535
Houston, TX 77094
www.aclaa.net

Association of Legal Administrators
75 Tri-State International, Suite 222
Lincolnshire, IL 60069-4435
(847) 267-1252
http://www.alanet.org/home.html

International Paralegal Management Association
P.O. Box 659
Avondale Estates, GA 30002-0659
(404) 292-2976
www.paralegalmanagement.org

NALS
8159 East 41st Street
Tulsa, OK 74145
(918) 582-5188
www.nals.org

National Association of Legal Assistants
1516 S. Boston, Suite 200
Tulsa, OK 74119
(918) 587-6828
www.nala.org

National Federation of Paralegal Associations
P.O. Box 2016
Edmonds, WA 98020
(425) 967-0045
www.paralegals.org

National Paralegal Association
Box 406
Solebury, PA 18963
(215) 297-8333
www.nationalparalegal.org

State and Local Associations

Alabama

Alabama Association of Paralegals, Inc. (formerly known as Alabama
   Association of Legal Assistants) (NALA)
P.O. Box 55921
Birmingham, AL 35255-5921
www.aala.net

Gulf Coast Paralegal Association (NFPA)
P.O. Box 66706
Mobile, AL 36660
http://groups.msn.com/gcpa/_homepage.msnw?pgmarket = en-us

Alaska

Alaska Association of Paralegals (NFPA)
P.O. Box 101956
Anchorage, AK 99510-1956
(907) 646-8018
www.alaskaparalegals.org/main.htm

Arizona

Arizona Paralegal Association (NALA)
P.O. Box 392
Phoenix, AZ 85001
www.azparalegal.org

Legal Assistants of Metropolitan Phoenix (NALA)
P.O. Box 13005
Phoenix, AZ 85002
www.geocities.com/azlamp/

Tucson Association of Legal Assistants (NALA)
P.O. Box 257
Tucson, AZ 85702
http://www.azstarnet.com/nonprofit/tala/index.html

Maricopa County Bar Association, Paralegal Division
(662) 262-0888
www.maricoaparalegals.org

Arkansas

Arkansas Association of Legal Assistants (NALA)
400 W. Capitol Avenue, Suite 2700
Little Rock, AR 72201
(501) 372-6175

California

California Alliance of Paralegal Associations
P.O. Box 1089
San Leandro, CA 94577-0126
www.caparalegal.org

California Association of Legal Document Assistants
www.calda.org

Inland Counties Association of Paralegals (NALA)
P.O. Box 143
Riverside, CA 92502-0143
www.icaparalegal.org/

Los Angeles Paralegal Association (NALA)
P.O. Box 71708
Los Angeles, CA 90071
(310) 921-3097
www.lapa.org

Orange County Paralegal Association (NALA)
P.O. Box 8512
Newport Beach, CA 92658
(714) 744-7747
www.ocparalegal.org

Paralegal Association of Santa Clara County (NALA)
P.O. Box 26736
San Jose, CA 95159-6736
(408) 235-0301
www.sccparalegal.org

Sacramento Valley Paralegal Association (NFPA)
P.O. Box 453
Sacramento, CA 95812-8317
(916) 286-8317
www.svpa.org

San Diego Paralegal Association (NFPA)
P.O. Box 87449
San Diego, CA 92138-3488
www.sdparalegals.org

San Francisco Paralegal Association (NFPA)
P.O. Box 2110
San Francisco, CA 91426-2110
(415) 777-2390
www.sfpa.org

San Joaquin Association of Legal Assistants (NALA)
P.O. Box 28515
Fresno, CA 93729-8515
www.fresnoparalegal.org

Santa Barbara Paralegal Association (NALA)
1224 Coast Village Circle
Suite 32
Santa Barbara, CA 93108
www.sbparalegals.org

Sequoia Paralegal Association
P.O. Box 3884
Visalia, CA 93278-3884
(559) 737-4422
www.sequoiaparalegals.org

Ventura County Association of Legal Assistants (NALA)
P.O. Box 24229
Ventura, CA 93002
www.vcparalegal.org

Colorado

Colorado Association of Professional Paralegals and Legal Assistants (NALA)
www.cappla.org

Rocky Mountain Paralegal Association (serving Colorado, Nebraska, Utah, and Wyoming) (NFPA)
P.O. Box 481864
Denver, CO 80248-1864
(303) 370-9444
www.rockymtnparalegal.org

Connecticut

Central Connecticut Paralegal Association, Inc. (NFPA)
P.O. Box 230594
Hartford, CT 06123-0594
www.paralegals.org/associations/2270/files/home154.html

Connecticut Association of Paralegals, Inc. (NFPA)
P.O. Box 134
Bridgeport, CT 06601-0134
(203) 382-8471
www.paralegals.org/associations/2270/files/home159.html

New Haven County Association of Paralegals, Inc. (NFPA)
P.O. Box 862
New Haven, CT 06504-0862
www.paralegals.org/associations/2270/files/home167.html

Delaware

Delaware Paralegal Association
P.O. Box 1362
Wilmington, DE 19899-1362
(302) 426-1362
www.deparalegals.org

District of Columbia

National Capital Area Paralegal Association (NFPA)
P.O. Box 27607
Washington, DC 20038-7607
www.ncapa.com

Florida

Central Florida Paralegal Association, Inc. (NALA)
P.O. Box 1107
Orlando, FL 32802
(407) 672-6372
www.cfpainc.com/pages/718816/index.htm

Gainesville Association of Paralegals, Inc.
P.O. Box 2519
Gainesville, FL 32602
(904) 462-2249
www.afn.org/~gala/

Northeast Florida Paralegal Association, Inc. (NALA)
221 North Hogan Street
Box 164

Jacksonville, FL 32202
www.nefpa.org

Northwest Florida Paralegal Association (NALA)
P.O. Box 1333
Pensacola, FL 32502
www.nwfpa.com

Paralegal Association of Florida, Inc. (NALA)
P.O. Box 7073
West Palm Beach, FL 33403
(800) 433-4352
www.pafinc.org

South Florida Paralegal Association (NALA)
P.O. Box 31-0745
Miami, FL 33231-0745
(305) 944-0204
www.sfpa.info

Southwest Florida Paralegal Association, Inc. (NALA)
P.O. Box 2094
Sarasota, FL 34230-2094
www.swfloridaparalegals.com/

Tampa Bay Paralegal Association, Inc. (NFPA)
P.O. Box 2840
Tampa, FL 33601
www.tbpa.org

Volusia Association of Paralegals (NALA)
P.O. Box 15075
Daytona Beach, FL 32115-5075
www.volusiaparalegals.com/

Georgia

Georgia Association of Paralegals, Inc. (NFPA)
1199 Euclid Avenue, N.E.
Atlanta, GA 30307
(404) 522-1457
www.gaparalegal.org

Southeastern Association of Legal Assistants (NALA)
www.seala.org/index2.html

Hawaii

Hawaii Paralegal Association (NFPA)
P.O. Box 674
Honolulu, HI 96809
www.hawaiiparalegal.org

Idaho

Idaho Association of Paralegals
P.O. Box 1254
Boise, ID 83701
www.idahoparalegals.org

Illinois

Central Illinois Paralegal Association (NALA)
P.O. Box 1948
Bloomington, IL 61702
www.hometown.aol.com/cipainfo/myhomepage/club.html

Illinois Paralegal Association (NFPA)
P.O. Box 452
New Lenox, IL 60451-0452
(815) 462-4620
www.ipaonline.org

Indiana

Indiana Paralegal Association, Inc. (NFPA)
P.O. Box 44518
Indianapolis, IN 46204
www.indianaparalegals.org

Michiana Paralegal Association, Inc. (NFPA)
P.O. Box 11458
South Bend, IN 46634
www.paralegals.org/associations/2270/files/home165.html

Northeast Indiana Paralegal Association, Inc. (NFPA)
P.O. Box 13646
Fort Wayne, IN 46865
www.paralegals.org/associations/2270/files/home169.html

Iowa

Iowa Association of Legal Assistants (NALA)
P.O. Box 93153
Des Moines, IA 50393
www.ialanet.org

Kansas

Heartland Association of Legal Assistants (NALA)
P.O. Box 12413
Overland Park, KS 66282-2413

(913) 477-7625
www.accesskansas.org/hala

Kansas Association of Legal Assistants (NALA)
P.O. Box 47031
Wichita, KS 67201
www.accesskansas.org/kala

Kansas Paralegal Association (NFPA)
P.O. Box 1675
Topeka, KS 66601
www.accesskansas.org/ksparalegals/

Kentucky

Kentucky Paralegal Association
P.O. Box 2675
Louisville, KY 40201-2675
www.kypa.org

Greater Lexington Paralegal Association, Inc. (NFPA)
P.O. Box 574
Lexington, KY 40589
www.paralegals.org/associations/2270/files/contactus.htm

Louisville Association of Paralegals
www.loupara.org

Louisiana

New Orleans Paralegal Association (NFPA)
P.O. Box 30604
New Orleans, LA 70190
(504) 467-3136
www.paralegals.org/associations/2270/files/home206.html

Louisiana State Paralegal Association, Inc. (NALA)
www.la-paralegals.org

Maryland

Maryland Association of Paralegals, Inc. (NFPA)
550 M. Ritchie Highway
PMB #203
Severna Park, MD 21146
(410) 576-2252
www.paralegals.org/associations/2270/files/home202.htm

Massachusetts

Massachusetts Paralegal Association, Inc. (NFPA)
P.O. Box 1381
Marblehead, MA 01945
(800) 637-4311
www.passparalegal.org

Central Massachusetts Paralegal Association (NFPA)
Centralmassachusetts@paralegals.org

Western Massachusetts Paralegal Association, Inc. (NFPA)
P.O. Box 30005
Springfield, MA 01103
www.paralegals.org/associations/2270/files/home200.html

Michigan

Grand Rapids Bar Association — Legal Assistant Section
535 Fountain Street, N.E.
Grand Rapids, MI 49503
(616) 458-9400
www.firms.findlaw.com/grbala/

Legal Assistants Association of Michigan (NALA)
P.O. Box 80125
Lansing, MI 48908-0125
www.laamnet.org

State Bar of Michigan Legal Assistants Section
www.michbar.org/legalassist

Minnesota

Minnesota Paralegal Association (NFPA)
1711 W. County Road B, #300N
Roseville, MN 55113
(651) 633-2778
www.mnparalegals.org

Mississippi

Mississippi Association of Legal Assistants, Inc. (NALA)
P.O. Box 966
Jackson, MS 39205
www.mslawyer.com/mala

Missouri

Kansas City Paralegal Association (NFPA)
1912 Clay Street
N. Kansas City, MO 64116
(816) 421-0302
www.paralegals.org/associations/2270/files/home207.html

Missouri Paralegal Association
P.O. Box 1016
Jefferson City, MO 65102-1016
www.missouriparalegalassoc.org

St. Louis Association of Legal Assistants (NALA)
P.O. Box 69218
St. Louis, MO 63169-0218
www.slala.org

Montana

Montana Association of Legal Assistants (NALA)
P.O. Box 9016
Missoula, MT 59807-9016
www.malanet.org

Nebraska

Nebraska Association of Legal Assistants (NALA)
P.O. Box 24943
Omaha, NE 68124
www.neala.org

Rocky Mountain Paralegal Association (serving Colorado, Nebraska,
  South Dakota, Utah, and Wyoming) (NFPA)
P.O. Box 481864
Denver, CO 80248-1864
(303) 370-9444
www.rockymtnparalegal.org

Nevada

Paralegal Association of Southern Nevada (NFPA)
P.O. Box 1752
Las Vegas, NV 89125
www.nvparalegal.net

New Hampshire

Paralegal Association of New Hampshire (NALA)
P.O. Box 728
Manchester, NH 03105-0728
www.panh.org/

New Jersey

Legal Assistants Association of New Jersey (NALA)
P.O. Box 142
Caldwell, NJ 07006
www.laanj.org/pages/1/index.htm

South Jersey Paralegal Association (NFPA)
P.O. Box 355
Haddonfield, NJ 08033
www.paralegals.org/associations/2270/files/home203.html

New Mexico

State Bar of New Mexico Paralegal Division
http://www.nmbar.org/Template.cfm?Section = Paralegals_Legal_Assistants

New York

Capital District Paralegal Association, Inc. (NFPA)
P.O. Box 12562
Albany, NY 12212-2562
www.cdpa.info

Empire State Alliance of Paralegal Associations
http://www.timesunion.com/communities/cdpa/

Long Island Paralegal Association (NFPA)
LongIsland@paralegals.org

Manhattan Paralegal Association, Inc. (NFPA)
P.O. Box 4006
Grand Central Station
New York, NY 10163
(212) 330-8213
www.paralegals.org/associations/2270/files/home162.html

Paralegal Association of Rochester, Inc. (NFPA)
Attn: Membership Committee
P.O. Box. 40567
Rochester, NY 14604
(585) 234-5923
http://par.itgo.com/index.html

Western New York Paralegal Association (NFPA)
P.O. Box 207
Niagara Square Station
Buffalo, NY 14201
(716) 635-8250
www.wnyparalegals.org

North Carolina

Metrolina Paralegal Association (NALA)
P.O. Box 26260
Charlotte, NC 28236
www.charlotteareaparalegals.com/

North Carolina Paralegal Association (NALA)
P.O. Box 36264
Charlotte, NC 28236-6264
(800) 479-1905
www.ncparalegal.org

North Dakota

Red River Valley Paralegal Association (NALA)
P.O. Box 1954
Fargo, ND 58107
www.rrvpa.org

Western Dakota Association of Legal Assistants (NALA)
www.wdala.org

Ohio

Cincinnati Paralegal Association (NFPA)
P.O. Box 1515
Cincinnati, OH 45201
(513) 244-4122
www.cincinnatiparalegals.org/index.htm

Cleveland Association of Paralegals, Inc. (NFPA)
P.O. Box 14517
Cleveland, OH 44114-0517
(216) 556-5437
www.capohio.org

Greater Dayton Paralegal Association, Inc. (NFPA)
P.O. Box 515
Mid-City Station
Dayton, OH 45402
www.paralegals.org/associations/2270/files/home188.html

Paralegal Association of Central Ohio (NFPA)
P.O. Box 15182
Columbus, OH 43125-0182
(614) 224-9700
www.pacoparalegals.org

Toledo Association of Legal Assistants (NALA)
P.O. Box 1322
Toledo, OH 43603-1322
www.tala.org

Oklahoma

Oklahoma Paralegal Association (NALA)
714 Maple Drive
Weatherford, OK 73096
www.okparalegal.org

Tulsa Association of Legal Assistants (NALA)
P.O. Box 1484
Tulsa, OK 74101-1484
www.tulsatala.org/

Oregon

Oregon Paralegal Association (NFPA)
P.O. Box 8523
Portland, OR 97207
(503) 796-1671
www.oregonparalegals.org

Pennsylvania

Central Pennsylvania Paralegal Association (NFPA)
P.O. Box 11814
Harrisburg, PA 17108
www.paralegals.org/associations/2270/files/home158.html

Lycoming County Paralegal Association (NFPA)
Lycoming@paralegals.org

Montgomery County Paralegal Association (NFPA)
P.O. Box 1765
Blue Bell, PA 19422
www.paralegals.org/associations/2270/files/home215.html

Philadelphia Association of Paralegals (NFPA)
P.O. Box 59179
Philadelphia, PA 19102-9179

(215) 255-8405
www.philaparalegals.com

Pittsburgh Paralegal Association (NFPA)
P.O. Box 2845
Pittsburgh, PA 15230
(412) 344-3904
www.pghparalegals.org

Chester County Paralegal Association
P.O. Box 295
West Chester, PA 19831-0295
www.chescoparalegal.org/

Rhode Island

Rhode Island Paralegals Association (NFPA)
P.O. Box 1003
Providence, RI 02901
www.paralegals.org/associations/2270/files/home149.html

South Carolina

Charleston Association of Legal Assistants, Inc.
215 East Bay Street, Suite 404
Charleston, SC 29401
(843) 534-2628

Grand Strand Paralegal Association, Inc.
743 Hemlock Ave.
Myrtle Beach, SC 29577

Greenville Association of Legal Assistants, Inc.
PO Box 16135
Greenville, SC 29606
(864) 233-6224

Palmetto Paralegal Association (NFPA)
P.O. Box 11634
Columbia, SC 29211-1634
(803) 252-0460
www.paralegals.org/associations/2270/files/home210.html

Tri County Paralegal Association, Inc. (NALA)
PO Box 449
Charleston, SC 29402
(843) 722-6319

South Dakota

Rocky Mountain Paralegal Association (serving Colorado,
   Nebraska, South Dakota, Utah, and Wyoming) (NFPA)
P.O. Box 481864
Denver, CO 80248-1864
(303) 370-9444
www.rockymtnparalegal.org

South Dakota Paralegal Association, Inc. (NALA)
27328 Adrianna's Place
Tea, SD 57064
www.sdparalegals.com

Tennessee

Greater Memphis Paralegal Alliance, Inc. (NALA)
P.O. Box 3846
Memphis, TN 38173
(901) 527-6254
www.memphisparalegals.org/

Memphis Paralegal Association (NFPA)
P.O. Box 3646
Memphis, TN 38173-0646
www.paralegals.org/associations/2270/files/home189.html

Middle Tennessee Paralegal Association (NFPA)
P.O. Box 198006
Nashville, TN 37219
www.mtpaonline.com

Tennessee Paralegal Association (NALA)
3295 Highway 45 South
Jackson, TN 30301
(800) 727-0622
http://firms.findlaw.com/TPA/

Texas

Alamo Area Professional Legal Assistants, Inc.
P.O. Box 524
San Antonio, TX 78292
(210) 231-5791
www.aapla.org

Capital Area Paralegal Association (NALA)
P.O. Box 773
Austin, TX 78767
www.capatx.org

Dallas Area Paralegal Association (NFPA)
P.O. Box 12533
Dallas, TX 75225
(214) 991-0853
www.dallasparalegals.org

El Paso Paralegal Association (NALA)
P.O. Box 6
El Paso, TX 79940
www.elppa.org

Ft. Worth Paralegal Association
P.O. Box 17021
Ft. Worth, TX 76102
www.fwpa.org/default.asp

Houston Legal Assistants Association
Lyric Centre
440 Louisiana
Houston, TX 77002
(713) 236-7724
www.hlaa.net/index.html

Houston Paralegal Association
P.O. Box 6183
Houston, TX 77208-1863
www.houstonparalegalassociation.org/

Metroplex Association of Corporate Paralegals
P.O. Box 201592
Arlington, TX 76006
www.macp.net/default.asp

South Texas Organization of Paralegals, Inc. (NALA)
P.O. Box 2486
San Antonio, TX 78299-2486
(210) 554-9135
www.southtexasparalegals.org/index.html

Southeast Texas Association of Legal Assistants (NALA)
P.O. Box 813
Beaumont, TX 77704
www.setala.org

State Bar of Texas — Legal Assistants Division
Texas State Bar
P.O. Box 12487
Austin, TX 78711
(800) 204-2222
www.lad.org

Utah

Legal Assistants Association of Utah (NALA)
P.O. Box 112001
Salt Lake City, UT 84147-2001
www.laau.info

Rocky Mountain Paralegal Association (serving Colorado, Nebraska,
    South Dakota, Utah, and Wyoming) (NFPA)
P.O. Box 481864
Denver, CO 80248-1864
(303) 370-9444
www.rockymtnparalegal.org

Vermont

Vermont Paralegal Organization (NFPA)
P.O. Box 5755
Burlington, VT 05402
www.paralegals.org/associations/2270/files/home204.html

Virginia

Richmond Paralegal Association (NALA)
P.O. Box 384
Richmond, VA 23218-0384
www.ralanet.org

Roanoke Valley Paralegal Association (NALA)
P.O. Box 1505
Roanoke, VA 24007
www.rvpa.org

Washington

Washington State Paralegal Association (NFPA)
P.O. Box 58530
Seattle, WA 98138-1530
(866) 257-9772
www.wspaonline.com

West Virginia

Association of West Virginia Paralegals, Inc. (NALA)
www.lawv.org

Wisconsin

Madison Area Paralegal Association (NALA)
P.O. Box 2242
Madison, WI 53701-2242
www.madisonparalegal.org

Paralegal Association of Wisconsin, Inc.
P.O. Box 510892
Milwaukee, WI 53203-0151
(414) 272-7168
www.wisconsinparalegal.org

Wyoming

Legal Assistants of Wyoming (NALA)
P.O. Box 155
Caspar, WY 82602-0155
www.lawyo.com

Rocky Mountain Paralegal Association (serving Colorado, Nebraska, South Dakota, Utah, and Wyoming) (NFPA)
P.O. Box 481864
Denver, CO 80248-1864
(303) 370-9444
www.rockymtnparalegal.org

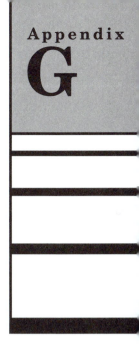

State and National Bar Associations

A number of Web sites provide direct links to state, national, and local bar associations, including the following:

www.abanet.org/barserv/stlobar.html
Links to state and local bar associations provided by ABA

www.palidan.com/statebar.htm
Links to state and local bar associations provided by Palidan Legal Resources

www.hg.org/northam-bar.htm
Web site of HG, general legal site, provides links to national, state, and local bar associations

www.findlaw.com/06associations/state.html
FindLaw, a general legal site, provides links to state and local bar associations

www.megalaw.com/orgs/orgs.php
MegaLaw, a general legal site, provides links to national, international, state, and local bar associations

Some National Bar Associations

American Association of Corporate Counsel
1025 Connecticut Avenue, N.W., Suite 200
Washington, DC 20036-5425
(202) 293-4103
www.acca.org

American Bar Association
321 N. Clark Street
Chicago, IL 60610
(312) 988-5000
www.abanet.org

Association of Trial Lawyers of America
1050 31st Street, N.W.
Washington, DC 20007
(800) 424-2725
www.atla.org

Federal Bar Association
2215 M Street, N.W.
Washington, DC 20037
(202) 785-1614
www.fedbar.org

National Bar Association
1225 11th Street, N.W.
Washington, DC 10001
(202) 842-3900
www.nationalbar.org

National Association for Public Interest Law
Equal Justice Works
2120 L Street, N.W., Suite 450
Washington, DC 20037-1541
(202) 466-3686
www.napil.org

National Association of Criminal Defense Lawyers
1150 18th Street, N.W.
Washington, DC 20036
(202) 872-8600
www.nacdl.org

National Lawyers Association
17201 E. 40 Highway, Suite 207
Independence, MO 64055
(800) 471-2994
www.nla.org

State Bar Associations

Alabama State Bar Association
415 Dexter Avenue
P.O. Box 671
Montgomery, AL 36101
(334) 269-1515
www.alaba.org

Alaska Bar Association
P.O. Box 100279
Anchorage, AK 99501
(907) 272-7469
www.alaskabar.org

Arizona State Bar Association
111 W. Monroe, Suite 1800
Phoenix, AZ 85003-1742
(866) 48- AZBAR (866-482-9227)
www.azbar.org

Arkansas Bar Association
400 West Markham
Little Rock, AR 78201
(800) 609-5668
www.arkbar.com

State Bar of California
180 Howard Street
San Francisco, CA 94105
(415) 538-2000
www.calbar.org

Colorado Bar Association
1900 Grant Street, Suite 900
Denver, CO 80203
(303) 860-1115
www.cobar.org

Connecticut Bar Association
30 Bank Street
P.O. Box 350
New Britain, CT 06050-0350
(860) 223-4400

Delaware State Bar Association
301 N. Market Street
Wilmington, DE 19801
(302) 658-5279
www.dsba.org

District of Columbia Bar Association
1250 H Street, N.W., Sixth Floor
Washington, DC 20005-5937
(202) 737-4700

The Florida Bar
651 E. Jefferson Street
Tallahassee, FL 32399-2300
(85) 561-5600
www.flabar.org

State Bar of Georgia
104 Marietta Street, N.W., Suite 100
Atlanta, GA 30303
(404) 527-8700
www.gabar.org

Hawaii State Bar Association
1132 Bishop Street, Suite 906
Honolulu, HI 96813
(808) 537-1868
www.hsba.org

Idaho State Bar and Idaho Law Foundation, Inc.
P.O. Box 895
Boise, ID 83701
(208) 334-4500
www2.state.id.us/isb/index.htm

Illinois State Bar Association
424 S. Second Street
Springfield, IL 62701
(800) 252-8908
www.illinoisbar.org

Indiana State Bar Association
230 East Ohio Street, Fourth Floor
Indianapolis, IN 46204-2199
(317) 639-5465
www.inbar.org

Iowa State Bar Association
521 East Locust
Des Moines, IA 50309-1939
(515) 243-3170
www.iowabar.org

Kansas Bar Association
1200 S.W. Harrison
Topeka, KS 66612-1806
(785) 234-5696
www.ksbar.org

Kentucky State Bar
514 W. Main Street
Frankfort, KY 40601-1883
(502) 564-3795
www.kybar.org

Louisiana State Bar
601 St. Charles Avenue
New Orleans, LA 70130-3404
(800) 421-5722
www.lsba.org

Maine State Bar Association
P.O. Box 788
Augusta, ME 04332-0788
(207) 622-7523
www.mainebar.org

Maryland State Bar Association
520 W. Fayette Street
Baltimore, MD 21201
(800) 492-1964
www.msba.org

Massachusetts Bar Association
20 West Street
Boston, MA 02111-1204
(617) 338-0500
www.massbar.org

State Bar of Michigan
306 Townsend Street
Lansing, MI 48933-2083
(800) 968-1442
www.michbar.org

Minnesota State Bar Association
600 Nicollet Mall, # 380
Minneapolis, MN 55402
(612) 333-1183
www.mnbar.org

The Mississippi Bar
P.O. Box 2168
Jackson, MS 39225-2168
(601) 948-4471
www.msbar.org

The Missouri Bar
P.O. Box 119
Jefferson City, MO 65102-0119
(573) 635-4128
www.mobar.org

State Bar of Montana
The Power Block
7 West 6th Avenue, Suite 2B
Helena, MT 59624
(406) 442-7660
www.montanabar.org

Nebraska State Bar Association
635 S. 14th Street
P.O. Box 81809
Lincoln, NE 68501
(800) 927-0117
www.nebar.org

Nevada State Bar
600 E. Charleston Boulevard
Las Vegas, NV 98104
(702) 382-2200
www.nvbar.org

New Hampshire Bar Association
112 Pleasant Street
Concord, NH 03301
(603) 224-6942
www.nhbar.org

New Jersey Bar Association
One Constitution Square
New Brunswick, NJ 08901-1520
(732) 249-5000
www.njsba.org

State Bar of New Mexico
P.O. Box 92860
Albuquerque, NM 87199-2860
(505) 797-6000
www.nmbar.org

New York Bar Association
1 Elk Street
Albany, NY 12207
(518) 463-3200
www.nysba.org

North Carolina Bar Association
P.O. Box 3688
Cary, NC 27519
(919) 677-0561
www.ncbar.org

State Bar Association of North Dakota
515 1/2 East Broadway, Suite 101
Bismarck, ND 58501
(701) 235-1404
www.sband.org

Ohio State Bar Association
1700 Lake Shore Drive
Columbus, OH 43204
(800) 282-6556
www.ohiobar.org

Oklahoma Bar Association
P.O. Box 53036
1901 N. Lincoln Avenue
Oklahoma City, OK 73152-3036
(405) 416-7000
www.okbar.org

Oregon State Bar
5200 SW Meadows Road
Lake Oswego, OR 97035-0889
(503) 620-0222
www.osbar.org

Pennsylvania Bar Association
100 South Street
P.O. Box 186
Harrisburg, PA 17105-0186
(717) 238-6715
www.pabar.org

Rhode Island State Bar
115 Cedar Street
Providence, RI 02903
(401) 421-5740
www.ribar.com

State Bar of South Carolina
950 Taylor Street
Columbia, SC 29202
(803) 799-6653
www.scbar.org

State Bar of South Dakota
222 East Capitol Avenue
Pierre, SD 57501
(800) 952-2333
www.sdbar.org

Tennessee Bar Association
221 Fourth Avenue North, Suite 400
Nashville, TN 37219
(615) 383-7421
www.tba.org

Texas State Bar Association
P.O. Box 12487
Austin, TX 78711
(800) 204-2222
www.texasbar.com

Utah State Bar
645 South 200 East
Salt Lake City, UT 84111
(801) 531-9077
www.utahbar.org

Vermont Bar Association
35-37 Court Street
P.O. Box 100
Montpelier, VT 05601-0100
(802) 223-2020
www.vtbar.org

Virginia State Bar
707 E. Main Street, Suite 1500
Richmond, VA 23219-2800
(804) 775-0500
www.vsb.org

Washington State Bar Association
2101 Fourth Avenue, Suite 400
Seattle, WA 98121-2330
(800) 945-9722
www.wsba.org

West Virginia State Bar
2006 Kanawha Boulevard East
Charleston, WV 25311-2204
(304) 558-2456
www.wvbar.org

State Bar of Wisconsin
5302 Eastpark Avenue
Madison, WI 53718-2101
(800) 728-7788
www.wisbar.org

Wyoming State Bar
500 Randall Avenue
P.O. Box 109
Cheyenne, WY 82003-0109
(307) 632-9061
www.wyomingbar.org

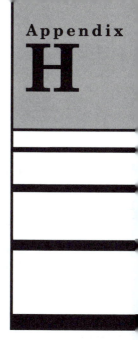
Paralegal Codes of Ethics

National Association of Legal Assistants (NALA) Code of Ethics and Professional Responsibility

Each NALA member agrees to follow the canons of the NALA Code of Ethics and Professional Responsibility. Violations of the Code may result in cancellation of membership. First adopted by the NALA membership in May of 1975, the Code of Ethics and Professional Responsibility is the foundation of ethical practices of paralegals in the legal community.

A paralegal must adhere strictly to the accepted standards of legal ethics and to the general principles of proper conduct. The performance of the duties of the paralegal shall be governed by specific canons as defined herein so that justice will be served and goals of the profession attained. (See Model Standards and Guidelines for Utilization of Legal Assistants, Section II.)

The canons of ethics set forth hereafter are adopted by the National Association of Legal Assistants, Inc., as a general guide intended to aid paralegals and attorneys. The enumeration of these rules does not mean there are not others of equal importance although not specifically mentioned. Court rules, agency rules and statutes must be taken into consideration when interpreting the canons.

Definition: Legal assistants, also known as paralegals, are a distinguishable group of persons who assist attorneys in the delivery of legal services. Through formal education, training and experience, legal assistants have knowledge and expertise regarding the legal system and substantive and procedural law which qualify them to do work of a legal nature under the supervision of an attorney.

In **2001**, NALA members also adopted the ABA definition of a legal assistant/paralegal, as follows:

A legal assistant or paralegal is a person qualified by education, training or work experience who is employed or retained by a lawyer, law office, corporation, governmental agency or other entity who performs specifically delegated substantive legal work for which a lawyer is responsible. (Adopted by the ABA in 1997.)

Canon 1.

A paralegal must not perform any of the duties that attorneys only may perform nor take any actions that attorneys may not take.

Canon 2.

A paralegal may perform any task which is properly delegated and supervised by an attorney, as long as the attorney is ultimately responsible to the client, maintains a direct relationship with the client, and assumes professional responsibility for the work product.

Canon 3.

A paralegal must not: (a) engage in, encourage, or contribute to any act which could constitute the unauthorized practice of law; and (b) establish attorney-client relationships, set fees, give legal opinions or advice or represent a client before a court or agency unless so authorized by that court or agency; and (c) engage in conduct or take any action which would assist or involve the attorney in a violation of professional ethics or give the appearance of professional impropriety.

Canon 4.

A paralegal must use discretion and professional judgment commensurate with knowledge and experience but must not render independent legal judgment in place of an attorney. The services of an attorney are essential in the public interest whenever such legal judgment is required.

Canon 5.

A paralegal must disclose his or her status as a paralegal at the outset of any professional relationship with a client, attorney, a court or administrative agency or personnel thereof, or a member of the general public. A paralegal must act prudently in determining the extent to which a client may be assisted without the presence of an attorney.

Canon 6.

A paralegal must strive to maintain integrity and a high degree of competency through education and training with respect to professional responsibility, local rules and practice, and through continuing education in substantive areas of law to better assist the legal profession in fulfilling its duty to provide legal service.

Canon 7.

A paralegal must protect the confidences of a client and must not violate any rule or statute now in effect or hereafter enacted controlling the doctrine of privileged communications between a client and an attorney.

Canon 8.

A paralegal must disclose to his or her employer or prospective employer any pre-existing client or personal relationship that may conflict with the interests of the employer or prospective employer and/or their clients.

Canon 9.

A paralegal must do all other things incidental, necessary, or expedient for the attainment of the ethics and responsibilities as defined by statute or rule of court.

Canon 10.

A paralegal's conduct is guided by bar associations' codes of professional responsibility and rules of professional conduct.

National Federation of Paralegal Associations (NFPA) Model Code of Ethics and Professional Responsibility and Guidelines for Enforcement

Preamble

The National Federation of Paralegal Associations, Inc. ("NFPA") is a professional organization comprised of paralegal associations and individual paralegals throughout the United States and Canada. Members of NFPA have varying backgrounds, experiences, education and job responsibilities that reflect the diversity of the paralegal profession. NFPA promotes the growth, development and recognition of the paralegal profession as an integral partner in the delivery of legal services.

In May 1993 NFPA adopted its Model Code of Ethics and Professional Responsibility ("Model Code") to delineate the principles for ethics and conduct to which every paralegal should aspire.

Many paralegal associations throughout the United States have endorsed the concept and content of NFPA's Model Code through the adoption of their own ethical codes. In doing so, paralegals have confirmed the profession's commitment to increase the quality and efficiency of legal services, as well as recognized its responsibilities to the public, the legal community, and colleagues.

Paralegals have recognized, and will continue to recognize, that the profession must continue to evolve to enhance their roles in the delivery of legal services. With increased levels of responsibility comes the need to define and enforce mandatory rules of professional conduct. Enforcement of codes of paralegal conduct is a logical and necessary step to enhance and ensure the confidence of the legal community and the public in the integrity and professional responsibility of paralegals.

In April 1997 NFPA adopted the Model Disciplinary Rules ("Model Rules") to make possible the enforcement of the Canons and Ethical Considerations contained in the NFPA Model Code. A concurrent determination was made that the Model Code of Ethics and Professional Responsibility, formerly aspirational in nature, should be recognized as setting forth the enforceable obligations of all paralegals.

The Model Code and Model Rules offer a framework for professional discipline, either voluntarily or through formal regulatory programs.

§1. NFPA MODEL DISCIPLINARY RULES AND ETHICAL CONSIDERATIONS

1.1 A PARALEGAL SHALL ACHIEVE AND MAINTAIN A HIGH LEVEL OF COMPETENCE.

Ethical Considerations

EC-1.1(a)   A paralegal shall achieve competency through education, training, and work experience.

EC-1.1(b)   A paralegal shall aspire to participate in a minimum of twelve (12) hours of continuing legal education, to include at least one (1) hour of ethics education, every two (2) years in order to remain current on developments in the law.

EC-1.1(c)   A paralegal shall perform all assignments promptly and efficiently.

1.2 A PARALEGAL SHALL MAINTAIN A HIGH LEVEL OF PERSONAL AND PROFESSIONAL INTEGRITY.

Ethical Considerations

EC-1.2(a)   A paralegal shall not engage in any ex parte communications involving the courts or any other adjudicatory body in an attempt to exert undue influence or to obtain advantage or the benefit of only one party.

EC-1.2(b)   A paralegal shall not communicate, or cause another to communicate, with a party the paralegal knows to be represented by a lawyer in a pending matter without the prior consent of the lawyer representing such other party.

EC-1.2(c)   A paralegal shall ensure that all timekeeping and billing records prepared by the paralegal are thorough, accurate, honest, and complete.

EC-1.2(d)   A paralegal shall not knowingly engage in fraudulent billing practices. Such practices may include, but are not limited to: inflation of hours billed to a client or employer; misrepresentation of the nature of tasks performed; and/or submission of fraudulent expense and disbursement documentation.

EC-1.2(e)   A paralegal shall be scrupulous, thorough and honest in the identification and maintenance of all funds, securities, and other assets of a client and shall provide accurate accounting as appropriate.

EC-1.2(f)   A paralegal shall advise the proper authority of non-confidential knowledge of any dishonest or fraudulent acts by any person pertaining to the handling of the funds, securities or other assets of a client. The authority to whom the report is made shall depend on the nature and circumstances of the possible misconduct, (e.g., ethics committees of law firms, corporations and/or paralegal associations, local or state bar associations, local prosecutors, administrative agencies, etc.). Failure to report such knowledge is in itself misconduct and shall be treated as such under these rules.

1.3   A PARALEGAL SHALL MAINTAIN A HIGH STANDARD OF PROFESSIONAL CONDUCT.

Ethical Considerations

EC-1.3(a)   A paralegal shall refrain from engaging in any conduct that offends the dignity and decorum of proceedings before a court or other adjudicatory body and shall be respectful of all rules and procedures.

EC-1.3(b)   A paralegal shall avoid impropriety and the appearance of impropriety and shall not engage in any conduct that would adversely affect his/her fitness to practice. Such conduct may include, but is not limited to: violence, dishonesty, interference with the administration of justice, and/or abuse of a professional position or public office.

EC-1.3(c)   Should a paralegal's fitness to practice be compromised by physical or mental illness, causing that paralegal to commit an act that is in direct violation of the Model Code/Model Rules and/or the rules and/or laws governing the jurisdiction in which the paralegal practices, that paralegal may be protected from sanction upon review of the nature and circumstances of that illness.

EC-1.3(d)   A paralegal shall advise the proper authority of non-confidential knowledge of any action of another legal professional that clearly demonstrates fraud, deceit, dishonesty, or misrepresentation. The authority to whom the report is made shall depend on the nature and circumstances of the possible misconduct, (e.g., ethics committees of law firms, corporations and/or paralegal associations, local or state bar associations, local prosecutors, administrative agencies, etc.). Failure to report such knowledge is in itself misconduct and shall be treated as such under these rules.

EC-1.3(e)   A paralegal shall not knowingly assist any individual with the commission of an act that is in direct violation of the Model Code/Model Rules and/or the rules and/or laws governing the jurisdiction in which the paralegal practices.

EC-1.3(f)   If a paralegal possesses knowledge of future criminal activity, that knowledge must be reported to the appropriate authority immediately.

1.4   A PARALEGAL SHALL SERVE THE PUBLIC INTEREST BY CONTRIBUTING TO THE IMPROVEMENT OF THE LEGAL SYSTEM AND DELIVERY OF QUALITY LEGAL SERVICES, INCLUDING PRO BONO PUBLICO SERVICES.

Ethical Considerations

EC-1.4(a)   A paralegal shall be sensitive to the legal needs of the public and shall promote the development and implementation of programs that address those needs.

EC-1.4(b)   A paralegal shall support efforts to improve the legal system and access thereto and shall assist in making changes.

EC-1.4(c)   A paralegal shall support and participate in the delivery of Pro Bono Publico services directed toward implementing and improving access to justice, the law, the legal system or the paralegal and legal professions.

EC-1.4(d)   A paralegal should aspire annually to contribute twenty-four (24) hours of Pro Bono Publico services under the supervision of an attorney or as authorized by administrative, statutory or court authority to:

1. persons of limited means; or
2. charitable, religious, civic, community, governmental and educational organizations in matters that are designed primarily to address the legal needs of persons with limited means; or
3. individuals, groups or organizations seeking to secure or protect civil rights, civil liberties or public rights.

The twenty-four (24) hours of Pro Bono Publico services contributed annually by a paralegal may consist of such services as detailed in this EC-1.4(d), and/or administrative matters designed to develop and implement the attainment of this aspiration as detailed above in EC-1.4(a) B (c), or any combination of the two.

1.5 A PARALEGAL SHALL PRESERVE ALL CONFIDENTIAL INFORMATION PROVIDED BY THE CLIENT OR ACQUIRED FROM OTHER SOURCES BEFORE, DURING, AND AFTER THE COURSE OF THE PROFESSIONAL RELATIONSHIP.

Ethical Considerations

EC-1.5(a)   A paralegal shall be aware of and abide by all legal authority governing confidential information in the jurisdiction in which the paralegal practices.

EC-1.5(b)   A paralegal shall not use confidential information to the disadvantage of the client.

EC-1.5(c)   A paralegal shall not use confidential information to the advantage of the paralegal or of a third person.

EC-1.5(d)   A paralegal may reveal confidential information only after full disclosure and with the client's written consent; or, when required by law or court order; or, when necessary to prevent the client from committing an act that could result in death or serious bodily harm.

EC-1.5(e)   A paralegal shall keep those individuals responsible for the legal representation of a client fully informed of any confidential information the paralegal may have pertaining to that client.

EC-1.5(f)   A paralegal shall not engage in any indiscreet communications concerning clients.

1.6 A PARALEGAL SHALL AVOID CONFLICTS OF INTEREST AND SHALL DISCLOSE ANY POSSIBLE CONFLICT TO THE EMPLOYER OR CLIENT, AS WELL AS TO THE PROSPECTIVE EMPLOYERS OR CLIENTS.

Ethical Considerations

EC-1.6(a)   A paralegal shall act within the bounds of the law, solely for the benefit of the client, and shall be free of compromising influences and loyalties. Neither the paralegal's personal or business interest, nor those of other clients or third persons, should compromise the paralegal's professional judgment and loyalty to the client.

EC-1.6(b)   A paralegal shall avoid conflicts of interest that may arise from previous assignments, whether for a present or past employer or client.

EC-1.6(c)   A paralegal shall avoid conflicts of interest that may arise from family relationships and from personal and business interests.

EC-1.6(d)   In order to be able to determine whether an actual or potential conflict of interest exists a paralegal shall create and maintain an effective recordkeeping system that identifies clients, matters, and parties with which the paralegal has worked.

EC-1.6(e)   A paralegal shall reveal sufficient non-confidential information about a client or former client to reasonably ascertain if an actual or potential conflict of interest exists.

EC-1.6(f)   A paralegal shall not participate in or conduct work on any matter where a conflict of interest has been identified.

EC-1.6(g)   In matters where a conflict of interest has been identified and the client consents to continued representation, a paralegal shall comply fully with the implementation and maintenance of an Ethical Wall.

1.7   A PARALEGAL'S TITLE SHALL BE FULLY DISCLOSED.

Ethical Considerations

EC-1.7(a)   A paralegal's title shall clearly indicate the individual's status and shall be disclosed in all business and professional communications to avoid misunderstandings and misconceptions about the paralegal's role and responsibilities.

EC-1.7(b)   A paralegal's title shall be included if the paralegal's name appears on business cards, letterhead, brochures, directories, and advertisements.

EC-1.7(c)   A paralegal shall not use letterhead, business cards or other promotional materials to create a fraudulent impression of his/her status or ability to practice in the jurisdiction in which the paralegal practices.

EC-1.7(d)   A paralegal shall not practice under color of any record, diploma, or certificate that has been illegally or fraudulently obtained or issued or which is misrepresentative in any way.

EC-1.7(e)   A paralegal shall not participate in the creation, issuance, or dissemination of fraudulent records, diplomas, or certificates.

1.8   A PARALEGAL SHALL NOT ENGAGE IN THE UNAUTHORIZED PRACTICE OF LAW.

Ethical Considerations

EC-1.8(a)   A paralegal shall comply with the applicable legal authority governing the unauthorized practice of law in the jurisdiction in which the paralegal practices.

§2.   NFPA GUIDELINES FOR THE ENFORCEMENT OF THE MODEL CODE OF ETHICS AND PROFESSIONAL RESPONSIBILITY

2.1   BASIS FOR DISCIPLINE

2.1(a)   Disciplinary investigations and proceedings brought under authority of the Rules shall be conducted in accord with obligations imposed on the paralegal professional by the Model Code of Ethics and Professional Responsibility.

2.2 STRUCTURE OF DISCIPLINARY COMMITTEE

2.2(a) The Disciplinary Committee ("Committee") shall be made up of nine (9) members including the Chair.

2.2(b) Each member of the Committee, including any temporary replacement members, shall have demonstrated working knowledge of ethics/professional responsibility-related issues and activities.

2.2(c) The Committee shall represent a cross-section of practice areas and work experience. The following recommendations are made regarding the members of the Committee.

1) At least one paralegal with one to three years of law-related work experience.
2) At least one paralegal with five to seven years of law related work experience.
3) At least one paralegal with over ten years of law related work experience.
4) One paralegal educator with five to seven years of work experience; preferably in the area of ethics/professional responsibility.
5) One paralegal manager.
6) One lawyer with five to seven years of law-related work experience.
7) One lay member.

2.2(d) The Chair of the Committee shall be appointed within thirty (30) days of its members' induction. The Chair shall have no fewer than ten (10) years of law-related work experience.

2.2(e) The terms of all members of the Committee shall be staggered. Of those members initially appointed, a simple majority plus one shall be appointed to a term of one year, and the remaining members shall be appointed to a term of two years. Thereafter, all members of the Committee shall be appointed to terms of two years.

2.2(f) If for any reason the terms of a majority of the Committee will expire at the same time, members may be appointed to terms of one year to maintain continuity of the Committee.

2.2(g) The Committee shall organize from its members a three-tiered structure to investigate, prosecute and/or adjudicate charges of misconduct. The members shall be rotated among the tiers.

2.3 OPERATION OF COMMITTEE

2.3(a) The Committee shall meet on an as-needed basis to discuss, investigate, and/or adjudicate alleged violations of the Model Code/Model Rules.

2.3(b) A majority of the members of the Committee present at a meeting shall constitute a quorum.

2.3(c)   A Recording Secretary shall be designated to maintain complete and accurate minutes of all Committee meetings. All such minutes shall be kept confidential until a decision has been made that the matter will be set for hearing as set forth in Section 6.1 below.

2.3(d)   If any member of the Committee has a conflict of interest with the Charging Party, the Responding Party, or the allegations of misconduct, that member shall not take part in any hearing or deliberations concerning those allegations. If the absence of that member creates a lack of a quorum for the Committee, then a temporary replacement for the member shall be appointed.

2.3(e)   Either the Charging Party or the Responding Party may request that, for good cause shown, any member of the Committee not participate in a hearing or deliberation. All such requests shall be honored. If the absence of a Committee member under those circumstances creates a lack of a quorum for the Committee, then a temporary replacement for that member shall be appointed.

2.3(f)   All discussions and correspondence of the Committee shall be kept confidential until a decision has been made that the matter will be set for hearing as set forth in Section 6.1 below.

2.3(g)   All correspondence from the Committee to the Responding Party regarding any charge of misconduct and any decisions made regarding the charge shall be mailed certified mail, return receipt requested, to the Responding Party's last known address and shall be clearly marked with a "Confidential" designation.

2.4 PROCEDURE FOR THE REPORTING OF ALLEGED VIOLATIONS OF THE MODEL CODE/DISCIPLINARY RULES

2.4(a)   An individual or entity in possession of non-confidential knowledge or information concerning possible instances of misconduct shall make a confidential written report to the Committee within thirty (30) days of obtaining same. This report shall include all details of the alleged misconduct.

2.4(b)   The Committee so notified shall inform the Responding Party of the allegation(s) of misconduct no later than ten (10) business days after receiving the confidential written report from the Charging Party.

2.4(c)   Notification to the Responding Party shall include the identity of the Charging Party, unless, for good cause shown, the Charging Party requests anonymity.

2.4(d)   The Responding Party shall reply to the allegations within ten (10) business days of notification.

2.5 PROCEDURE FOR THE INVESTIGATION OF A CHARGE OF MISCONDUCT

2.5(a)   Upon receipt of a Charge of Misconduct ("Charge"), or on its own initiative, the Committee shall initiate an investigation.

2.5(b)   If, upon initial or preliminary review, the Committee makes a determination that the charges are either without basis in fact or, if proven, would not constitute professional misconduct, the Committee shall dismiss the allegations of misconduct. If such determination of dismissal cannot be made, a formal investigation shall be initiated.

2.5(c)   Upon the decision to conduct a formal investigation, the Committee shall:

1) mail to the Charging and Responding Parties within three (3) business days of that decision notice of the commencement of a formal investigation. That notification shall be in writing and shall contain a complete explanation of all Charge(s), as well as the reasons for a formal investigation and shall cite the applicable codes and rules;

2) allow the Responding Party thirty (30) days to prepare and submit a confidential response to the Committee, which response shall address each charge specifically and shall be in writing; and

3) upon receipt of the response to the notification, have thirty (30) days to investigate the Charge(s). If an extension of time is deemed necessary, that extension shall not exceed ninety (90) days.

2.5(d)   Upon conclusion of the investigation, the Committee may:

1) dismiss the Charge upon the finding that it has no basis in fact;

2) dismiss the Charge upon the finding that, if proven, the Charge would not constitute Misconduct;

3) refer the matter for hearing by the Tribunal; or

4) in the case of criminal activity, refer the Charge(s) and all investigation results to the appropriate authority.

2.6 PROCEDURE FOR A MISCONDUCT HEARING BEFORE A TRIBUNAL

2.6(a)   Upon the decision by the Committee that a matter should be heard, all parties shall be notified and a hearing date shall be set. The hearing shall take place no more than thirty (30) days from the conclusion of the formal investigation.

2.6(b)   The Responding Party shall have the right to counsel. The parties and the Tribunal shall have the right to call any witnesses and introduce any documentation that they believe will lead to the fair and reasonable resolution of the matter.

2.6(c)   Upon completion of the hearing, the Tribunal shall deliberate and present a written decision to the parties in accordance with procedures as set forth by the Tribunal.

2.6(d)   Notice of the decision of the Tribunal shall be appropriately published.

2.7   SANCTIONS

2.7(a)   Upon a finding of the Tribunal that misconduct has occurred, any of the following sanctions, or others as may be deemed appropriate, may be imposed upon the Responding Party, either singularly or in combination:

   1) letter of reprimand to the Responding Party; counseling;

   2) attendance at an ethics course approved by the Tribunal; probation;

   3) suspension of license/authority to practice; revocation of license/authority to practice;

   4) imposition of a fine; assessment of costs; or

   5) in the instance of criminal activity, referral to the appropriate authority.

2.7(b)   Upon the expiration of any period of probation, suspension, or revocation, the Responding Party may make application for reinstatement. With the application for reinstatement, the Responding Party must show proof of having complied with all aspects of the sanctions imposed by the Tribunal.

2.8   APPELLATE PROCEDURES

2.8(a)   The parties shall have the right to appeal the decision of the Tribunal in accordance with the procedure as set forth by the Tribunal.

DEFINITIONS

"Appellate Body" means a body established to adjudicate an appeal to any decision made by a Tribunal or other decision-making body with respect to formally-heard Charges of Misconduct.

"Charge of Misconduct" means a written submission by any individual or entity to an ethics committee, paralegal association, bar association, law enforcement agency, judicial body, government agency, or other appropriate body or entity, that sets forth non-confidential information regarding any instance of alleged misconduct by an individual paralegal or paralegal entity.

"Charging Party" means any individual or entity who submits a Charge of Misconduct against an individual paralegal or paralegal entity.

"Competency" means the demonstration of: diligence, education, skill, and mental, emotional, and physical fitness reasonably necessary for the performance of paralegal services.

"Confidential Information" means information relating to a client, whatever its source, that is not public knowledge nor available to the public. ("Non-Confidential Information" would generally include the name of the client and the identity of the matter for which the paralegal provided services.)

"Disciplinary Hearing" means the confidential proceeding conducted by a committee or other designated body or entity concerning any instance of alleged misconduct by an individual paralegal or paralegal entity.

"Disciplinary Committee" means any committee that has been established by an entity such as a paralegal association, bar association, judicial body, or government agency to: (a) identify, define and investigate general ethical considerations and concerns with respect to paralegal practice; (b) administer and enforce the Model Code and Model Rules and; (c) discipline any individual paralegal or paralegal entity found to be in violation of same.

"Disclose" means communication of information reasonably sufficient to permit identification of the significance of the matter in question.

"Ethical Wall" means the screening method implemented in order to protect a client from a conflict of interest. An Ethical Wall generally includes, but is not limited to, the following elements: (1) prohibit the paralegal from having any connection with the matter; (2) ban discussions with or the transfer of documents to or from the paralegal; (3) restrict access to files; and (4) educate all members of the firm, corporation, or entity as to the separation of the paralegal (both organizationally and physically) from the pending matter. For more information regarding the Ethical Wall, see the NFPA publication entitled "The Ethical Wall—Its Application to Paralegals."

"Ex parte" means actions or communications conducted at the instance and for the benefit of one party only, and without notice to, or contestation by, any person adversely interested.

"Investigation" means the investigation of any charge(s) of misconduct filed against an individual paralegal or paralegal entity by a Committee.

"Letter of Reprimand" means a written notice of formal censure or severe reproof administered to an individual paralegal or paralegal entity for unethical or improper conduct.

"Misconduct" means the knowing or unknowing commission of an act that is in direct violation of those Canons and Ethical Considerations of any and all applicable codes and/or rules of conduct.

"Paralegal" is synonymous with "Legal Assistant" and is defined as a person qualified through education, training, or work experience to perform substantive legal work that requires knowledge of legal concepts and is customarily, but not exclusively performed by a lawyer. This person may be retained or employed by a lawyer, law office, governmental agency, or other entity or may be authorized by administrative, statutory, or court authority to perform this work.

"Pro Bono Publico" means providing or assisting to provide quality legal services in order to enhance access to justice for persons of limited means; charitable, religious, civic, community, governmental and educational organizations in matters that are designed primarily to address the legal needs of persons with limited means; or individuals, groups or organizations seeking to secure or protect civil rights, civil liberties or public rights.

"Proper Authority" means the local paralegal association, the local or state bar association, Committee(s) of the local paralegal or bar association(s), local prosecutor, administrative agency, or other tribunal empowered to investigate or act upon an instance of alleged misconduct.

"Responding Party" means an individual paralegal or paralegal entity against whom a Charge of Misconduct has been submitted.

"Revocation" means the recision of the license, certificate or other authority to practice of an individual paralegal or paralegal entity found in violation of those Canons and Ethical Considerations of any and all applicable codes and/or rules of conduct.

"Suspension" means the suspension of the license, certificate or other authority to practice of an individual paralegal or paralegal entity found in violation of those Canons and Ethical Considerations of any and all applicable codes and/or rules of conduct.

"Tribunal" means the body designated to adjudicate allegations of misconduct.

Glossary

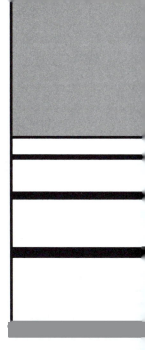

Advocate: One who argues or pleads for another person

Affirmative defense: Allegation by a defendant that negates a plaintiff's right to relief

Alternative dispute resolution: Method of resolving disputes without trial; often called *ADR*

Arbitration: Process by which a neutral third party renders a decision affecting disputing parties

Associate: A junior attorney

Bar association: Organization administered by a state; licenses attorneys and provides assistance to its member attorneys and to the public

Bates® stamp: An implement that assigns sequential numbers to pages and documents; may be done manually or electronically

Billable hours: Time that can be charged to a client for work performed

Blind ad: Advertisement that does not identify the person or firm that placed it

Boutique firm: Law firm that handles only one type of case

Chinese wall: Efforts taken to prevent an employee who has a conflict of interest from participating in a certain case(s); also called *screens* or *cones of silence*

Chron file: A chronological file of all documents prepared by an employee in a law office

Class action: A lawsuit in which a specific number of people sue on behalf of an entire group

Client number: Unique number assigned to a client by a law firm

Codicil: Something added or changed with regard to a will

Confidentiality: Duty to maintain information in secrecy; a duty owed by those in the legal profession to their clients

Conflicts check: Review of firm files and client lists to ensure a conflict of interest does not exist

Conflict of interest: A real or seeming incompatibility between the interests of a lawyer's clients, such that the lawyer is disqualified from representing both clients if the dual representation adversely affects either client or if the clients do not consent

Contingency fee: Fee paid to a law firm by the client only if the firm is successful in recovering money for the client

Contract attorney: Nonemployee attorney who works for a firm on a project basis; *see also* Freelance paralegal

Copyright: The exclusive right, for a limited amount of time, to print, copy, or sell an original work

Debtor: One who owes a debt, usually money

Deposition: Out-of-court examination of a witness or party under oath

Director: The manager of a corporation

Discovery: Investigation conducted by parties before trial to obtain information from each other

Dissolution: The act of canceling a legal relationship, such as a marriage

Docket: Law firm's calendar of its pending matters and related deadlines (same term is also used to refer to a court's schedule of its cases)

Due diligence: A reasonable effort to carry out a duty or direction, usually with regard to the review of documents for a transaction

Equity partner: A partner who owns business assets

Escrow: Property (money, instructions, or deeds) held by a third party until a transaction is completed

Exit interview: Final interview of an employee who is voluntarily resigning; designed to inform the employer of workplace problems

Extranet: Computer network within an office that allows some limited access by those outside the office

Flat fee: Fee paid to a law firm by a client for a certain legal task or matter, regardless of the time it takes to complete the task or matter

Freelance paralegal: A self-employed paralegal who works as an independent contractor for attorneys on an as-needed basis; also called *contract paralegal*

General counsel: The most senior in-house attorney in a corporation

General partnership: A business structure with shared decision making and personal liability for its partners

General practice: A law firm that handles a wide variety of cases

Headhunter: A recruiter who places candidates for employment

Hidden job market: Those positions that are not announced or advertised publicly

Hourly fee: Fee paid to a law firm by a client for each hour spent working on a client's matter

Independent paralegal: A paralegal who works directly for consumers (generally, completing forms) without supervision by an attorney

Informational interview: Interview set up by prospective job seeker to obtain information about a practice field or job

Infringement: An invasion of a right or the unauthorized use of another party's copyrights, trademarks, or patents

In-house counsel: Attorney employed directly by a company to perform its legal work

In-house legal department: Group within a company that performs legal work for the company

Internship: Placement of an individual, usually a student, in a work setting for the purpose of gaining work experience; internships are usually unpaid

Interrogatories: Written questions asked by one party of another party in a lawsuit

Intranet: Internal computer network within an office that allows workers to share documents

Joint and several liability: Liability for an entire debt

Jurisdiction: The power of a court to hear a case

Lateral hire: Attorney, usually experienced, hired by one firm from another

Legal administrator: Individual who manages nearly all aspects of a law firm and its personnel

Legal nurse consultant: *See* Nurse paralegal

LEXIS: A fee-based legal research computer service; a computerized system used for legal research

Lien: A claim against property for settlement of a debt

Limited liability company (LLC): Business structure that protects its members from unlimited personal liability; a new form of business that combines features of partnerships and corporations

Limited liability partnership (LLP): Type of partnership that protects partners from liability for each other's wrongful acts

Litigation: A contest in a court of law; usually refers to civil trials

Lunch interview: An interview conducted at a restaurant over lunch

Managing partner: A partner who directs or manages a partnership

Matter number: Unique number assigned to each individual matter handled by a firm for a client

Mediation: Process by which a neutral third party attempts to help parties resolve their differences

Mock interview: A practice interview, held with someone familiar, to assist in preparing for an actual interview

National Association of Legal Assistants (NALA): A professional organization for individual paralegals

National Federation of Paralegal Associations (NFPA): A professional organization for state and local paralegal associations and individual members

No reference rule: The policy of most employers to provide only basic information about terms of employment rather than discussing an employee's performance

Notary public: A person licensed by the state to administer oaths and witness the signing of important documents

Nurse paralegal: A registered nurse who is trained as a paralegal; also called a *legal nurse consultant*

Of counsel: Term usually assigned to older or semi-retired attorneys, although sometimes used to refer to senior attorneys

One-on-one interview: Interview in which candidate meets with interviewers separately rather than as a group

Panel interview: An interview conducted by a group of individuals

Paralegal association: Professional organization for individual paralegals; may be local, regional, state, or national

Paralegal coordinator: *See* Paralegal manager

Paralegal manager: Paralegal who manages other paralegals; sometimes also called a *paralegal coordinator*

Partner: The owner of a firm or business operating as a partnership

Partnership track: A firm's established course to become a partner or owner of the firm

Permanent associate: An attorney who will remain an employee of a firm rather than an owner; also called *senior attorney, staff attorney, nonequity partner,* or possibly *of counsel*

Personal liability: Liability extending beyond what one invests in a business to one's personal assets

Placement agency: Company or person that places legal professionals in law firms and other legal settings

Preliminary interview: A short interview designed to weed out unqualified candidates; also called a *screening interview*

Probate: The settlement of an estate

Pro bono: Legal services that are provided for the public or those in need without charge

Professional corporation: A corporation organized to provide professional services, such as legal services

Rainmaking: Attracting new business and clients

Redact: Striking out of material in a document, usually for confidentiality reasons

Rescission: The act of cancelling a contract

Retainer: Initial fee paid to attorney or a firm to engage legal services

Screening interview: *See* Preliminary interview

Senior paralegal: Experienced paralegal who generally has at least five years of experience

Settlement conference: Meeting held before trial (usually with a judge) to attempt to settle a lawsuit without a trial

Shadowing: The act of following another person during the work day with the intent of gaining knowledge about the person's job or duties

Shareholder: An owner of a corporation

Sole practitioner: An attorney who practices by himself or herself

Telephone interview: An interview conducted exclusively by telephone

Tickler system: A method of providing reminders to individuals of tasks that need completion or that have pending deadlines

Timekeeping: Method of tracking and entering time spent on client and other work

Traditional paralegal: A paralegal who works under the supervision of an attorney, usually in a law firm, corporate law department, or government agency

Transactional work: Work that is not related to litigation

Trust: A document that provides for the handling and disposition of property, either during a person's lifetime or after death

Unauthorized practice of law: The practicing of law by one without a license to do so; usually called *UPL*

UPL: *See* Unauthorized practice of law

Vicarious disqualification: Disqualification of all the lawyers of a firm or in an office because one of the lawyers is ethically disqualified from representing the client at issue

Westlaw: A fee-based legal research computer service; a computerized system of doing legal research

Will: A document that provides the details of estate disposition

Work study: Academic programs that enable students to gain work experience in exchange for a salary or academic credit while simultaneously continuing their studies

Index